Designing Research in the
Social Sciences

SAGE has been part of the global academic community since 1965, supporting high quality research and learning that transforms society and our understanding of individuals, groups, and cultures. SAGE is the independent, innovative, natural home for authors, editors and societies who share our commitment and passion for the social sciences.

Find out more at: **www.sagepublications.com**

Connect, Debate, Engage on Methodspace

Connect with other researchers and discuss your research interests

Keep up with announcements in the field, for example calls for papers and jobs

Discover and review resources

Engage with featured content such as key articles, podcasts and videos

Find out about relevant conferences and events

Connecting the Research Community

www.methodspace.com

brought to you by

Designing Research in the Social Sciences

Martino Maggetti
Fabrizio Gilardi
Claudio M. Radaelli

Los Angeles | London | New Delhi
Singapore | Washington DC

Los Angeles | London | New Delhi
Singapore | Washington DC

SAGE Publications Ltd
1 Oliver's Yard
55 City Road
London EC1Y 1SP

SAGE Publications Inc.
2455 Teller Road
Thousand Oaks, California 91320

SAGE Publications India Pvt Ltd
B 1/I 1 Mohan Cooperative Industrial Area
Mathura Road
New Delhi 110 044

SAGE Publications Asia-Pacific Pte Ltd
3 Church Street
#10-04 Samsung Hub
Singapore 049483

Editor: Katie Metzler
Assistant editor: Anna Horvai
Production editor: Ian Antcliff
Copyeditor: Richard Leigh
Proofreader: Emily Ayers
Marketing manager: Ben Griffin-Sherwood
Cover design: Francis Kenney
Typeset by: C&M Digitals (P) Ltd, Chennai, India
Printed and bound by CPI Group (UK) Ltd,
Croydon, CR0 4YY

MIX
Paper from
responsible sources
FSC® C013604
www.fsc.org

Library of Congress Control Number: 2012939231

British Library Cataloguing in Publication data

A catalogue record for this book is available from
the British Library

ISBN 978-1-84920-500-9
ISBN 978-1-84920-501-6 (pbk)

Contents

Ad Alexandra ed Eliana (CR)
A Erika, Viola e Zeno (FG)
A Valentina (MM)

About the authors

Martino Maggetti is a lecturer at the Institut für Politikwissenschaft (University of Zurich) and senior researcher at the Institut d'Etudes Politiques et Internationales (University of Lausanne). He participates in the project 'Internationalization, mediatization and the accountability of regulatory agencies', funded by the Swiss National Science Foundation, and teaches Comparative Regulatory Governance and Comparative Methods. His research interests include comparative politics, public policy, public administration, regulation and transnational governance. His research articles have appeared, among others, in the journals *Business & Society*, *European Political Science Review*, *Journal of European Public Policy*, and *Regulation & Governance*.

Fabrizio Gilardi is associate professor at the Department of Political Science of the University of Zurich, Switzerland. His work on regulatory institutions and policy diffusion has been published in journals such as the *American Journal of Political Science*, *Comparative Political Studies*, the *Journal of European Public Policy*, and the *Journal of Theoretical Politics*, among others. He is also the author of a book on independent regulatory agencies in Europe (Edward Elgar, 2008), and the co-editor of a volume on delegation in contemporary democracies (Routledge, 2006).

Claudio M. Radaelli is professor of political science at the University of Exeter, where he directs the Centre for European Governance, a Jean Monnet Centre of Excellence. His research interests lie in the theory of the policy process, learning in public policy, regulatory reform, governance and Europeanization. He is the co-editor of the *European Journal of Political Research*. He edited (with Theofanis Exadaktylos) *Research Design in European Studies* (Palgrave, 2012). His research is published in major political science journals. He is currently directing a four-year project funded by the European Research Council on learning in regulatory governance.

Acknowledgements

We are grateful to the doctoral students at the University of Exeter who contributed with their encouragement and ideas to the development of this book by taking part in a module on Research Design taught by Maggetti and Radaelli. Susan Banducci taught one edition of our module on Research Design with us and shaped our thinking about the issues discussed in the book. We thank her and hope there will be future opportunities to teach together again.

Some draft chapters were also piloted as compact module on Research Design at the University of Agder, Kristiansand, where Claudio Radaelli teaches on the PhD programme in Public Administration. Radaelli wishes to thank the Politics faculty at the University of Agder for providing an ideal environment for research and doctoral training. Fabrizio Gilardi wishes to thank Olivier Baumann, Katharina Füglister, Dominik Hangartner, and Fabio Wasserfallen for helpful comments on draft chapters and the University of Zurich for financial support. Martino Maggetti thanks Michael James for excellent copy-editing, Christian Ewert for invaluable research assistance and his students at the University of Zurich for engaging discussions and challenging remarks.

We wish to thank the Sage team, who provided superb editorial guidance and support throughout the writing process, in the persons of Patrick Brindle, Anna Horvai and Katie Metzler. Finally, we owe a great debt to the anonymous reviewers for their encouragement and for providing insightful revision suggestions.

Foreword

This volume is the product of a truly collective effort implying a close dialogue between us. Working on this volume has been a constructive process based on the confrontation of our points of view, which in many cases were the same and in other cases were different. In line with our conception of research design, the outcome is a pluralistic but unified and – we hope – coherent account of existing choices and trade-offs when designing an empirically oriented research project in the social sciences. However, Radaelli has primary responsibility for Chapters 1 and 2; Maggetti for Chapters 3, 5 and 6; Gilardi for Chapters 4 and 7. The conclusion was mainly written by Maggetti and Radaelli.

SAGE is delighted to be IPG Academic and Professional Publisher of the Year 2012

The judges from the Independent Publishers Guild commented:

SAGE won this category with a thoroughly professional publishing programme, wide-ranging digital activity, high production standards and sharp global strategies. Judges also noted its ability to attract and retain outstanding staff and authors, and said it had retained a strong sense of independence while growing into a big player. "SAGE knows its market and does what it does phenomenally well. It consistently attracts top talent and is very dynamic internationally."

"We are delighted that the IPG has recognized SAGE with this award," said *Ziyad Marar, Global Publishing Director, SAGE*. "We are very proud of our independence, which enables us to focus on the broad publishing needs of our communities and to make decisions for the long term. We passionately believe that education and scholarship are intrinsically valuable, and that publishers play a key role in shaping and disseminating ideas. To be recognized as the **IPG Academic and Professional Publisher of the Year** stands as testament to our authors and our talented and committed people across the company, who put this vision into practice every day."

ONE

Social sciences and research design

Demand and supply

A book is a complex entity made up of inspiration, vision and ideas that, although generated by different kinds of teaching and research experience, find a single home in a text. It can be seen as the product of a truly independent mind, or as the result of writing with a specific reader looking over the author's shoulder. That is, writing in anticipation of the reaction of some type of reader that matters to the author – for most of us, this means writing with a set of expectations about the readership in mind.

Granted that we did not write for ourselves but with specific expectations about our readers, who then is the reader looking over our shoulder?[1] Who do we think 'you', our readers, are? Our book, we hope, is the result of a productive encounter between demand (or what 'you' want) and supply (or what we offer). In our experience as university lecturers involved in modules on methods and design, as well as when we talk informally, wearing our researchers' hats, to young members of the profession, we have found that there is demand for a volume on research design in the social sciences that treats the reader as a competent person capable of making responsible choices: a grown-up social scientist, so to speak. All too often, however, those who set out to write a new research project or enter a course on research design and methods looking for inspiration and guidance seem frustrated. They do not seem to find what they want. Typically, when we look on the library shelves for books on how to design research, we are provided with either a cookbook (with precise instructions about what ought to

---

[1] *The Reader Over Your Shoulder* (Graves and Hodge, 1944) is a time-honoured handbook for 'writers of English prose' that still contains valuable suggestions for those who write up their research in professional journals.

be done), or a somewhat bewildering collection of extremely diverse propositions about the nature of scientific inquiry and its methods. It is all very well to say, paraphrasing Mao Zedong, 'let a hundred flowers blossom', but there is a point beyond which the reader starts to suspect that the flowers are in different greenhouses that do not communicate with one another. Pluralism is a virtue, but this degeneration – we argue – is not what readers are looking for.

Let us say a few words about pluralism, which seems (and indeed is, up to a point) a genuinely good, honest, reasonable approach. Of course we all accept that there are different approaches, each of them particularly strong in some respects and weaker in others. The problems arise when pluralism first turns into incommensurability, and then degenerates into sectarian thinking. Being pluralist does not mean that approaches are always incommensurable with one another, that we cannot move between traditions, that paradigms should never speak to one another. Neither should this kind of argument lead us to close our minds to what others do – quite the opposite, in fact. Yet we have met researchers who say 'I am a rational choice theorist' or 'I am a Chicago school of sociology person' – they tend to use these paradigmatic assertions as blinkers. They feel that there is no need to move beyond or outside their paradigm-bound world. The suspicion is that these researchers live in their protective paradigmatic shells and do not want to hear anything that may disturb or challenge their core beliefs.

This is understandable: it is comforting to feel at home inside our approach, and claim that we do not have to look at what others do, because what they do 'is incommensurable' with what we do. But, epistemologically, it is wrong. Even if we buy into only moderate doses of analytic eclecticism (Sil and Katzenstein, 2010; we will return to this later in this chapter) we have to accept that there has been genuine progress – in the sense of 'understanding and explaining better' – in taking intuitions, conjectures and mechanisms developed within one approach and using them to increase the leverage of another approach. To illustrate, our knowledge of what exactly institutions 'do' to social behaviour can be used to control for institutional variables in an approach that does not start from institutional premises.

There is also a vast area where we can still be pluralist but accept that two approaches are truly in competition, so that if one is right the other is wrong. It is possible to say whether, for example, a certain kind of behaviour in a given process by an individual actor (say, a political party during an election campaign) is better explained by a rational calculation of the effects of expected consequences or by the decision to conform to the identity and roles that are expected by the environment surrounding the actor. It is therefore important to determine whether two given domains of the social sciences are ontologically or epistemologically incommensurable, whether they are commensurable and therefore compete for the explanation of the same type of behaviour, and so on.

What we take issue with is not the academic debate in the philosophy of the social sciences, but rather the more mundane behaviour of researchers and doctoral students. Some scholars mentally translate the contents of books where traditions are presented one after the other in rigid, separate compartments into the (wrong) conventional wisdom that 'anything goes provided that you back up your choices with a decent justification'.[2] Thus, we have heard students say 'I have decided to study Germany and France and will find a justification later on, but these are going to be my cases because I speak German and French'. Again, we all understand why someone may be keen on exploiting language skills (why not?), but there is nothing scientific in choosing cases before the skeleton of a research design has materialized.

As mentioned, the opposite of the loosely pluralist book is the cookbook version. Here the reader is given a very passive role in the master's kitchen. The chef provides instructions, long lists of criteria to follow, tables of what can and should be done and what must be avoided at all costs, and the steps that, although not at all realistic, in a world where 'everything else is constant' will provide the perfect solution to the researcher's problems. True, recipe books for social scientists always come with the caveats that research is a process of going back and forth to the evidence, that research questions are formulated in a process of scientific inquiry rather than in a one-shot fashion, and other soothing rhetorical devices. But the substance is a pedagogical model in which the novice has nothing to contribute to the cooking experience, while the chef possesses 100 per cent of the knowledge necessary to produce fine food.

In the 'let a hundred flowers blossom but in separate greenhouses' approach and its more extreme 'anything goes' version, the readers are told that we live in a truly diverse, if not Balkanized, social scientific world. Very few people talk to each other, and do so only within their cluster or field. Perhaps it is not true that anything goes in the social sciences – only the approaches included in the given volume are 'good' and 'trustworthy'. Yet the very idea of providing a coherent approach to research design is presented to the reader as definitively 'early modern', connected to Hempel's visionary (but today regarded as flawed) notion of unity

---

[2]That 'anything goes' is the only truth shared by the disciples of Feyerabend (1975), who in the philosophy of the social sciences has established the most relativistic position we are aware of. The problem with the epistemological anarchism of Feyerabend is that it does not tell us anything about quality criteria – how to discriminate between 'high-quality' and 'low-quality' research. We may or may not like it, but shared notions of quality and demands for quality research exist out there in the real world, no matter how deep a philosophical critique may be. These quality criteria determine our careers and reputations as researchers: why did that journal reject my article but publish that other article? Why was this project funded and that project not? What was that funding body thinking when it turned down my application last month?

in science,[3] if not historically passé. The problem with this approach is that the reader is often offered several options that contradict each other. One cannot believe in rationality in Chapter 3 and denigrate rationality in Chapter 4! The reader can only come to the conclusion that the volume must have been written by people who were not in the same room when the project was discussed, or agreed to write the chapters only by stipulating that they should not read and comment on each others' drafts. Indeed, this is how peace in some departments is kept: people on different sides of the corridor do not speak to each other.

Thus, we think that you, the reader looking over our shoulder, are a grown-up. We believe that you want to make responsible choices. You are looking for a relatively coherent approach to design behind the diversity of individual methods and techniques. After all, the majority of funded research projects within a social scientific discipline have similar characteristics, and the major journals publish articles on the fundamental aspects of research design that acknowledge and build on each other.

After the demand has been sketched, the supply is pretty straightforward, consisting of a coherent product based on the assumption that researchers are reflective human beings who live in the real world of research funding bodies, journals, and PhD programmes rather than imaginary kitchens or on the moon. What we offer (the supply) insists on choices and trade-offs, not on definitively right and definitively wrong decisions in the research process. We also give equal consideration to problems of concept formation and problems of measurement. When we piloted our volume on two cohorts of doctoral students in political science, we found that for most of our students the notion of research design is nowadays practically very similar to the issue of what methods should be chosen. In contrast, we believe that to design a research project includes both conceptual aspects and the choice of one or several methods. It is important to be aware of whether we are making a choice about problems and concepts or a choice of methods or techniques. There is no leverage in locking horns over the problem-driven versus methods-driven choice. Successful projects deal with both problems and methods. Essentially, we would like to pitch this volume after your cookbook but before your book on methods. The simple cookbook tells you what should really be avoided in a research project. It also tells you what to do, but often with an unrealistic, idealistic approach to real-world research in the social science. The cookbook is more useful in pointing to possible mistakes than in guiding the reader. Thus, what we say is: read it but do not believe it entirely. And we add: do not jump into the methods before you give proper consideration

---

[3]Carl Hempel (1965) was one the strongest advocates of the unity of science, but one can go back to Kant, who believed in the unity of science not because there is unity in nature but because of the unifying functions or character of human reason and concepts.

to research design. Hence our claim that this volume in a sense comes after the cookbook but before the treatment of methods.

More importantly still, let us consider what research is all about. The craft of research is about tying claims, arguments and evidence (Booth et al., 2008). Becker (1998) defines the research process in terms of imagery, sampling, concepts and logic. This is the precious stuff of research. We use theories to make claims. The claims are true because of an argument we find in the theory. The evidence is decisive in corroborating the argument or in directing our attention towards something else. We can, for example, claim that governments perform better in terms of policy reforms in the first part of their mandate. This claim is supported by the argument that after elections governments enjoy a honeymoon period with their electorate in which they can push the boundaries of the possible and produce policy change. The evidence comes from a cross-section and time-series data about Latin American democracies. As this claim–argument–evidence chain makes clear, there is no point in trying to decide whether it is measurement or concepts that are decisive: they both are but for different reasons. Perfect measurement of a wrong concept pushes back science (Brady and Collier, 2010); concepts that cannot be operationalized and measured by the evidence do not tell us whether the argument supporting the claim is empirically valid or not.

Choice, responsibility and trade-offs

To achieve our vision in which demand and supply meet, we emphasize responsibility, choice and trade-offs. These are three important concepts for our volume. Let us introduce them one by one.

Responsibility means that we approach the demand of readers by treating them as responsible researchers who co-produce knowledge with their mentors and instructors. We do not subscribe to a pedagogical model where the instructor has all the knowledge needed to 'cook' the dish, and the reader's skills are essentially all about following the instructions. Readers come with their knowledge of their field, the substantive knowledge of problems they want to address, and their previous experience of research and university modules. They have to interact with – rather than execute – the message and the detailed suggestions presented by their teachers. Responsible researchers have to make choices; their key task is not to follow instructions.

However, these choices should be informed by an understanding of what is at stake in a specific project and in its execution. More often than not, the grand epistemological debates are silent about the design aspects of a project (Gerring, 2001). One implication of responsibility is therefore the need to make informed choices. With this volume we hope to increase the amount of information and, overall, the awareness you need to make this type of choice. To illustrate: design and methods are contingent on notions of causality. In turn, causality raises issues of ontology, but it also directs us towards the search for mechanisms (although mechanisms are not universally present in all conceptions of causal analysis). Finally, mechanisms must connect the sphere of individual behaviour to the logic of macro explanation. This is the logic of explanation in research design. Coherent choices respect this logic.

Trade-offs are essential to this vision of how demand and supply meet. A trade-off is an inverse relationship between two equally desirable (or equally undesirable) outcomes. While there is still a sort of conventional wisdom – at least in the groups of doctoral students we talked to when preparing our volume – that research design choices are about the stark contrast between one approach or tradition and another, the reality is that we have to compromise on something to achieve something else. Our trade-offs are not the high-level divides of so many heated debates among students and faculty, nor the greenhouses that never communicate but let their flowers blossom in isolation.

Let us take a very concrete example. How many times have we heard students and faculty talk about the divide between qualitative and quantitative research (for an in-depth analysis of the divide see Mahoney and Goertz, 2006)? Or that between social constructivists and those who give priority to material interests? Yet many truly exciting projects published in major journals are produced by scholars who write across the qualitative–quantitative divide (for an example, see Ross, 2008; see also Creswell, 2009, on mixed-methods designs). Social constructivists and institutional-organizational theorists do not have to engage in tribal wars – they can talk about scope conditions instead (Olsen, 2001). A rich debate on mixed and multi-method research has moved the boundaries beyond this classic divide (Creswell, 2008). Some of the techniques we use, such as meta-analysis of case studies or qualitative comparative analysis, embody elements of the qualitative tradition in causal analysis and quantitative techniques (Jensen and Rodgers, 2001). So the language of the qualitative–quantitative divide or the 'rational' versus the 'socially constructed' is no longer valid, if it ever was. It does not match what social scientists do – at least, it does not match what social scientists like us do (cf. Mahoney and Goertz, 2006). To be clear, we are not persuaded that there is a general trade-off between quantitative analysis and qualitative analysis. There are trade-offs about establishing causality, but not at this level of thinking qualitatively or quantitatively, for the reasons to do with multi-method research we mentioned above and the arguments we put forward later in the book (for a different opinion, see Mahoney and Goertz, 2006).

In a similar fashion, we have taken part in doctoral training programmes that spend weeks on the 'value-laden' nature of the social sciences and the ontological–epistemological divide.[4] Again, this is not what we have in mind when we speak of trade-offs. Let us briefly look at these issues in turn. In a sense, most aspects of the social sciences are value-laden, including the choice of topic: why study governance and not government? Actually the same can be said of some choices made by natural scientists. Be that as it may, we have quality criteria in the social sciences that enable us to say that one piece of research is closer to evidence than another. Howard Becker (1998: 79) explains that the 'value-laden' dimension of research

> does not mean that there aren't degrees of interpretation, that some descriptions can't be less interpretive (or perhaps we should say less conventionally interpretive) than others. We might even say that some descriptions require less inference than others. To say that someone looks like he is hurrying home with his shopping requires an inference about motivation that saying he is walking rapidly doesn't.

With Becker's words in mind, we are ready to turn to the thorny issue of ontology and epistemology. We have heard in our own PhD classes that a social ontology – that is, the fact that a phenomenon or entity exists only in the realm of social representations – calls for a post-positivist epistemology. This ignores the simple fact that a social ontology is compatible with an objective epistemology. We certainly believe that a piece of paper with some numbers and pictures printed on it is 'money' and has 'value' only because of shared social representations. Yet we count and study money (in short, we gather valid knowledge) with an objective epistemology, and central banks identify with some precision the quantity of money available in a given country (Searle, 1995). By the same token, electoral volatility or party competition does not exist 'out there' in the physical world. They are constructs created by political scientists with their mental representations of elections and party systems. This has not deterred generations of scholars from proposing and using indexes of volatility and measures of party competition.

This is not true only of social objects. For a social scientist, even physical objects exist because of their socially constructed nature. Becker (1998: 158) draws on the notion of the classic sociologist George Herbert Mead that 'an object is constituted by the way people are prepared to act toward it'.[5] Becker

---

[4]Epistemology sets the criteria we use to generate scientific knowledge about the objects we study. Ontology refers to our assumptions about the nature of reality.

[5]Thus, the main difference between physical objects and social objects lies somewhere else. An important distinction is that physical objects do not have intentionality. Social objects such as a soldier or an army have individual and collective intentionality. For a discussion along the lines of Searle of the epistemological and ontological problems of intentionality, see Gallotti (2012).

provides another instructive example about musical instruments. To most of us, it is clear that a guitar is a guitar. However,

> a musical instrument, for all its indubitable physical reality, is the physical embodiment of all the experiments in acoustics that made it possible, but also of the choices made by many, many generations of performers and composers to compose for and play the instrument in a certain way, of the listeners who accepted the resulting sounds as music, and of the commercial enterprises that made all that possible. (Becker, 1998:47)

It follows that we should be aware of the interaction between physical properties and social definitions – as Becker would say, 'things' are just people acting together. But it does not follow that we cannot count the number of musical instruments in different museums, or try to explain variation in their values across time and space.

We can even go a bit further. We argue that rather than pigeonholing the young members of our profession into social scientific 'sects' or non-communicating 'schools', we should liberate them. We have already mentioned analytic eclecticism. This is useful to those who work at the shop-floor level, that is, in specific empirical projects. Analytic eclecticism assembles substantive and theoretical aspects of scholarship originating in different research traditions. It is different from, and more than, the operation of drawing on different methods to address causation and inference (see Chapters 3 and 4). Essentially, this approach 'seeks to extricate, translate, and selectively integrate analytic elements – concepts, logics, mechanisms, and interpretations – of theories or narratives that have been developed within separate paradigms but that address related aspects of substantive problems that have both scholarly and practical significance' (Sil and Katzenstein, 2010: 10). Thus, instead of segregating researchers, we should be open to the possibility of selectively and intelligently importing major conceptual findings from different traditions. We cannot deny that rationality explains a lot of the variation about compliance: if there are speed cameras in a street, drivers tend to comply with the limits and the same drivers tend to drive faster when in a country lane with no speed limits. Governments make calculations before they decide whether to implement international obligations or to ignore them. Yet we account for other aspects of non-compliance by looking at mechanisms of trust, collective identities and historical memories when we compare the efficacy of speed limits and compliance with international obligations across countries. We all know that Moscow is not Stockholm, as a famous article by Rothstein (2000) puts it, because citizens hold different collective memories in the two countries. Instead of wasting time building walls between one paradigm and another, we should direct researchers towards the exploration of scope conditions that tell us when one logic applies and when the other applies (Olsen, 2001).

To sum up, the thrust of our volume is to move beyond these stark contrasts and paradigm-bound visions and to acknowledge trade-offs. The presence of trade-offs makes the cookbook approach less useful than it seems prima facie. When there is a trade-off, strictly speaking, it is not between a group of choices that are right and another group that are wrong.[6] These trade-offs can be eased of course – this is one of the key motivations for writing the substantive chapters in this volume. But the trade-offs do not disappear. Some have to do with the limitations of a single research project: for example, in a one-year project it is impossible to give equal weight to concept formation and measurement, so there will be a trade-off between, say, discussing the concept of the authoritarian personality and measuring it in a sample of candidates for elections. Other trade-offs are more sophisticated, for example, that between focusing a project on the causal explanation of a phenomenon (such as variation in the levels of taxation between two neighbouring countries) and looking at the consequences of an important factor we have highlighted, such as actors with veto power. One can either study the causes of war, and in this context pay some attention to emotions, or study how emotions influence different aspects of world politics. It is important to be aware of whether we are pursuing one type of explanation or the other, otherwise we will most likely publish results that do not stand up in terms of causal analysis (see Chapter 3).

What is research design?

We have just mentioned the importance of being aware of where one stands in terms of trade-offs. But this can be generalized to the whole of research design. Even those who claim they are interested only in methods have made implicit choices about research design. Indeed, research design can be a real problem if one ignores it. We still find many articles that say nothing about research design; that is to say, they are not clear about what they seek to explain; they do not justify the cases; they do not say how the findings corroborate theories or support this or that middle-range model (for a review of these problems in the field of European Studies, see Exadaktylos and Radaelli, 2009). These are the publications that are most likely to be found deficient by other authors working in the field, and in consequence will gather few citations.

We also have direct experience of editing journals and special issues of them. Our impression is that reviewers tend to wear their research design spectacles

---

[6]The effects of trade-offs are discussed in a very important volume titled *Rethinking Social Inquiry: Diverse Tools, Shared Standards* that has now been published in two editions (Brady and Collier, 2004, 2010).

when they peer-review papers, so it is becoming increasingly hard to neglect this aspect of research. It is better to be explicit about research design choices and trade-offs than to be accused by a reviewer of having made the wrong implicit choice.

This brings us to the question of what research design is. There are different answers, of course, but it is useful to concentrate on a minimalist answer and a more elaborate response. Basically, social science research is a map of reality. It is not reality itself. Indeed, we want a map precisely because it helps us to understand some elements of reality that we need to understand – for example, because we need to travel from Golders Green to Stockwell on the London Underground. All studies contain bias, the most classic bias being about measuring reality with indicators – even the best indicator will capture only a dimension of the rich fabric that makes up reality.

Research design – this is the minimalistic definition – is a set of decisions we take in order to reduce or control bias. We like this definition because it is humble. It does not say that research design cooks the perfect dish. It only controls for, and hopefully contains, bias. However, it does not say much about the specific dimensions of research design. It is also true that bias is only one dimension of a research project. This is why we turn to more textured definitions. For John Creswell (2008: 3), author of an influential textbook on the subject, research designs are 'plans and the procedures for research that span the decisions from broad assumptions to detailed methods of data collection and analysis'. Creswell talks about three broad families of research designs: qualitative, quantitative, and mixed-methods – though in so doing arguably does not differentiate sufficiently between 'design' and 'methods'.

Broadly speaking, we follow John Gerring (2001) and identify the following elements of research design:

- Theoretical framework
- Concept formation
- Types of propositions, such as generalizations, classifications, predictions, and causal propositions
- Research questions
- Causality, especially using evidence to draw causal inference
- Selection of cases
- Variables
- Explanation (what is the type of explanation we are seeking with a research project, an article?, etc.)
- Mechanisms
- Methods

Today, it is indispensable to add ethics to Gerring's list. In several countries, social science funding councils have their own ethical requirements that grant-holders have to comply with. To illustrate, ethical issues arise around the following: rights of those who participate in our research projects, professional integrity, legitimacy of data, safety and risk. Researchers have obligations to people who come to be involved in the research project (as informants, interviewees, subjects of experiments). But they also have obligations to themselves and their research associates, in terms of distress in response to participant's disclosures, physical intimidation, and antagonism from authorities in foreign countries.

Another important element is the communication strategy. As will be explained in the final chapter, we write research for different audiences, in different contexts. We have to be aware that when we write for our university's press office, we are addressing an audience that is not generally able to discern the difference between a statistical test and fully fledged proof of causation. When we communicate to policy-makers there is often more interest in 'what should be done' than in how our findings were generated. Some of us also communicate findings during the research project via Twitter, Facebook, websites, blogs and podcasts. This is where our communication strategy intersects with ethical issues: in a short post to a blog on a political issue it may be difficult to spend time separating our findings from the more general opinion we have on the issue, but it is indispensable. When we talk to the media it is vital to distinguish what 'we think' from what we actually found in our research project.

One word on the status of methods in research design is now in order. While some students still ask for 'more training on the methods' at the beginning of the academic year, and they certainly have a point, we see methods at the end of the research design choices. This is because the decision to go for one method rather than another is informed by previous thinking about cases, variables, mechanisms and, in a deeper sense, explanation and the type of causality we wish to establish. We do not assign a chapter to each of these elements of research design, but they will be our fellow-travellers throughout the book. To illustrate, we will return to causality in different chapters. Given that we are interested in shop-floor practice, we take seriously the notion that researchers move back and forth between the various elements of research design. Becker (1998) argues that researchers are hectic travellers moving back and forth between their imageries, the cases they use, the concepts they employ, and logic. Some order is needed – as mentioned, one cannot choose the cases before everything else. But the research process is a process of iteration and discovery. It is also a process of constantly redrafting – writing 'yet another draft' is intrinsically connected to the process of scientific discovery (for the presentation of this argument, see Booth et al., 2008).

Two other questions are in our view connected to research design, although they are not design criteria in the sense of Gerring (2001). We call them the *so what* and *who cares* questions. We often speak to people who are in the early stages of their research project or doctoral students saying that they feel very strongly about a given topic. They want to study something that is subjectively important for them. We have heard students asking to write a PhD on a directive of the European Union, or on why their country has not embraced certain tools of the new public management. These subjective motivations fuel the research project. But the *so what* question alerts us to the fact that projects must contribute to a specific field in our disciplines. Thus, a given directive may or may not be the right focus for a project. It may be if, for example, the project is about the quality of law-making in the European Union or an ethnographic study of how officers evoke roles in their daily management of proposals. Colleagues will be interested in the project not because it is a well-documented study of a directive (often journalistic sources and websites will most likely provide more details on this than academic articles) but because it contributes to the field of legislative studies or is about bureaucratic roles in supranational settings such as the European Commission.

The same happens when we try to publish our findings at the end of a project. It is important to report on our substantive empirical findings, but we also have to convince our colleagues in our discipline: why should they cite our findings? Why should a good journal publish our research on case A and not someone else's paper on case B? How do our findings help colleagues – who are not engaged with the empirical details of our study but are working on common puzzles in a given field of the discipline? How does our work fare in terms of the quality standards shared by the discipline, or at least by the major journals?

The *who cares* question is difficult to handle. We do not offer any predetermined answers. We have already mentioned that for most of us an idea (at least) or, better, a plan of how we want to communicate our findings is a component of design. If we plan to communicate, then we expect someone out there to care about our findings. In some countries, however, researchers have to show that public funding of the social sciences leads to findings that can be utilized for reasons other than the training of a new generation of academics – or 'the production of paper by means of paper', as cynical observers are fond of saying by way of paraphrasing the title of the economist Piero Sraffa's (1960) book, *Production of Commodities by Means of Commodities*. In the UK, the Research Excellence Exercise, a major exercise that determines the level of public funding for individual universities and departments, has an explicit emphasis on the 'impact' of research (in the social sciences, but also in the humanities, arts and natural sciences). Universities have to demonstrate with case studies that their research has produced observable impacts if they want their research to be funded by the taxpayer.

True, the range of what we could explore has no limits. There are millions of things we do not know in the social sciences. The unknowns vastly overwhelm the knowns. When we propose to study something we do not yet know about, we can do that for reasons internal to our field (*so what*) but we may also wish to think about the relevance or topicality of our research choice. It is easy to find an answer to *who cares* if the project is in public management, the transplantation of legal constructs such as contracts from one country to others, and so on, but less so if we are trying to answer some fundamental questions about learning, reflexivity in law, and the types of discourses in bureaucratic representations. Yet in the end if the fundamental questions are answered properly, many more people and organizations will care – precisely because fundamental 'answers' are applicable to many different domains.

What looks like a rather curious and abstract type of inquiry, such as finding the mechanisms that lead people to free-ride on the funding and provision of public goods, scores high in terms of *who cares* because there are thousands of situations in which the free-riding syndrome operates. In short, we find it difficult to believe that a good piece of social science research is not relevant to anybody, except the few people in the world who can use the paper to train the next generations of academics on an esoteric topic. In the end, questions about external impact and *who cares* in general are contingent on the type of professional researcher one wants to be.

The social sciences: an autonomous field of knowledge

It is intrinsically difficult to speak of 'results' in the social sciences, at least in some disciplines such as international relations or comparative politics, and perhaps less so in social psychology, public policy analysis, and education. This is why researchers often talk about their 'evidence' rather than 'results' – arguably an indication of how they feel about the possible usage of their findings outside academia. There is also a lively debate about what constitutes an explanation in the social sciences, with different schools of thought, particularly those who argue for interpretivist approaches as alternatives to 'explanatory' approaches. Hedström (2005), among others, reminds us that research arguments we commonly refer to as 'explanations' (no matter how interpretivist we are) are after all truths (or 'statements', if you prefer) about subjects (actors, political parties, movements, and so on), because of reasons, based on evidence. Here we have the holy trinity of social scientific explanation, namely, subject-related truths or statements, reasons and evidence. On this basis, we can distinguish between explanatory arguments, covering-law explanations, statistical generalizations, mechanism-based explanations and, perhaps, mechanism-based generalizations. Explanatory arguments are explanations of certain facts, because of reasons, based on evidence. When we have an explanation of facts in terms of laws we have a covering-law explanation. In statistical world views, there is an explanation of a dependent variable because of middle-range theorizations, based on data. A mechanism-based explanation is concerned with cases, often events, in terms of theorized mechanisms, based on conditions and occurrences (that is, facts). Finally, the mechanism-based generalization is a generalizing statement we make about processes, in terms of theorized mechanisms, based on explanations of cases.

So far, we have avoided solemn declarations about what the social sciences are or should be. Instead, we have tried to illuminate the corner of the social science in which we operate as researchers in our daily professional life. No matter how wide our angle of observation is, we cannot claim to represent in a single volume all the traditions in the profession today. Neither it is up to us to lecture on what the social sciences ought to be. What we aim for in this volume is a coherent vision of the social sciences, certainly not the only vision that exists in the current debate, but a coherent one. This is our way of handling the trade-off between being ecumenical and being coherent, without running into the problem of Balkanization we mentioned earlier. The problem with saying that there are myriad approaches to explanation and to the very definition of the social sciences is that we cannot establish why one paper should be more useful or relevant to the people out there than another: we can only say 'it depends on your research tradition'. Remember that we are pluralists, but we are not saying that pretty much anything goes! If we accept incommensurability among the strands and traditions, we end up with a position where we have nothing to offer in terms of addressing the *who cares* question – as Gerring (2001) rightly observes.

To be more explicit and to summarize, we do not believe that the social sciences are just a (perhaps poor) cousin of the natural sciences. Neither do we believe that the social sciences are yet another branch of the humanities. Instead, they exist because they are neither the humanities nor the natural–physical sciences, and cannot be reduced to 'something else'.

In the domain of research design, questions of ontology and epistemology over which first-year doctoral students regularly agonize are not a priority. Philosophy of science is a preliminary step but it does not answer the key questions of research design. Ontological puzzles should liberate researchers, not paralyse them. We cannot simply state 'I am an objectivist in epistemology' to know how exactly we design a project on peace-building missions; we can only say that our epistemology will guide us towards some types of questions rather than others. Thus, we argue that research design is not predominantly about epistemology: indeed, we have two different terms in our vocabulary, 'research design' and 'epistemology'!

Arguably, it all depends on the perspective one adopts. We are not interested in how social scientists talk about their research but in how they 'do' their research, that is, as we said earlier, in the shop-floor practice. Studies of scientists at work (Latour and Woolgar, 1979) have revealed that scientists talk about their research in formal language that has little to do with their shop-floor practice, that is, what they really do. We suspect that a similar kind of hypocrisy affects social scientists, too. While handbooks used in doctoral training in countries such as the UK suggest that the research process is informed by theoretical discussions about structure and agency, ontology and epistemology, and the like (Marsh and Stoker, 2010), those who draft applications for funding and carry out successful projects deal with a completely different set of intellectual problems (as argued by Becker, 1998: 5).

What are the social sciences, then? In the end, we agree with Gerring's (2001: xv) proposition that social scientists study human action and relationships 'in a systematic, rigorous, evidence-based, generalising, non-subjective and cumulative fashion'. What is systematic and rigorous depends on intersubjective understandings among a community of professionals, that is, the 'shared standards' of Brady and Collier (2010). The role of evidence distinguishes the vast majority of social scientific projects from philosophical investigations, with the exception of modellers (like game theorists) and some types of political theorist concerned with the history of ideas (although these projects do make use of their own textual evidence to relate a body of work to the intellectual climate of an era, for example). The generalizing fashion indicates that individual cases, personal narratives, oral accounts do matter, but because they contribute to more general conjectures about people, or some political parties, communities, schools, cities and so on.

This is not to be taken as primitive positivism – we all know that we are studying social behaviour that responds to the fact of being observed. But, first of all, this happens only with some treatments (such as a negative income tax administered in a region of the country, to which citizens respond by calculating the likely policy effects of their responses[7]), not with others – a political system does not respond to the fact of being observed via panel data of electoral results across years and constituencies. Second, 'non-subjective' means that precisely because we all know there is bias in our observations, we can use validity and reliability tests – which tells us whether our measure really reports on what is being measured or on something else, and whether two different researchers would come to the same value of the measure if they were to use it independently. Thus, we are

---

[7]Citizens who know they are part of a negative income tax experiment may react by using the additional disposable income made available by the negative tax to invest in education for their children. Once the experiment and the observers are gone, however, they may spend the money on drink! This is called the Hawthorne effect (after Hawthorne Works, near Chicago, where experiments on factory workers were carried out between 1924 and 1932), and it is a classic source of observation bias.

back in research design. For us, research design is a device to control for bias and an attempt to reduce it in a (definitively) disenchanted, sceptical world of tough peer reviewers and journals where it is hard to publish.

Organization of the volume

In the next chapter we turn to concepts and categories. What are the constructs through which we 'think' our objects of analysis? How do we create concepts? How do they differ? We start from a simple, yet useful, benchmark for conceptual analysis and then explore trade-offs and violations of the conditions behind the benchmark. Concepts have to be organized. Consequently, we introduce typologies as a tool for conceptual analysis (and explanation, thus establishing the link between concept formation and explanation). Specifically on explanation, we go through the so-called bathtub to show how concepts at different levels can be connected in an explanatory social scientific model.

In Chapter 3 we introduce the main theories of causation and the main strategies of causal analysis in the social sciences. The clarification of these conceptual foundations is the first step in making informed decisions about how to conduct a research project. The chapter shows that there is no general consensus about the definition of causal arguments, and there is no stable agreement on the methodologies of causal explanation. The different existing approaches to causal analysis should be recognized so that this diversity can be handled in a proficient way. There are four main conceptual approaches to causal analysis: regularity, probabilistic, counterfactual and manipulative. It follows that different strategies of causal analysis in empirical research follow different research goals and types of data: experiments, comparative case studies, statistical analysis, process analysis and set-relations analysis. Methodological pluralism is useful for improving causal analysis and to provide the right answers to distinct research questions. In fact, empirical research has already gone beyond the sharp divide between 'qualitativists' and 'quantitativists'. Social scientists tend to think in an integrated way about data analysis. Qualitative and quantitative techniques are frequently combined. What is more, recent advances in social science methodology demonstrate that different methods can be not only juxtaposed but also integrated in a coherent theoretical and empirical analytical framework.

In Chapter 4 we turn to statistical research designs for causal inference. The key to these approaches is the identification or construction of comparable treatment and control groups. For example, if we are interested in the effects of quotas on women's representation in parliament, the ideal set-up is one in which we can compare two groups of countries (or other units) which are similar in all respects except that in one countries have quotas and in the other they do not.

Setting aside practical and ethical constraints (see the above discussion on ethics), the best way to enable such a comparison is through 'randomization', that is, the randomized assignment of treatment (quotas) to units. This feature is the hallmark of experiments. In experiments proper, randomization is undertaken by researchers themselves, whereas if it happens thanks to circumstances outside researchers' control we speak of quasi-experiments. Both have been used with increased frequency in the social sciences. Because they rely on statistical techniques, these research designs obviously have a strong quantitative component. However, successful experiments and quasi-experiments usually require important qualitative information. For instance, extensive fieldwork similar to that of typical qualitative case studies is carried out in the context of certain types of experiments, while quasi-experiments often need archival work and other types of qualitative research to access data and back up the assumption that the study actually has the characteristics of an experiment. Thus, the usual quantitative–qualitative dichotomy is of limited use here – back to one of the key themes of this book! Like any other approach, statistical research designs for causal inference involve trade-offs. Experiments and quasi-experiments ensure internal validity (the causal relationship can be measured precisely in the sample) but have problems of external validity (to what extent can the findings be generalized?). Moreover, the strict requirements of these designs may lead researchers to focus on narrow, tractable questions at the expenses of big, complex problems.

In Chapter 5 we invite you to reflect with us on time. Temporality is a foundational concept for causal analysis because causal relationships unfold over time and become observable only after a certain lapse of time. Above all, time is a crucial dimension of variation for empirical research. Time-related variables can be studied in different ways. Examples are historical case studies, descriptive statistics, simulations and the analysis of sequences. In this chapter you learn how to connect specific research goals about temporality to appropriate research designs and to methods to operationalize it. For instance, psychologists may want to study the effect of psychological therapies and treatments on the duration of depressive episodes; economists may want to assess abnormal fluctuations in stock market returns and possibly make predictions on future variations of stock prices; lawyers may try to explain the variation in the duration of civil and criminal trials in different jurisdictions; sociologists may seek to compare the family–career balance of a cohort of respondents over time; political scientists may want to interpret the persistence of social welfare policies in advanced democracies in a context of economic globalization. It is thus possible to examine the duration of social phenomena with historical or simulative methods. The description and the analysis of a tendency make it possible to characterize the overall trend of social phenomena and unexpected deviations and anomalies. Other research designs can operationalize the causal effect of the temporal ordering of events or the impact of the transitions from one social state to another. Finally, the concept of path dependence allows us to make sense of the stability and inertia of social phenomena.

Chapter 6 opens the door to the world of heterogeneity, that is, the fact that social phenomena present dissimilar features, behave differently from each other and constitute diverse classes of things. In many cases social phenomena are deeply heterogeneous at many levels of scale, and you may be interested precisely in exploring these levels to make sense of this heterogeneity. You first encounter heterogeneity across individuals or social groups. Individuals vary in their socio-economic status, motives, ideational frameworks, emotions and behaviour. Similarly, social groups can display different degrees of internal and external heterogeneity as regards their composition, function, role and resources. Second, you find the heterogeneity of causal relations. Social phenomena are commonly the result of a combination of conditions that is highly contingent. The explanations of social phenomena are also frequently equifinal, that is, a different set of factors may explain the same outcome. Third, there is heterogeneity in the particular cases that you have examined. In fact, some 'special' features may be discovered within the categories of things and events that are investigated, such as students, organizations, cities, religions, democracies and social movements. This chapter presents research strategies and methods for examining these different forms of heterogeneity. Different approaches exist for grouping variables and for the examination of the variation between and among samples. Complex causation can be operationalized with comparative configurational methods, namely with qualitative comparative analysis (QCA). Case selection techniques for the investigation of special cases conclude the chapter.

Chapter 7 takes you through interdependence. Interdependence is a central feature of the social world. It has been studied in most social science disciplines, such as sociology, political science, international relations, public policy analysis, communication and economics. Many questions are related to this topic. For instance, is someone more likely to give up smoking if many of his or her friends are or have become non-smokers? Are sub-national units more likely to adopt a policy if it has been successful elsewhere in the country? To what extent are states influenced by other states with which they compete for trade or foreign direct investment, or which participate in the same international organizations? Social network analysis is a first way to study these questions. It is a method that allows a precise description of the connections that exist between units and can be combined with various research designs. For instance, it can be used to construct 'connectivity matrices' that are employed in quantitative approaches such as spatial regression. Another quantitative approach to interdependence is dyadic analysis, in which units of analysis are pairs of units. This approach allows us to focus directly on the connections between units, such as whether they share a border or a language. Quantitative research designs offer quite powerful ways to measure interdependence, but usually they are less appropriate when it comes to identifying the precise nature of interdependence. Qualitative approaches have the opposite characteristics. They cannot demonstrate conclusively that interdependence is a general pattern, but they can describe precisely how it operates in individual cases. A general problem in the analysis of interdependence is 'homophily', namely, the fact that stronger contacts tend to be established among units that are more similar. Therefore, it is quite difficult to establish whether units become more alike because they are connected, or become more connected because they are alike. However, ignoring the problem of interdependence is certainly no better a solution than analysing it with the best tools that we currently have, even though they are imperfect.

Finally, in Chapter 8 we reflect on what we have learned. The volume follows a pattern of logic from concepts to interdependence, but you may wish simply to read the individual chapters you feel are closer to your research interest and motivation.

Checklist

- The craft of research is about tying claims, arguments and evidence.
- Research design is about responsibility, choice, and trade-offs.
- A design is a plan covering theory, concept formation, types of propositions we wish to establish, research questions, a given approach to causality, case selection, variables, mechanisms, type of explanation, and methods.
- Ethics and communication plans are components of research design.
- Research design is concerned with identifying and controlling bias.
- Strong research projects address the questions *so what* and *who cares.*
- Pluralism does not mean incommensurability and sectarian thinking.
- The social sciences are neither a branch of the humanities nor a strand of natural sciences. They have an autonomous paradigm, internally varied but different from the paradigms of humanities and natural sciences.

 ## Questions

1 Why do you think you are a social scientist?
2 Are you worried about bias in your project? Where can bias come from?
3 What do you plan to write about research design in your project?
4 What is the relationship between the different components of research design?
5 What do you plan to do to address bias in your project?
6 Can you persuade your reader (or funding body) that your project will survive the *who cares* and *so what* tests?

7   Illustrate how your project will effectively exercise responsibility, choice and address trade-offs.
8   Write a 200-word press release about your new project: 'Today, Dr X (you!) has kicked off a new research project on …'
9   How have you coped with ethical issues in your previous projects? Did you learn any lesson from the experience?
10 Do you plan to communicate during the research project, and, if so, how?

▮▮ Further reading ▮

Becker, H.S. (1998) *Tricks of the Trade: How to Think about Your Research While You're Doing It*. Chicago: University of Chicago Press.
Booth, W.C., Colomb, G.C. and Williams, J.M. (2008) *The Craft of Research*, 3rd edn. Chicago: University of Chicago Press.
Brady, H.E. and Collier, D. (eds) (2010) *Rethinking Social Inquiry: Diverse Tools, Shared Standards*, 2nd edn. Lanham, MD: Rowman and Littlefield.
Creswell, J.W. (2008). *Research Design: Qualitative, Quantitative and Mixed-Method Approaches*, 3rd paperback edn. London: Sage.
Gerring, J. (2001) *Social Science Methodology: A Criterial Framework*. Cambridge: Cambridge University Press.

TWO

Conceptual analysis

Introduction

Without concepts, we would have only specific statements of fact. These statements would apply to particular countries, or people, or schools, or public organizations. They would not travel. They would not enable us to develop middle-range models and theories. Rather than statements of fact, we need 'generalized statements about whole classes of phenomena' (Becker, 1998: 109). We need concepts that travel (Sartori, 1970, 1991). This is particularly important if we are concerned with comparative research. But it is a general feature of the social sciences that we prefer concepts that are valid beyond the individual example or the single statement of fact.

This brings us immediately to the trade-off between idiographic studies and nomothetic sciences.[1] Idiographic research digs deep into the single case to understand it, without the aim of making generalizations. By contrast, a nomothetic approach has the aim of making at least some kinds of generalization, beyond the statement of fact. In turn, generalization may be limited to a set of historical cases or a family of countries. Our knowledge in the social sciences is often bound or limited to a given context; in some cases it can even be an individual organization or a neighbourhood of a city. Yet the way a social scientist looks at the individual case is informed by concepts that travel beyond the case under examination.

---

[1]'Nomothetic' comes from a Greek word meaning law (*nomos*), hence it is connected to a vision of scientific enterprise as the construction of generalizations. By contrast, the Greek word *idios* means one's own, private. For a discussion of the tension between the two in the field of psychology, see Franck (1982).

Social science concepts are developed either by observing a large class of events or cases (for example, the concept of political culture arose out of the analysis of cross-country attitudes towards government, parties and the political system) or by drilling down into intuitions about 'what is going on' in a given episode or event. An ethnographer immersed in the description of a ceremony may come up with a new conjecture about the social mechanism at work. In 1967, Barney Glaser and Anselm Strauss proposed to create sociological concepts from the data rather than developing them deductively, from abstraction – this is part of their vision of 'grounded theory'. An example is the concept of 'chronic pain': it is better to extract the meaning of this concept from people's private experience rather than from an abstraction (Strauss and Corbin, 1997, chapter 1). Today, grounded theory is used in accounting, education, nursing, social work and, of course, sociology.

Concepts are adopted by a community of social scientists because they travel – either from the large class of events to a new case (imagine a researcher using the general concept of political culture and then applying it to a newly formed democracy) or from the ethnographic study to another class of projects on symbols and ceremonies. Grounded theory, for example, draws on in-depth comparison (Strauss and Corbin, 1997, provides a useful reader).

Both approaches (intuition from an episode or a large class of events) have advantages in terms of innovation in social scientific research. Yet typically, albeit not uniquely and with variation across fields as diverse as social psychology, political science and ethno-methodology, social scientists work with context-bound generalizations, often of a probabilistic nature. Thus, there is an important distinction between context-bound generalizations and law-like generalizations in the natural sciences. Gravitation laws are not valid everywhere (as shown by astronauts walking on the moon) but certainly they are more similar to general law-like statements of the type 'if X happens … then Y will happen' than any social science law (which are most likely to work only in some systems, for example societies with universal suffrage and competitive elections, but not totalitarian systems, and only at certain times, such as after World War II but not before).

In this chapter you will learn about conceptual analysis. At the outset, we stress that concepts are not simply labels we need to describe events – this is the conventional, ordinary meaning of concepts. In the second section we shall see how this has a limited role to play in the nominalistic view of social science concepts. We may say 'what do you mean when you say you do not understand' to elicit more information about the learning process of a friend who looks puzzled by what we just said. In the social sciences, to devise, define and utilize concepts is a special form of analysis. So, to press this point, it would be limiting to think of concepts as 'all the definitions we need at the beginning of a research paper'.

Concept formation is *analysis* within the research process, not before or above it. In the third section we explain the benchmarks used for classification, and introduce the notion of the ladder of abstraction to move among conceptual categories. This benchmark, however, needs to be extended and modified to cope with the cases of radial concepts and family resemblances (fourth section). In the fifth section we connect concepts to explanation, and briefly conclude in the final section. Throughout the chapter, we shed light on trade-offs and choices that give shape to our research projects, and discuss their pros and cons.

Concepts and categorical analysis[2]

What are concepts? Why do we need them? How do they differ? There are different answers to these questions, pointing to trade-offs and explicit choices that researchers have to make and explain to their peers and readers.

Let us start with the first question. At one extreme we find nominalist positions, at the other realistic understandings of what concepts are. For a nominalist, concepts are just labels that scholars need to communicate – more or less as in ordinary language. As Gary Goertz (2006a: 4) says in his magisterial work on social science concepts, the nominalist view draws on semantics: meanings are not intrinsically connected to empirical evidence, but vary depending on our lenses and interpretation. If this view is taken to its extreme yet logical consequences – Goertz (2006a: 4) goes on – we end up in (thinking of Lewis Carroll's *Through the Looking-Glass*) the Red Queen's camp 'on the issue of meaning and what determines it'. It is fair to recognize that in some areas of research, meaning will always play a role, albeit that perhaps most of us would not like to transform the social sciences into a context of Red Queens!

To illustrate, international organizations have invested in programmes for 'high-quality regulation' since around 1990. But this is a tricky concept. It blends a noun (regulation) with an adjective (quality) (we shall return to concepts with adjectives later). Indeed, the meaning of regulatory quality is contested (Radaelli, 2005). Regulatory quality means one thing to a trade union leader and another thing to an advocate of the unfettered forces of global capitalism. Put differently, it depends on whether one interprets quality as efficiency, conformity to rules, consensus, protection from risk, or participation – or combinations of these. Clearly, there are different rationales for regulation. Consequently, different stakeholders, even different social scientists, will most likely not agree on a single rationale. Although an extreme nominalistic position is not acceptable

---

[2]Following Collier and Mahon (1993: fn. 1) we treat concepts and categories as similar.

unless we want to turn the social sciences into the Tower of Babel, in some fields researchers accept that concepts depend in crucial ways on interpretation. When this happens, we suggest maximum transparency and explicit references to the rationales embraced by a researcher in a given project.

The other choice on this trade-off has become popular in the methodological discussion in political science and sociology (Becker, 1998; Brady and Collier, 2010). We can call it the realistic perspective on concepts, categories and definitions (Goertz, 2006a: 5). According to Howard Becker (1998: 128), 'concepts are not just ideas, or speculations, or matters of definition. In fact, concepts are empirical generalizations, which need to be tested and refined on the basis of empirical research results – that is, of knowledge of the world'. Thus Becker, like most social scientists, links concepts to evidence. Concepts are not produced somewhere in the mind of the researchers; they arise out of, and are in constant dialogue with, empirical research. For a nominalist, a concept is never right or wrong since definitions come from interpretive lenses and concepts are a matter of semantics. For Becker and other 'realists', in contrast, a concept is so anchored to evidence that can be tested. Indeed, a concept should be refined (we are using Becker's words) if an empirical test shows that the initial definition was flawed.

Goertz has widened the realist perspective by adding two other categories to our understanding of concepts. He proposes a view of concepts that is ontological and causal as well as realist. According to Goertz (2006a: 5), 'concepts are theories about ontology: they are theories about the fundamental constitutive elements of a phenomenon'. The concepts of democracy and the welfare state are ontological because they tell us what reality is. Or, to put it differently, a democracy *is* what the concepts say about this political reality. 'To *be* a welfare state *is* to provide these goods and services' (Goertz, 2006a: 5; emphasis in original). Hence, 'ontological' here refers to what constitutes a phenomenon or a portion of reality we are interested in. In turn, ontological attributes (what democracy *is*, to continue with the example) play a key role in causal hypotheses originating in theories. It is because of certain causal hypotheses we embed in our concept of democracy (or the concept of welfare state, war, conflict and so on) that we can venture into explanation. It follows that (from this perspective) the constitutive attributes of a concept are selected because they have a causal function in explanation. When we follow this approach, we join concepts to theories and explanation rather than leaving them in a semantic limbo. It is for this reason that the realist, ontological and causal perspective has become so popular in recent years among qualitative and quantitative sociologists and political scientists. It also sheds light on an important principle, namely, that *concept formation comes before measurement.*

The notion that concept formation is preliminary to measurement (Brady and Collier, 2010; Sartori, 1970) seems almost common sense: why on earth would we jump to measurement without having thought about the concepts? We need to establish what we are interested in and what we are not interested in at the start of a project. We often begin research projects by collating some evidence, but evidence without categories does not speak. Quite often we can establish only what we do not want to know. Yet this is a good starting point. We can assert that X does not interest us because we have a fairly good idea of what would interest us: 'Naming the object of interest is the beginning of conceptualization' (Becker, 1998: 122). The necessary priority of concept formation over measurement provides a good answer to the second question we posed at the beginning of this section, that is, why we need concepts: we need them so that we can 'do' our job of looking at evidence and reducing bias in our measurement. In fact, flawed concepts produce artefacts and bias (Becker, 1998).

However, there are different situations in which this principle of 'concepts first' is violated. Sometimes there is only a pragmatic reason: in a given research project, one cannot invest equal time in measurement and concept formation. For pragmatic reasons (such as a funding body interested in generating new data on migration, addiction, crime or other pressing social problems), researchers give priority to measurement – thus importing possible sources of bias into their analysis of what constitutes a migrant, an addict, or a crime. Or, yet again pragmatically, in fields where much conceptual work has already been undertaken, most researchers will engage in measurement until someone comes up with a critical analysis of the concepts in use and proposes something radically new. Put differently, the preference for either conceptual analysis or measurement may be the result of the maturity of the field – we expect new, emerging fields to be mostly dedicated to conceptual work, although the reality of the sociology of social sciences is often messy, and there are fields where measurement has led to deep interrogations about concepts that did not exist in the first place.

In other circumstances, for example because of the ambiguities of a given theoretical framework and the qualitative nature of your project, you may want to go for grounded theory and start from your empirical material to develop concepts through appropriate coding procedures (Glaser and Strauss, 1967; Strauss and Corbin, 1997). Or you may be facing a huge gap between the concept you plan to work with and the available measures. For several years, researchers in education and psychology have grappled with highly abstract concepts such as 'intelligence' or 'personality' (Goertz, 2006a: 14–15). On the one hand, these concepts are abstract and context-bound, meaning that 'intelligence' denotes different things across time, space and cultures. On the other hand, more often than not researchers cannot draw on sophisticated indicators. Although the application of neuroscience to social phenomena has made considerable progress in recent years, until recently we could not look into the brain and find indicators of what 'intelligence' or 'emotion' or other concepts might be. We could examine only the responses given by people to large-scale questionnaires. For these reasons, researchers in education and psychology tended first to consider the available indicators, and then develop measures of latent variables via factor analysis (Blalock, 1982, cited by Goertz, 2006a: 14; see also Chapter 6, this volume).

Factor analysis is a standard statistical technique that, by considering correlations among a set of indicators, produces variables and indexes. We can thus reduce a large number of indicators to a few variables, each made up of several indicators. Researchers then label these variables in ways that are reminiscent of concepts. For example, instead of defining high-quality regulation, one could examine a large data set of regulatory indicators across countries, extract variables via factor analysis, and then name the first dimension (the one that explains most of the variance) 'regulatory transparency', the second 'efficiency', and the third 'participation'. One would thus define the concept, albeit indirectly.

As mentioned, however, the factor-analytic approach is used with abstract conceptual problems, such as defining intelligence or the authoritarian personality. Becker (1998: 110) provides yet another interesting case by citing research on the concept of 'attitude'. He describes the process of determining indirectly what attitude means by using the term 'operationalization':

> Many researchers assumed that people had thoughts or dispositions or ideas (or something) – summarized as attitudes – inside them, waiting to be released by the appropriate stimulus or situation. What an attitude was wasn't clear. Scientists argued about the definition. But their inability to define an attitude didn't prevent them from inventing attitude measurement, a procedure in which people's answers to a long list of questions produced a number that 'measured' their attitude towards movies or foreigners or schools or political parties. (Becker, 1998: 110)

For operationalization to make sense, one must assume that indicators are linked to unmeasured concepts. But to do so one needs a causal model where the assumptions about indicators and concepts are explicit. Note, however, that in political science and sociology (especially if we follow Goertz) the core idea of the factor-analytic school is not valid (Goertz, 2006a: 15). There is something like 'intelligence' that causes the high scores on IQ tests. But competitive elections do not 'cause' democracy. They define an important aspect of what democracy *is*. Consequently, Goertz insists on the constitutive, ontological view of many social science concepts.

To recapitulate, we have introduced concepts as a fundamental organizing step in social research. To name something is to say what we are interested in. We need to qualify this by noting that some concepts are more mature or 'definitive' – they truly give us prescriptions about what to see. But, depending on the field, you may also encounter looser concepts that lack strong specification and attributes, but suggest directions along which to look. These, following Blumer (1954), are called sensitizing concepts. We have then introduced a trade-off between realist and nominalist perspectives, and illustrated the differences between measurement-driven approaches to highly abstract concepts and the more classic constitutive approach employed in political science and sociology.

We now introduce another important trade-off in concept formation. Should the conceptual category define our case? Or should we let the case(s) define the concept? Becker explains that:

> we let the category define the case by saying what we have studied is a case of x, let's say of bureaucracy or modernization or organization or any of the other common concepts we use to understand the social world. Doing that leads us (not necessarily, but often enough in practice) to think that everything that is important about the case is contained in what we know about the category. (Becker, 1998: 123)

Prima facie, the former approach – whereby the conceptual category defines the case – seems to have more leverage. It is intuitive to clarify categories at the outset, and then allocate each case to one of our conceptual boxes. Categories can be organized hierarchically, so to speak, from the more general (or basic) categories to the more specific (or secondary) categories. We do not want our research to be excessively idiographic, and most of us aspire to some nomothetic social sciences (to repeat, in the sense of enabling some context-bound generalizations). In consequence, there is a rationale for putting each case into a category defined prior to empirical analysis via a classificatory exercise. In turn, the generation of concepts draws on theoretical frameworks that are elaborated before measurement starts.

Adcock and Collier (2001) suggest four levels. At the more general level, we find the background concept. This is the broad range of meanings and understandings associated with a concept. To illustrate, a basic category such as 'Europeanization' covers a broad range of meanings, from the early routes of medieval pilgrimages that traced the first paths connecting European people of a common faith to the contemporary rise of a transnational public sphere in Europe – think of how Europeans debate the issues of migration, public scandals and public debt in different countries.

But communities of scholars tend to rely on narrower, more explicit meanings. To illustrate, when political scientists deal with Europeanization, they look at the effects of the European Union on domestic politics and public policy (Exadaktylos and Radaelli, 2012). This is what Adcock and Collier call a background concept – or the second level. Concepts like this are operationalized in social science projects – the third level. Operationalization means that these concepts generate measures and operational definitions to classify cases. The fourth level of analysis consists of the scores that individual cases generate. These are the values of individual cases, be it numerical or qualitative statements such as 'high' or 'less' (Adcock and Collier, 2001).

So far, so good. But as Becker (1998: 124) notes, this strategy 'comes at a price: we don't see and investigate those aspects of our case that weren't in the description of the category we started with'. This problem is compounded by sampling errors: if the original classification is too narrow we end up sampling the wrong cases. Let us see why this may happen. Becker recalls a famous episode in the history of sociology: Edwin Sutherland's presidential address to the American Sociological Association in 1940. Sutherland was concerned with the sociology of crime. At that time, research had converged on explanations of crime based on correlations between, on the one hand, age, race, broken homes and level of education, and, on the other, trials and imprisonment data. Sutherland attacked the socially approved prejudice that was embedded in the conventional concept of crime. Because the conventional concept of crime was based on the social stereotype of robberies, physical assaults and so on, the description of the concept was not equipped to capture white-collar crime. White-collar crimes are less often reported, for various reasons. They lead to imprisonment in fewer cases than do robberies – after all, the government wants white-collar criminals to stop tampering with the mail, not to send them to jail. Corporations manage to avoid criminal prosecution by settling cases within civil law (Becker, 1998: 118).

If the original definition of crime is not open to the full range of crimes, including white-collar crimes, we have a definitional artefact with flawed results. As Becker concludes:

> if you decided not to include the crimes rich people and corporations committed when you calculated your correlations, you guaranteed the result that crime was correlated with poverty and its accomplishments. Not because it really was, but because you were using a flawed concept, one that pretended to contain all members of a given class, but actually left out a large number of those members on the uninspected grounds of social prestige. You didn't have an empirical finding, you had a definitional artefact. (Becker, 1998: 117)

Thus, the strategy of letting the case define the concept is not necessarily weak – it is a trade-off. Indeed, we can imagine a researcher finding that banking regulations are manipulated in a way that makes it difficult for prosecutors to find out what happened – and the researcher would be right to use this case to build a category of 'crime'. The sample of cases would not be censored in this instance. Some interesting questions would be raised in the course of this research project, and some conventional wisdom would be challenged.

We can make the same point about cases defining concepts in a different way. Suppose you have gathered evidence. This evidence will always be specific:

it will be about implementation of some laws, or the quality of teaching in some schools, or trade among some nations, or decision-making processes in some organizations. A 'cases define concepts' researcher would take the evidence and ask the question: 'what is it that I have found, can I describe my evidence without using any of the identifying characteristics of the actual case?' For Becker, this is indeed one of the most useful tricks of the trade in the social science profession: he calls it 'Bernie Beck's trick after sociologist Bernard Beck (Becker, 1998: 126).

Yet another way to think about concepts on the basis of the cases – Becker argues – is to look at relations. The concepts we use in the social sciences are relational (Becker, 1998: 132). Once we have a case, we need to situate this case in the system of relations to which it belongs. Some systems may be cultural (for example, calculating abilities are more rewarded in some cultures than in others) or historical (each system of production tends to privilege some skills over others). Even a physical characteristic such as 'being tall' is contingent on age (one can be relatively 'tall' at 12 but become a person of average height later) and country (Becker, 1998: 133). The point about the relational qualities of concepts is actually valid whether we start from evidence or from abstract definitions: it is a general characteristic of social science concepts.

A benchmark for conceptual analysis...

As mentioned, the classic approach to conceptual analysis, at least in disciplines such as international relations and political science, is to build concepts from the more general down to the more specific. Giovanni Sartori (1970), drawing on the essential properties of logic, shows that this approach is exactly the same approach to classification *per genus et differentiam* used for centuries to classify animal species and plant varieties. 'To classify is to order a given universe into classes that are mutually exclusive and jointly exhaustive' (Sartori, 1991: 246).

Sartori coined the expression 'ladder of abstraction' to show how we can move up and down a classificatory scheme. The movements up and down the ladder are based on extension and intension. These are two fundamental properties of concepts. Intension denotes the features or properties of the concepts. Extension refers to the cases covered by the concept. Intension and extension are in inverse relation. If we build a concept with many properties, there will be few cases matching all the properties, and vice versa. Thus, there is a trade-off between extension and intension. A case of zero extension is the Weberian ideal type (Goertz, 2006a: 83). Bureaucracy is an ideal type. As Weber noted, empirical cases that match all the properties of an ideal-typical bureaucracy are hard to find. But this does not mean that bureaucracies do not exist; it simply means that given *n* features of an ideal-typical bureaucracy we will not find cases with value 1 on all the variables (Goertz, 2006a).

It is important to keep in mind the motivation that led Sartori to propose his ladder of abstraction. He was concerned with concepts that 'do not travel', as he put it: too many studies – he argued – are not truly comparative, but are based on characteristics of specific countries or contexts. We should instead use concepts that are not contingent on specific evidence. To exemplify, we would not like to start a study of French politics with a kind of ad hoc theory of the 'French political system'. We would prefer to start with concepts that define government, parliament, institutions, elections and the like in any contemporary political context (French or not) and then apply it to the case of France. This is not too far away from Bernie Beck's trick mentioned above, that is, describing a case without relying on the identifying characteristics of the specific sample or cases to hand.

The second motivation behind Sartori's approach was to avoid errors of classification. Degreeism is a case in point. Imagine you are looking at political regimes and find that democracies are regimes with variable degrees of civil liberties, rule of law, and regular elections with universal suffrage. You may end up classifying systems with low scores on civil liberties, rule of law and regular elections as democratic. This would stretch the concept of democracy where ordinary citizens would disagree with the social scientist's definition of case X as 'a democratic system'. To avoid this – Sartori argued – one has to start with a high-level concept of 'electoral regime' and then break it down into two different categories, one of which is 'democracy' and the other 'authoritarian regime'. Sartori illustrated this problem with the famous cat-dog example, which is worth quoting at length:

> Mr Doe is ready for his dissertation, but he must be original and must have, he is insistently told by his advisers, a hypothesis. His subject is the cat-dog (one cannot be original, nowadays, just with cats or just with dogs), and his hypothesis, after much prodding, is that all cat-dog emit the sound 'bow wow'. The adviser says 'interesting', and a foundation gives him $100,000 for world-wide research. Three years later Mr Doe shows up in great dismay and admits: many cat-dogs do emit the sound 'bow wow', but many do not – the hypothesis is disconfirmed. However, he says, I now have another hypothesis: all cat-dogs emit the noise 'meow meow'. Another three years go by, another $100,000 are dutifully spent in researching, and yet, once again, the hypothesis is not sustained: many cat-dogs do emit the noise 'meow meow' but many do not. In deep despair Mr Doe visits, in her cave, at dusk, the oracle of Delphi, who on that day had grown tired of making up sibylline responses. My friend, the oracle says, to you I shall speak the simple truth, which simply is that the cat-dog *does not exist.* (Sartori, 1991: 247)

Sartori went on to criticize the parochialism of those who end up with cat-dogs because of their narrow concepts – 'single-country studies *in vacuo*', in

Sartori's (1991: 247) words – and concept-stretching which ends up in ridicule, as in the cat-dog story. Pseudo-classes and mislabelling also generate cat-dogs. China, India and Mexico have for a long time been one-party states, but this concept collapses three entirely different regimes into a single animal – Sartori submitted that this is the cat-dog-bat! Pluralism can be stretched to the assertion that all countries contain some form of pluralism. But then propositions such as 'pluralism falls and stands with democracy' can no longer be tested (Sartori, 1991).

Majone (1980, 1996) added another item to the list of conceptual problems. This is the error of assuming that a higher-level unit necessarily has the properties of the lower-level units. Majone cited the example of the European Union. Although the European Union is constituted by states, it does not follow that it has the properties of a state. In fact, the member states have developed the functions of taxation and redistribution, while the European Union has not. When this type of conceptual error is taken for granted by a community of scholars, we have a pitfall (Majone, 1980). According to Majone, a pitfall, unlike a fallacy or a simple error, can be understood as:

> a conceptual error into which, because of its specious plausibility, people frequently and easily fall. It is 'the taking of a false logical path' that may lead the unwary to absurd conclusions, a hidden mistake capable of destroying the validity of an entire argument. (Majone, 1980: 7)

To avoid these problems – Sartori concluded – one has to follow basic Aristotelian logic in building classificatory schemes, respect the inverse rule between intension and extension when moving up and down the ladder of abstraction, and limit 'degreeism' by using mutually exclusive categories so that we can determine whether a system is a democracy or an authoritarian regime (a system is either a 'dog' or a 'cat', it cannot be both). To avoid concept stretching, researchers should not add properties to a concept – otherwise the dog becomes a cat-dog! Instead, they ought to move up the ladder towards concepts that, because they have fewer defining characteristics, fit a larger number of cases.

... and beyond the benchmark

Since 1990 or thereabouts, the approach that Sartori suggested has been redefined. For us, it is still a useful benchmark. However, by taking into consideration developments in the philosophy of language and the cognitive sciences, social scientists have identified types of concepts that, in different ways, do not follow Sartori's logic, or call for extensions and modifications.

One important extension concerns radial categories and diminished subtypes. Radial categories are well known to cognitive scientists. These categories do not fit Sartori's logic, based as it is on the notion that we differentiate a higher-level category into lower-level categories by adding to the common properties of, say, being a pet, the specific properties of either a cat or a dog, thus augmenting extension.

As Collier and Mahon (1993) explain, radial cases have a special relation with their higher-level concept. The authors observe that 'in the process of cognition, the central subcategory functions as a gestalt, in that it is constituted by a bundle of traits that are learned together, understood together, and most quickly recognized when found together' (Collier and Mahon, 1993: 848). In their example, the classic concept of dog follows the classic rules of a taxonomy. We have different types of dogs, but they all share the same basic attributes A, B and C (Figure 2.1). The attributes of the different types occur in addition to A, B, and C. So to have a spaniel we need the three core attributes of a dog (A, B and C) plus property E.

However, when we consider the category of mother, here conventionally defined as female, providing 50 per cent of the genetic make-up, giving birth to the child, providing nurturance and being married to father, we observe that the properties of the different mothers in Figure 2.1 are contained in the primary category rather than occurring 'in addition to' (as in the case of the dog types).

If now we substitute 'authoritarianism' for 'dog' and 'democracy' for 'mother', we can see the difference between classical and radial categories. Both populist and bureaucratic authoritarianism share properties of the higher-level type. They have additional properties that distinguish them and that are not contained in the primary category. In a sense, they behave like the dog types in Figure 2.1.

Democracies, in contrast, come in different types (think of liberal, participatory, popular and so on) whose differentiating properties are contained within the primary category – like the mother types in Figure 2.1. The consequences for conceptual travelling are not trivial. When we move to a broader set of cases in the discussion of bureaucratic and populist authoritarian regimes, we do so by dropping adjectives and moving up the ladder to 'authoritarianism'. This way we avoid concept stretching. When we move to a broader set of cases in radial categories, we add adjectives. As Goertz (2006a) explains, this is made by moving sideways. This violates the assumption Sartori made that in a taxonomy one can move only up and down the ladder.

In later work, Collier and Levitsky (1997) extended their discussion of radial categories to the substantive topic of 'diminished types'. Their motivation for diminished types is to account for types of democracy that are different from the classic parliamentary democracy. Instead of moving up and down the ladder, Collier and Levitsky move sideways and generate other types, such as the illiberal type of Guatemala (Figure 2.2). So, although Guatemala is not a democracy in

Classical catogory: Dog

Category	Components					
Primary Category							
Dog	A	B	C			
Secondary Categories							
Retriever	A	B	C	D		
Sheepdog	A	B	C		E	
Spaniel	A	B	C			F

Note: Differentiating characteristics of secondary categories are *in addition* to those of the primary category.

A, B, and C = Hypothetical set of general attributes of dogs
D, E, and F = Hypothetical attributes that differentiate specific types of dogs

Radial Category: Mother

Category	Components				
Primary Category					
Mother	A	B	C	D	E
Secondary Categories					
Genetic mother	A	B			
Birth mother	A		C		
Nurturing mother	A			D	
Step mother	A				E

Note: Differentiating characteristics of secondary categories are contained within the primary category.

A = Female
B = Provides 50% of genetic makeup
C = Gives birth to child
D = Provides nurturance
E = Married to father

Figure 2.1   Classical and radial categories

Source: Reprinted from Collier and Mahon (1993: 849)

the full sense of a parliamentary democracy like Britain and the USA, it is radially (so to speak) anchored to the concept of democracy. Note that in Figure 2.2 the dashed line shows that an illiberal democracy is something less than a democracy; it is in fact a diminished type.

The radial categories tend to have more extension than the original, primary category of democracy. This would never happen with classical categories. However, as Collier and Mahon (1993: 852) noted, 'this very flexibility [of radial categories] can lead to major scholarly disputes about whether the category fits the cases under study'. Indeed, one may wonder why we still relate 'illiberal democracies' to the concept of democracy and not to something else.

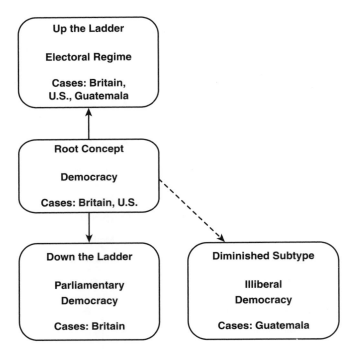

Figure 2.2 Diminished types

Source: Reprinted from Collier and Levitsky (1997: 439)

Goertz (2006a) provides a solution to this problem by noting that diminished types make more sense in a kind of horizontal continuum rather than in relation to the ladder of abstraction. Forget for a moment the whole ladder of abstraction. Concentrate on the definition of democracy. If the definition is logically correct – Goertz reasons – we conceptualize democracy as one pole of a continuum at whose opposite pole we find authoritarianism. An illiberal democracy is a case on the authoritarianism–democracy continuum where some core attributes of the 'democracy' pole are missing, such as civil liberties. If we also take out properties such as full and open contestation and competitive elections, we reach the other pole of the authoritarian regime. In short, for Goetz the whole discussion on diminished types has been trapped by the 'vertical' ladder metaphor but it should be situated on a horizontal continuum (Goertz, 2006a: 82). However, if we go back to the reason why Sartori proposed his dichotomous vertical taxonomy (either 'dog' or 'cat', otherwise go up one level and say 'pet'), Goertz's solution comes full circle: we started with a problem of degreeism, Sartori solved it with the ladder of abstraction, the diminished types created a new source of ambiguity, and Goertz suggested a continuum where individual political systems have some properties typical of an authoritarian regime and some properties of a

Cases	Distribution of Attributes					
A	1	2	3	4	5	
B	1	2	3	4		6
C	1	2	3		5	6
D	1	2		4	5	6
E	1		3	4	5	6
E		2	3	4	5	6

Figure 2.3 Family resemblance

* All cases have five of the six attributes, and each of the six cases lacks a different attribute.

Source: Adapted from Collier and Mahon (1993: 847).

democracy. We suspect that, for a 'pure' Sartorian at least, this may look like the reinvention of degreeism. The reality is that we have found yet another trade-off in building categories: we can reason vertically or use horizontal continua, provided that we are clear on how we take taxonomic steps and that we understand whether our categories are classical, radial, or, to introduce the new type, family resemblances.

Indeed, family resemblance, a phenomenon originally elaborated by Ludwig Wittgenstein, is quite common in the social sciences. As Becker (1998: 128) observes, the concepts that interest social scientists have multiple criteria. In a family resemblance case, however, the relationship among criteria is peculiar. In Figure 2.3, the cases from A to F have strong commonalities. Even visually, one can see they belong to the same family. Yet they do not have a single attribute (from 1 to 5) that is common to all cases from A to F. Thus it is impossible to follow the logic of the ladder of abstraction and say that there is a set of criteria common to all cases (the set defining the higher-level concept), which then differ among each other because of other attributes. If we follow Sartori, we have to conclude that the category binding together cases A to F does not exist, and should be abandoned (Collier and Mahon, 1993: 847). Yet dropping the category seems premature. Think of our use of the concept 'bureaucracy' in the social sciences: we observe organizations that resemble the ideal-typical case of the Weberian bureaucracy even if our specific cases do not have a single property in common. As Collier and Mahon argue, to see the category of bureaucracy one has to consider all the cases simultaneously. Categories are analytic constructs, after all; they are never a perfect description of a case. When we look at the members of a human family, we can see that together they form a family, although father and son may share some characteristics of the nose and the jaw while mother and daughter may both be very tall, and so on. To see these people as a family

does not mean that we are stretching a concept. The error of dropping a potentially useful category, according to Collier and Mahon (1993: 852), is avoided by:

> self-consciously thinking in terms of ideal types, by using a system-specific
> approach to applying categories in particular contexts, or by adopting other
> techniques that do not depend on the assumption that members of a category
> share a full set of defining attributes.

Organizing concepts

Concepts are the building blocks of research. But they have to be organized if they
are to provide explanation. In this section we consider the connection between
conceptual analysis and explanation. We have already seen that logic provides the
basic rules for organizing concepts, and devices such as the ladder of abstraction.

Plenty of work on typologies has been undertaken in the social sciences since
the 1950s at least (Lazarsfeld and Barton, 1951).[3] Colin Elman (2005) has linked
typological analysis to explanation. His model of explanatory typologies provides
some useful rules to pack and unpack concepts in taxonomies. His approach is
reminiscent of Sartori's ladder of abstraction, but it is more directly linked to the
explanatory aims of research. We can distinguish descriptive, classificatory and
explanatory purposes in the social sciences. Description revolves around the
question of what constitutes a type. Classification, in contrast, takes a country
like Guatemala or an organization such as a regulatory agency and raises the
question 'what is this a case of?' Finally, explanation is typically concerned
with questions such as 'if my theoretical expectations are correct, what should I
find in my evidence? And do I actually 'see' what I expect to observe, given my
theory and the observable implications I can draw from it?'

Thus, an explanatory typology draws on a pre-existing theory. Let us imagine
a simple classificatory scheme based on four cells in a matrix. In an explanatory
typology, the researcher draws on theory to generate the two variables that make
up the property space. For example, in a conceptual paper on learning in public
policy, Dunlop and Radaelli (2013) use theories of the policy process to generate
two dimensions, and build four types of learning around these dimensions. Their
two dimensions are the social certification of actors (such as whether a given actor
is seen as competent, trustworthy, and a reliable source of knowledge) and the level
of tractability of the policy problems – or level of uncertainty. This way, we map the
territory of learning in public policy into four cells of reflexivity, bargaining, learning via experts (the 'epistemic community' cell) and learning in a hierarchical or

---

[3]Lazarsfeld's early writings on typologies date from the 1930s.

	Low	High
Low	Reflexive learning	Epistemic learning
High	Learning through bargaining	Learning in the shadow of hierarchy

Problem tractability (rows: Low, High)

Certification of actors (columns: Low, High)

Figure 2.4 Mapping policy learning on two dimensions

Source: Dunlop and Radaelli (2013)

rule-bound context (Figure 2.4). Reflexive learning occurs when actors engage in truth-seeking communication and modify their preferences. In epistemic learning situations, the constellation of actors dealing with a given policy problem operates under conditions of uncertainty – but networks of experts with shared causal beliefs about policy and a common sense of direction (in short, an epistemic community) reduce uncertainty and make problems amenable to human action. Under 'bargaining' we find a given system of actors that uses negotiation as predominant mode of interaction. Learning is often a by-product of negotiation. Finally, learning can occur in hierarchical settings, where political institutions or courts issue instructions and regulations.

Elman adds that typologies can also be used to compress or expand the property space – an analytical move that was originally made by Lazarsfeld. An expansion of the property space transforms a given category into four categories. The procedure can indeed be repeated more than once if it is theoretically justifiable to dig deeper into a given category.

To continue with the example of learning, one can take the cell of epistemic communities, expand the property space, and consider different roles experts can play in public policy. Indeed, experts can act as 'hired guns' or 'teach' policy-makers in a more disinterested way. To expand the property space of the cell 'epistemic communities', Dunlop and Radaelli use theory yet again, this time theories of knowledge from adult education. The expansion generates the four shaded cells of Figure 2.5, replacing the single 'epistemic learning' cell of Figure 2.4.

Another way to organize concepts in order to provide explanations is the well-known bathtub put forward by sociologist James Coleman (1990). This is a device you may wish to use to explore relationships at different levels (macro and micro) in your research project.

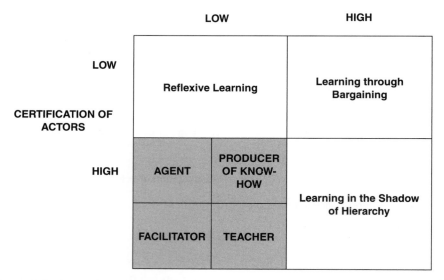

Figure 2.5 Expanding the property space in the 'epistemic learning' cell into four cells (shaded)

Source: Adapted from Dunlop and Radaelli (2013)

Typically, we find evidence at the level of relationships between variables measuring aggregate concepts. That would be the macro–macro relation in Figure 2.6. Imagine the classic pattern showing a relationship between economic variables and elections. It is almost a tenet of conventional wisdom that when the economy is growing, the incumbent government benefits electorally. To postulate a relation between two concepts such as economic growth and electoral success, however, is not to provide an explanation, even if there is a statistical correlation between the two variables. In Coleman's approach, once a macro–macro relation has been established, we need to explore the micro-foundations of the phenomenon that shows up in our statistics.[4] Why do people behave the way they do? Why do they reward the incumbent, for example? To investigate the micro-foundations, in this case at least, we need a theory of voting: not any theory of voting that predicts the behaviour observed in the data, but a particular theory of voting, especially

---

[4]The term 'micro-foundations' is popular in economics (where it refers to the link between macro-economic models and micro-economics) and in sociology. Generally speaking, micro-foundations are the relationships between an aggregate variable and the individual variables. Individual variables may refer to the single individual as a unit, or to organizations, states, parliaments and so on. The relationship between macro-phenomena and their micro-foundations sheds light on how individual behaviour has unintended and often inefficient consequences at the micro level. To illustrate with a famous example, individuals take individual decisions about where to live that seem efficient, but at the aggregate level the decisions may produce segregation. This phenomenon is also called 'emergence', that is, individual behaviour generates emergent properties at the macro level (Schelling, 1978).

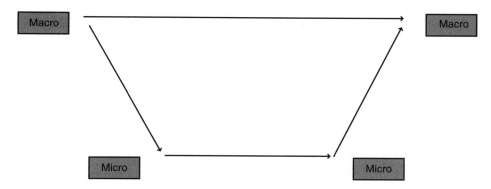

Figure 2.6 The bathtub

Source: Adapted from Coleman (1990)

a theory of economic voting, arguing that citizens (or crucial segments of the electorate such as the swing voters) vote on the basis of economic considerations rather than class, socio-economic cultures, habit or other variables. We then need to compose the micro–micro effects. The theory of voting is valid for an abstract, isolated individual. What about the relationship between individuals? Once we have theorized interaction among *n* individuals, we need to move back up in the bathtub, but this time we ride up towards the right of Figure 2.6. The link between micro and macro is about aggregation. How is behaviour aggregated in such a way to show up in electoral results? Why should something valid for the individual show up in macro-data about elections? We may need to add theoretical considerations about the structure of so-called popularity functions (Bellucci and Lewis-Beck, 2011) to explain this micro–macro linkage.

Conclusions

In this chapter you have learned about conceptual analysis. We have argued that concept formation comes before measurement, although in practice there are trade-offs between conceptual analysis and measurement in a single project. Nominalist and 'realist' notions of concepts diverge. Although there are rationales for one approach or the other, we found that realist, ontological and causal approaches to concepts are more useful in the social sciences. We use terms such as 'welfare state' and 'democracies' – to be a welfare state, we said, *is* to provide certain goods and services, hence the definition is ontological.

Logic provides the benchmark for conceptual classification. There is a trade-off between intension and extension, and movements up and down the ladder of abstraction follow rules that should avoid the problems of degreeism. Another important trade-off is that between letting the case describe the concept and using the concepts first and then finding and examining the cases.

This benchmark, however, needs to be critically discussed when we deal with radial concepts and family resemblances. The next step is to connect classification with explanation. One way to do this within conceptual analysis is to work with explanatory typologies, by expanding and compressing the property space. The bathtub reminds us that concepts perform at different levels, such as macro–macro relations, micro-foundations, and aggregation. To observe a statistical relationship between democracies and war is not to explain the origin of wars! We need to dig into the micro-foundations of war and explain how democracies relate to each other before we turn yet again to what happens, statistically speaking, to a group of democracies over time, that is, whether they go to war or not.

Checklist

- As a general rule, concept formation is a step preliminary to measurement. Grounded theory is an exception to this rule.
- Concepts can be examined at different levels: (a) background; (b) systematized; (c) operationalized and (d) measured on individual levels.
- Concepts that have reached maturity in a given field contain prescriptions of 'what we should see'; however, curiosity and innovation in social research also necessitate 'sensitizing concepts' (read Blumer, 1954).
- Standard concepts can be analysed in terms of their intention and extension.
- Radial categories are used to examine so-called diminished types, for example 'diminished' forms of democracy.
- Family resemblance is a special case of categorical analysis.
- Concepts can be usefully organized in classificatory schemes and typologies. Typologies may or may not be explanatory, depending on the presence or absence of causal logic.
- The so-called bathtub organizes three types of relations: from macro to micro, micro–micro, and from micro to macro. It is used to uncover the explanatory force of a macro–macro relation.

Questions

1 Can you describe your research project in a 300-word abstract using Bernie Beck's trick? Can you now take the project of a colleague (or student) and transform it by using the same trick?
2 Why is it often argued that concepts in the social sciences are 'ontological' and 'causal'?

3 Choose a concept that plays an important role in your project: can you describe how extension and intension work in this concept? How would you move up and down the ladder of abstraction?

4 Can the cases define the concept in your project?

5 What is degreeism?

6 Select 10 successful articles in your special field of research (such as 'international tax competition' or 'anti-poverty programmes'): how many of them would sit comfortably in Coleman's bathtub?

7 What are the micro-foundations of your project?

8 How do we distinguish a classification from an explanatory typology?

_____■■ **Further reading** ■_____

Becker, H.S. (1998) *Tricks of the Trade: How to Think about Your Research While You're Doing It.* Chicago: University of Chicago Press, Chapter 4.

Blumer, H. (1954) What is wrong with social theory? *American Sociological Review*, 18: 3–10. Available at http://www.brocku.ca/MeadProject/Blumer/Blumer_1954.html.

Elman, C. (2005) Explanatory typologies in qualitative studies of international politics. *International Organization*, 59 (2): 293–326.

Goertz, G. (2006) *Social Science Concepts: A User's Guide.* Princeton, NJ: Princeton University Press.

Sartori, G. (1991) Comparing and miscomparing. *Journal of Theoretical Politics*, 3 (3): 243–57.

THREE

Causal analysis

Introduction

Most empirical research in the social sciences is directed at establishing and understanding causal relationships among social phenomena. The aim of this chapter is to present the different strategies of causal analysis that are commonly used in the social sciences, constituting the common ground of discussion for the 'research design trade-offs' that will be presented in the rest of this book. The clarification of the conceptual foundations of different approaches to causal analysis is the first step in making informed decisions about how to conduct a research project. To some extent, inductive causal thinking is constantly experienced in everyday life, so that the definition of cause seems self-evident. As a matter of fact, we normally consider that excessive speed causes car accidents, or that doing mathematics exercises explains students' success in their final exams. However, as we will see in the rest of this chapter, there is no general consensus in the philosophy of science about the definition of causal arguments, and there is no stable agreement on the methodologies of causal explanation. The different existing approaches to causal analysis should be recognized so that this diversity can be handled in a proficient way. The next section reviews the four main conceptual approaches to causal analysis: regularity, probabilistic, counterfactual and manipulative. Then, different strategies of causal analysis in empirical research are presented, in accordance with different research goals and types of data: experiments, comparative case studies, statistical analysis, process analysis, and set-relations analysis. The conclusion points to the need for a unified theoretical framework of causation while recognizing that methodological pluralism is indispensable for providing the answers to distinct research questions.

Causation in the social sciences

The study of causation focuses on the causal relationship between one event (a cause) and another (its effect). The examination of this relationship involves explaining how the first event causes the second event to happen, with the help of empirical direct or indirect observations, in line with the scientific method advanced by Hempel and Popper. All causal relationships share some general properties.

- Causation is usually considered transitive: when A is a cause of B and B is a cause of Z, then A is also a cause of Z.
- Causation is usually considered non-reflexive: an event cannot cause itself.
- Causation is usually considered asymmetric: if A is a cause of Z then Z is not a cause of A.
- Causation is usually considered directed: causes precede their effects in time.
- Causation can be multiple: the effect Z can have more than one cause, A, B, C.
- Causation can be conjunctural: the effect Z can be the consequence of a joint set of causes, A1, A2, etc., none of which can produce Z alone.

However, in the social sciences, different paradigms coexist as regards the conceptual foundations and the analytical procedures to be applied to causal relationships. These paradigms are occasionally confused. For the sake of clarity, the three main conceptual approaches to causal analysis (regularity, probabilistic and counterfactual) are distinguished, with the addition of another perspective (the so-called manipulative), before their application and fruitful combination are discussed in later chapters.

Regularity approaches

Regularity represents the most intuitive approach to causal analysis. This approach analyses causation in terms of a constant coincidence between a cause and its effect. This line of attack was most famously developed by J.S. Mill (2002 [1843]), who stated that the cause 'is the sum total of the conditions positive and negative taken together ... which being realized, the consequent invariably follows'. Regularity means that a given causal factor, when present, leads invariably to a specified outcome. Typically, regularity approaches aim to fully explain the occurrence of specific events. A famous example is Theda Skocpol's study of social revolution in France, Russia and China, agrarian-bureaucratic states that were not formally colonized. In her work, two main variables lead to social revolution: 'peasant revolt' and 'state breakdown' (Goertz and Mahoney, 2005). It is generally considered that this approach implies a deterministic view of causation, an epistemological position that assumes that causes are always sufficient to produce the effect. Although absolute determinism is regarded quite sceptically, some authors consider that deterministic relations are vital to unpack causal arguments and to account for the transition from generic statistical associations to individual cases (Hesslow, 1976). Deterministic assumptions are usually relaxed in the course of empirical research, and their applicability is restricted to the certain contexts and to the presence of certain conditions. For instance, causal relationships where the cause leads 'almost always' to a certain effect can be considered to be consistent with a regularity-oriented view of causation (Ragin, 2000).

Moreover, it is commonly argued that plausible deterministic causal expressions are constituted by conjunctions of different causal factors. Therefore, individual causal factors can be considered as determinant only when they make up specific combinations, which may be quite complex, non-trivial and empirically relatively rare. An illustration is the unusually very high casualty rate of the sinking of the *Titanic* – 1,517 of the 2,223 passengers, as reported by Braithwaite and Drahos (2000). According to recent historiography, a full explanation of this disaster has to account not only for the violent collision with an iceberg that happened just before midnight on 14 April 1912, but also for the shortage of lifeboats carried by the ship, and for the fact that boats within 30 miles of the *Titanic*, which could have rescued the survivors, did not hear the distress calls because radio-operating procedures were not standardized. The deterministic explanation of this particular effect is thus composed of at least three individual conditions that constitute a 'causal recipe'. Therefore, a single condition in itself provides only a partial explanation of the phenomenon investigated. Mackie (1965) provided a systematic discussion of this point, by claiming that the typical explanatory factor in the real world consists of a particular type of deterministic cause, called an INUS condition: the so-called cause is an *i*nsufficient but *n*ecessary part of a condition which is itself *u*nnecessary but *s*ufficient for the result.

Another example is required to illustrate the use of INUS conditions. Following Mahoney and Goertz (2004), to say that unitary democracy is a cause of the welfare state is to say that unitary democracy is an INUS condition for the development of the welfare state in Western countries. It is an insufficient part of the explanation because it cannot explain the welfare state on its own: other conditions, such as working-class mobilization, or the presence of a Catholic government, should be present. And the whole combination, although sufficient, is not necessary, since some other conditions, such as the presence of a patriarchal state combined again with working-class mobilization, can produce the same outcome.

The regularity approach to causal analysis seems very reasonable. But its practical application entails a number of inconveniences that make it inappropriate for a number of research questions that are commonplace in the social sciences. Determinism assumes a level of certainty about relations among phenomena that is unlikely in many contexts, such as where the researcher lacks complete information and must deal with the complexity of representing social interactions among rationally bounded human beings. Some uncertainty about causal relations may stem from systematic measurement errors that can be reduced but hardly ruled out, from the 'randomness' of social phenomena or from the fundamental indeterminacy of causal effects. In particular, it is difficult to account for uncertainties under deterministic assumptions in studies involving a large number of cases, for which the researcher cannot acquire a substantial knowledge of each observation.

Probabilistic approaches

Unlike regularity, with probabilistic approaches the social world is fundamentally indeterministic, meaning that there are events that lack a discernible sufficient cause (Dowe and Noordhof, 2004). Probabilistic models are inexact by design so as to manage different kinds of fallibilities, such as coding errors, systematic and random measurement errors and missing data. However, they aim to offer powerful explanations and even, sometimes, predictions of social phenomena by relying on the statistical manipulation of data. This conception points to allowing us to adopt a more flexible epistemology, even if, as we will see, the solution to some problems opens up a new set of distinct issues to be taken into account.

Under a probabilistic approach, an event that 'genuinely' causes its effect must be conceived as follows (Suppes, 1970). The event A must occur before its effect Z and must increase its 'unconditional probability' of occurring, while there must be no evidence that would show that A is a spurious cause of Z. This formulation is quite simple, but its practical application is far from obvious. In particular, the notion of spuriousness is very important. It refers to the possible existence of an omitted, non-observed or undetermined condition that co-influences A and Z and increases exogenously the probability of their concomitant occurrence. For instance, David Hendry (1986) reported a very high correlation over time between inflation and cumulative rainfall in the UK, and yet a causal relation between the two variables is highly implausible. At any time, the risk of spuriousness cannot be completely dismissed, but the use of a theoretically sound causal model and careful research design will reinforce the plausibility of a 'genuine' causal relationship. Chapter 4 is devoted to this type of research design.

What is the main added value of probabilistic approaches? They are particularly suitable for estimating the average effect of independent variables on one or more dependent variables. In other words, their research goal is not to fully explain causal relations in particular cases, but to isolate the 'net effect' of one or more variables on the outcome of interest. Research strategies based on probabilistic assumptions are indeed variable-oriented, that is, they focus on different independent variables competing with each other to explain variation in the dependent variable. It is also possible to estimate the size of this effect by taking into account the error term. For instance, research in higher education studies suggested that the variable 'parents' education' influences the academic ability of students, in the sense of having an independent, linear, additive impact on the average academic achievement level of students. Of course, this model needs further specification, as the variable 'parents' education' is notoriously correlated with other sociological and psychological variables influencing children's school outcomes, such as income, parental involvement, social ties and social skills.

To conclude, a couple of reservations can be mentioned. First, probabilistic approaches in particular are plagued by the frequent situation of 'too few cases and too many variables' in the social world that makes some research questions very difficult to answer. Furthermore, one should recognize a growing mismatch between the increasing sophistication of existing statistical methodology and the availability of reliable data about social phenomena. Many statistical tools presuppose data quality and quantity that are unrealistic for the social sciences, and force us to use information which can reduce the internal and external validity of results by increasing the risk of selection bias and measurement error. In fact, depending on the topic, it is possible to examine only a quite limited number of cross-sectional cases, and reliable time-series data are relatively difficult to obtain in most disciplines.

Counterfactual approaches

According to the classical definition of Hume (2003 [1739]):

> we may define a cause to be an object followed by another, and where all the objects, similar to the first, are followed by objects similar to the second. Or, in other words, where, if the first object had not been, the second would never have existed.

While the first part of this definition is recurrently cited as representative of the 'causal law' thinking that characterizes the natural sciences, the second sentence opened up another route, that is, a counterfactual conception of causation, which is also very common in the social sciences (Lewis, 1973). As we will see, counterfactual approaches constitute a complement rather than an alternative to the approaches presented above. Counterfactual reasoning lies at the heart of the potential-outcomes approach to causal analysis to be presented in Chapter 4, which presupposes the comparison of outcomes in a given sample or population under different levels of treatment to ascertain what would happen when the cause of the event investigated is absent rather than present. However, it is convenient to start by illustrating the specificity of counterfactual reasoning as an approach to causal analysis.

Counterfactual reasoning considers causes as *sine qua non* conditions for their effects. In other words, when the cause A actually brings about the effect Z, then the counterfactual conditional 'if A had not occurred, Z would not have occurred' must be true (Woodward and Hitchcock, 2003). Of course, a double limitation of this reasoning is immediately evident. On the one hand, if we observe the occurrence of the positive case (the effect Z is present), we are obliged to adopt a speculative position about the expected effect of the hypothetic absence of A. On the other hand, when we consider the negative case, and argue that because of the absence of A there is no Z, we are confronted with the problem of selecting the correct A among many possible instances (Fearon, 1991). In this sense, pure counterfactual reasoning remains a thought experiment.

In order to reframe this debate in more systematic terms, Tetlock and Belkin (1996) have developed six attributes of the process of counterfactual reasoning: (a) clarity, (b) logical consistency, (c) minimal-rewrite rule, (d) theoretical validity, (e) consistency with empirical evidence, and (f) projectability of implications. Clarity, logical consistency, theoretical validity, and empirical consistency are attributes of any argumentation expressed in scientific form. The two other criteria are less obvious and deserve a brief gloss.

First, according to the minimal-rewrite rule, the imaginary world in which the cause A does not occur and the effect Z does not occur must be the closest possible to the actual world where A and Z do occur, and, most importantly, it must be closer to it than any possible world where A does not occur but Z occurs (Woodward and Hitchcock, 2003). For instance, the proposition 'if Bosnians had been blue-nosed dolphins, NATO would not have allowed their slaughter', quoted by Tetlock and Belkin (1996), violates this assumption, while speculations about the occurrence of World War I if Gavrilo Princip had not shot and killed the Austrian Archduke Franz Ferdinand in Sarajevo on 28 June 1914 are consistent with this procedure (Lebow, 2000). In fact, in the former example the activation of the counterfactual hypothesis would require the rewriting of much conventional wisdom, while in the latter the counterfactual situation would have been easily realizable. As we all remember from high school, Princip's attack was indeed an individual action that was largely fortuitous, contingent and potentially preventable.

Second, the criterion of projectability relates to the extent to which it is possible to derive observable implications from the hypothetic pattern and to assess their plausibility in the light of contextual historical knowledge. In other terms, it is necessary to be able to discuss the consequences of the counterfactual and make sense of it with reference to other historical events. This point can be very demanding. It can be illustrated with a short example (Hassig, 2001). In February 1519, the governor Diego Velázquez de Cuéllar of Cuba, the initial political supporter of Captain Hernán Cortés's campaign in the Americas, tried to dismiss the captain from his command after he proved to be disloyal. However, the famous conquistador Cortés anticipated this move and sailed just before the decision could be implemented. In this context, any answer to the question of whether there would be an Aztec-derived state in Mexico – if Velázquez had acted more quickly and replaced Cortés with a more faithful captain who would have followed his orders to explore but not to subjugate the indigenous populations – must still take account of the subsequent course of Central American history, which gave birth to prosperous civilizations but was punctuated by severe internal conflicts and recurrent crises of food production.

To sum up, although quite elusive, counterfactuals are fundamental to all explanatory theories and interpretive narratives, and constitute a decisive component of causal inference (Collins et al., 2004). Following Elster (1978), any sound theory must be 'weak enough' to admit the counterfactual assumption, but 'strong enough' to permit a clear-cut conclusion. In 'large N' research, we can implement this reasoning by constructing a sample of comparable cases large enough to contain adequate variation of dependent and independent variables, and by posing the counterfactual of what would have happened if variables in the error term were altered (Lebow, 2000). Also, in studies involving a small number of observations, scholars can evaluate causal hypotheses by referring to counterfactual cases in which a hypothesized causal factor is supposed to be absent, even if in practice they often do so in an implicit and quite incomplete way (Fearon, 1991).

Other approaches

Other approaches to causal analysis exist that are less relevant to the social sciences but deserve to be mentioned. One of these, which will be briefly considered in this book, is the manipulability perspective. Manipulability approaches start from the idea that causes are not external to the observer but should be conceived of as means of producing effects. Therefore, these causes are purposely produced by human beings intervening in the course of events and exploiting event A in order to bring about event Z. In this sense, the term 'cause' simply denotes those things that humans can control or manipulate for their pragmatic ends. This view can be extended beyond causal relationships that can be manipulated and controlled, to include cases in which manipulation and control are impossible, but in which subsists a concern for what would happen in the event of purposeful variation of the factors involved in the relation: that is, counter-factuals. From an instrumentalist perspective, the manipulability approach is applied when researchers construct or mimic experimental research designs, as discussed in Chapter 4, where some intervention actually takes place, or where it is at least possible to figure out the situation as if some intervention had occurred (Goldthorpe, 2001). Conversely, following the subjectivist interpretation of this approach, different actors will emphasize different causal factors depending on their individual perspectives (Kurki, 2008). Take the example, cited by Woodward (2001), of what causes a car to accelerate. The casual driver will point to the pressure of his or her foot on the gas pedal, while the automotive engineer will refer to the functioning of the internal combustion engine.

Towards causal inference

The approaches presented above eventually aim to analyse causal relations and generalize results to some extent, that is, to make causal inferences. The methodology of causal inference in light of the potential-outcomes framework will be discussed systematically in Chapter 4. Nonetheless, it is worth anticipating here in general terms the difference between 'narrow' and 'broad' conceptions of inference.

Causal inference is defined narrowly as the study of the difference between units that received random treatment and units that did not. This difference corresponds to a 'fully generalizable' causal effect (Rubin, 1974). Therefore, strictly speaking, the conditions for deriving causal inference are quite demanding and require either an experimental setting or statistical manipulations that reproduce this setting. The difference between the outcome with the treatment and the outcome without it, representing the causal effect, should be measured for the same unit, which is conceptually and practically impossible. The best research device to approximate this situation would be an experimental design in which the researcher is able to artificially control the relationships among variables under investigation. In such experiments it is possible to compare groups that received the treatment with randomized control samples of the population. However, for practical and ethical reasons social scientists cannot always rely on this research design. Therefore, we must also use more indirect techniques for making causal inference, namely observational methods of data collection and statistical techniques of data analysis. In this setting, it is crucial that explanatory variables measure the same concept for all units and that units are not mutually interdependent – for example, their properties do not depend on the characteristics of other units. Even so, a major problem is that we must specify *ex ante* the type of relation between variables; this is largely based on assumptions such as linearity, and the need to rely on pre-formatted functional forms (for instance, logarithmic or quadratic functions). Therefore, results are highly dependent on model specifications.

As shown in Chapter 4, matching methods are designed to solve this problem by improving the balance between the treated and the control groups. It is possible to make the treated and the control groups as similar as possible as regards the distribution of cases and to get closer to an experimental situation, where functional forms are not predetermined (Ho et al., 2007). Nonetheless, this technique does not help to remedy a possible omitted-variables bias, which remains pervasive in all observational research studies, as we can never control everything for all the variables. There is no definitive solution for what social scientists cannot observe or measure. Observational studies in the social sciences lead to an additional problem that must be taken into account in scientific inquiries, which is sometimes called 'double subjectivity'. This means that, on the one hand, we cannot adopt an entirely value-free epistemological position, and, on the other, the object of any investigation – which is usually a set of human beings or groups of them – can respond to, dispute and even manipulate the research process.

However, causal inference can also be understood in a broader sense, and in this case more options are available. Here, to make a causal inference simply means to learn about causal effects from the observed data that go beyond the particular observations collected (King et al., 1994). This type of inferential process is more modest as it is not 'fully generalizable' but is limited by contextual factors, by historical periods and by scope conditions. Therefore, the causal relations uncovered can be confidently extended only to a limited number of comparable cases or to a specific population. This limited view of generalizability is more appropriate for a great variety of phenomena that are considered in the social sciences; and at the same time it is easier to be applied in empirical research. Both 'qualitative' and 'quantitative' data can be used for causal inference, even if the respective analytical procedures differ in important ways, which will be discussed later in this book. As King et al. (1994) remind us in their highly influential book on research design, inference constitutes a crucial goal of any research project with explanatory aims, although the scope of inference may range from a very limited scale to an ambitious quasi-universal generalization of theory and results. In particular, statistical macro-comparisons permit wider generalizations but are less precise, while case studies lead to even less generalizable results but concern a larger number of properties of the investigated concepts.

In fact, it must be acknowledged that when we do social science research we always try to broaden our view, implicitly or explicitly, by applying information derived from observations to unobserved phenomena. For instance, even the anthropologist Clifford Geertz – an exemplary exponent of ethnographic research who relied on 'singular' phenomena, 'grounded' direct observation and interpretive 'thick description' for data collection and data analysis – made inferences. Discussing the symbolic basis of cockfighting in a Balinese village in *The Interpretation of Cultures*, he intended to extend his findings beyond the mere chronicling of this particular event in order to develop a new conception of what culture is – culture as text – with broader implications for other cases, according to which 'the culture of a people is an ensemble of texts, themselves ensembles, which the anthropologist strains to read over the shoulders of those to whom they properly belong' (Geertz, 1973).

Summary of the approaches

So far, we have reviewed the different conceptual approaches to causation in the social sciences (Table 3.1). Regularity approaches usually adopt deterministic assumptions and aim to fully account for one or more particular phenomena or events. These phenomena or events typically correspond to peculiar or substantially important cases, such as the French Revolution or World War II. Probabilistic approaches are used to estimate the effect of independent variables on dependent variables with the help of statistical manipulation, whereby the analytical focus is on the net impact of selected variables. Counterfactual and manipulative approaches represent stand-alone philosophical positions but they are normally applied in conjunction with regularity and probabilistic approaches to strengthen the inferences made from causal analysis. Counterfactual approaches permit reflection upon the effect when the cause does not occur and vice versa, while manipulative approaches introduce the possibility of an external control of causal relationships through the manipulation of the research setting.

Table 3.1 Summary of approaches to causal analysis in the social sciences

	Regularity approaches	Probabilistic approaches	Counterfactual approaches	Manipulative approaches
Ontological assumptions	The social world is deterministic (even if probabilistic principles can be introduced to simplify social complexity)	The social world is indeterministic (many effects lack a sufficient cause, data errors are considered normal)	Speculations about other hypothetical social worlds have an epistemological value	The social world is understandable through subjective and/ or instrumental viewpoints

(Continued)

Table 3.1 (Continued)

	Regularity approaches	Probabilistic approaches	Counterfactual approaches	Manipulative approaches
Methodological assumptions	Causal expressions are usually constituted by conjunctions of causal factors	Hypothesis testing requires statistical manipulation to isolate the additive impact of variables	Causal arguments must be tested against consistent, valid, plausible counterfactuals	Human agency is required
Heuristic focus	Cases	Variables	Thought experiment	Actors
What is a cause?	An INUS condition	An event increasing the probability of its effect	A sine qua non condition of its effect	What actors can control or manipulate
What connects causes to effects?	A causal chain	A probabilistic relation	A counterfactual logical support	A deliberate action
Goal	To fully account for a (set of) effect(s) in (a number of) particular cases	To estimate the competing individual or interactive impact of one or more causes	To envisage the effect when the cause does not occur (and vice versa)	To highlight the consequences of human intervention
Main advantage	Permits 'thick' explanations	Permits generalizations	Is a component of causal inference	Operationalizes actors' room for manoeuvre
Disadvantages	Epistemologically rigid; sometimes unrealistic assumptions about information and relations among variables	Not appropriate for a small number of cases; sometimes misalignment between theory and methodology	Requires speculation about unobserved phenomena; is a complementary, not alternative, approach	Strictly speaking, has no explanatory power; should be applied in conjunction with other approaches

The study of causation in empirical research

The conceptual approaches to causal analysis presented in the previous section inform different strategies of empirical research. For instance, regularity approaches constitute the conceptual foundations of case-oriented historical research, while macro-comparative research typically relies on probabilistic approaches. However, more frequently than not, insights from these fundamental approaches to causal analysis are combined in empirical research. This section provides an overview of the operationalization of approaches to causation in empirical causal analysis.

The unit to be empirically analysed in social science research can be an individual, a group of people, an organization, an institution, a country, a region, or a city (this list is far from exhaustive). The investigated time span can range from an instantaneous snapshot to thousands of years. The analytical focus can be situated at the micro level, referring to the characteristics of individual actors; at the meso level, an intermediate stage of aggregation like that of groups and organizations; or at the macro level, when we assume that structures and systemic properties offer the highest analytical leverage for explaining social phenomena. The number of cases can range from one to many thousands. Empirical observations may concern a small sample or the whole population considered. The technique of data analysis can be qualitative (focusing on differences in kind), quantitative (focusing on differences in numbers), combined (that is, using one after another) or mixed (taking into account differences both in kind and in degree at the same time).

Each one of these parameters can vary from study to study and should inform, but does not determine, the choice of a strategy of empirical research, following a number of theoretical and practical rationales that will be tackled in this book. As we will see, the study of causal relations in empirical research can follow different pathways according to the research goal, the type of data to be collected, the availability of information, and the personal inclinations and methodological competencies of the researcher. In the rest of this chapter, the three main existing strategies for studying causal relationships in the social sciences are presented, namely comparative analysis (the most widespread), process analysis and set-relations analysis. The aim is to identify their distinctive traits and the complementarities between them, before discussing them in detail in the following chapters with reference to specific research questions, methodological issues and existing trade-offs.

Comparative methods

The typical way to analyse causal relations in the social sciences is through the adoption of a comparative design in order to conduct or approximate an experimental study. The goal is to isolate the impact of independent variables by creating an artificial situation of *ceteris paribus* conditions (Przeworski and Teune, 1970). Following this strategy, the logic of causal analysis is covariational. By following a covariational design, evidence of causation is derived from the systematic confirmation or exclusion of a relationship between one (or more) explanatory variables and a dependent variable, usually by excluding or controlling for other variables. The relationship between the two variables is commonly described in numerical terms as a correlation. Correlation indicates the extent to which values of the two variables are dependent to each other. Obviously, in order to implement this strategy, some variation in the variables under investigation is needed. Variation can be found within cases, across cases or both simultaneously, and may relate to space, time, or both. For instance, historical case studies are based on within-case comparisons over time, while cross-sectional comparative studies display synchronic cross-case variations (Gerring, 2007b).

Experiments

The prototypical way to make causal inferences is represented by direct experimentation. Experiments are discussed at length in Chapter 4 with reference to the potential-outcomes framework. Here we anticipate the underlying logic of causal analysis in order to situate other comparative methods in relation to this starting point. The standard procedure of experimentation is as follows. We create two or more equivalent groups of participants in the study, by randomization (the placement of each participant into one group or another on the basis of chance), matching (the assignment to each group of one of a pair of participants who share some characteristics that are deemed to influence the outcome), or elimination (the statistical control of the effect of some characteristics that may influence the dependent variable). Afterwards, we have to introduce different levels or types of treatment to each group of participants. Finally, we can simply measure the difference between the levels of the dependent variable in the groups that is expected to be causally connected to the treatment. Since there is an independent control on the explanatory variable related to the treatment, we are able to isolate its net causal effect on the dependent variable. In so-called quasi-experiments, the procedure is similar: the presumed cause is manipulated but there is either no randomization or no control condition.

At least three types of experimental designs exist in the social sciences. First, in laboratory experiments the investigator artificially controls the level of independent variables before measuring the level of dependent variables. For example, a series of experiments was set up to test some expectations related to a special case of 'fixation' in cognitive psychology, where reproductive responses produce problem-solving failure rather than success (Eysenck and Keane, 2005). A tested group and a control group were given a series of elementary arithmetical problems to solve. In a first step, the tested group received a series of problems that could be solved using the same solution method, while the control group received problems that had to be solved using different methods. Subsequently, both groups received a problem that could be solved using either a very simple method or the more complex method that the tested group had to apply before. The control group tended to use the simple method but the tested group opted for the more complex method. In fact, they did not see the simpler method because they remained 'fixated' on the more complex one.

Second, field experiments examine our interventions in the real world rather than in the laboratory that randomize units into treatment and control groups to compare outcomes between these groups. For instance, in order to study the impact of development assistance on 'democracy and governance' outcomes, some social scientists collaborated and gained support from international organizations such as the US Agency for International Development and the World Bank, and from local authorities, to introduce a randomized treatment in some political processes (Moehler, 2010). Other researchers (Vicente and Wantchekon, 2009) found that a randomized door-to-door leaflet campaign against vote buying in São Tomé and Príncipe increased negative perceptions of vote buying, but also reduced turnout in targeted census areas. Collier and Vicente (2008) investigated a campaign against political violence that was randomized across neighbourhoods and villages in six Nigerian states. They were able to observe that the campaign reduced electoral violence as recorded by perception surveys and independent data sources and, as a result, increased citizen turnout and reduced votes for violent opposition leaders.

Third, natural experiments make the most of random assignments of treatments that have been created 'by nature'. They are observational studies that reproduce experimental designs, and are increasingly common in economics and political science. An interesting example is Kern and Hainmueller's (2009) natural experiment to identify the impact of West German television on public support for the communist regime in East Germany. Data on West German television exposure (independent variable) and on expressed support for the East German regime (dependent variable) were retrieved from formerly classified survey data collected by the Zentralinstitut für Jugendforschung that became available after reunification. The comparison of the regime support of East Germans exposed to West German television with the regime support of East Germans not so exposed would not be very informative about the causal effect of West German television exposure, because of the well-known problem of the association between the selection into treatment and the outcomes. The standard solution would be to control for observable characteristics known to affect both selection into West

German television exposure and political attitudes, using some method of covariate adjustment (such as regression or matching). However, this solution would not rule out the possibility that East Germans were selected into West German television exposure based on unobservable characteristics. Hence, the authors followed another strategy: they used instrumental variables based on information about respondents' place of work, by exploiting the fact that, because of East Germany's topography, West German television broadcasts could be received in most but not all parts of the country. This naturally occurring variation permitted the estimation of average treatment effects for the subgroup of compliers, by inducing exogenous variation in the treatment. In other words, this design produces groups where the treatment, at aggregate level, can be considered as randomly assigned. Results are quite surprising. Against the conventional wisdom in the democratization literature that foreign mass media undermine authoritarian rule, it happens that East Germans exposed to West German television were more satisfied with life in East Germany and more supportive of the East German regime. The authors conclude that East Germans used West German television primarily as a source of entertainment.

Comparative case studies

Comparative case study is the standard method whereby we endeavour to study a handful of cases in depth, so that we rely on only a relatively small amount of observations. This is typically the case with research projects in comparative politics focusing on (some) EU member states, OECD countries, Latin American countries, and so on. Comparative case studies exploit within-case and cross-case variations in space or time. When cross-case synchronic and diachronic analyses are combined, the method is usually referred to as a comparative-historical case study. Within-case analysis typically focuses on variations across territorial units over time such as in the classic study of Italy, *Making Democracy Work* (Putnam et al., 1993). The baseline comparative case study methods are those derived from the British philosopher John Stuart Mill in 1843 (see Mill, 2002) and refined further by Przeworski and Teune (1970): the so-called 'most similar system design' and 'most different system design'. The aim of these authors is to mimic experimental designs with a 'second best' procedure based on the explicit selection of cases using information on independent and dependent variables. It should therefore be noted that the allegedly infamous process of 'selecting cases on the dependent variable' is actually correct when this type of research design is used.

The 'most similar system design' presupposes the selection of cases that are different on the dependent variable (Z), different on the independent variable(s)

(A), and similar on control variables. Thus, the logic of causal analysis is as follows: cases are similar except for one independent variable (A). When A is present, cases display the same phenomenon Z. When A is absent, cases do not display the phenomenon Z. Therefore, A explains Z. This design can be exemplified with a classic research study on social mobility in Great Britain and the United States. Kerckhoff et al. (1985) compared two societies that were considered extremely similar as regards macro-level variables such as economy, culture, values and historical trajectory, but in which there was an expected systematic difference in the levels of social mobility due to the variation of one crucial explanatory variable, namely the different types of educational system. Given the exclusive educational system, Great Britain exhibits more intergenerational stability of social position, while the USA is considered to be a more fluid society due to greater equality of opportunity in secondary and post-secondary education.

The 'most different system design', by contrast, requires cases that are similar on the dependent variable (Z), similar on the independent variable(s) (A), and different on control variables. So A explains Z when cases differ except for one variable (A) and they display the same phenomenon (Z). For example, a study comparing the media coverage of the war in Iraq in the USA and Sweden is built upon a most different systems design (Dimitrova and Strömbäck, 2005). The authors consider that the USA and Sweden are two most different countries among the advanced industrialized democracies, because they differ greatly in their political institutions, their media systems, and the organization of their political economies. Given this research design, the crucial variable that is expected to explain public attitudes is the only one that does not vary, that is, the relative shares of news coverage of quality newspapers and the popular press.

Statistical analysis

The covariational logic of experimental designs can also be replicated with the application of statistical techniques to a large sample or population. In fact, according to a similar logic to the qualitative comparative method discussed above, 'the statistical method … entails the conceptual (mathematical) manipulation of empirically observed data – which cannot be manipulated situationally as in experimental design – in order to discover controlled relationships among variables' (Lijphart, 1971).

Mahoney and Goertz (2006) consider this design especially relevant when empirical research focuses on the estimation of the average effect of independent variables and when we want to maximize the generalizability of our results.

The main underlying assumptions are that all observations are mutually independent, equally important and display some predetermined distributions – for instance, a normal distribution – which can be properly described, compared and analysed (Landman, 2003). In this view, much importance is attached to issues related to measurement and indicators. Suitable data are usually collected through document analysis or survey inquiries to provide a numeric description of trends, attitudes, or opinions of a population by studying a sample of that population (Creswell, 2009). Four types of survey inquiry can be identified: self-administered or web-based questionnaires; interviews; record reviews to collect information; and structured observations. After data collection, it is vital to assess the validity and reliability of the scores obtained. When analysing data, it is important to establish a transparent rationale for the choice of the statistical test and to spell out the underlying assumptions. The final step of data analysis is to present the results in tables or figures and interpret them convincingly. Interpreting results means that we have to draw conclusions from the results relating to the research questions and hypotheses, and identify the broader implications of our results.

As an illustration of statistical design, the sociologists Peterson and Kern (1996) examined Anglo-Saxon tastes with multiple regression analysis, where a set of independent variables explained a proportion of the variance in a dependent variable, that is, cultural tastes. They detected an extension of the tastes of highly educated Anglo-Saxons from 'snob' tastes (such as appreciation of fine art) in the late nineteenth century to more eclectic, 'omnivorous' tastes in recent years (for instance, football and popular culture). In order to explore this relation, the authors pooled a series of questions extracted from national surveys undertaken in 1982 and 1992 on taste-related attitudes and behaviour, for instance about respondents' attendance of performances of plays, ballet, classical music, musicals, and opera, and visits to art galleries. They found that in 1992, on average, highly educated persons were more omnivorous than they were in 1982 and had become even more omnivorous than others. Following the statistical analysis, this effect is significantly linked to cohort replacement and to changes during the 1980s among highly educated persons of all ages, reflecting above all modifications of the social structure and generational conflicts.

Process analysis

A common alternative to covariational techniques as a way to conduct causal analysis is the study of causal mechanisms. This research strategy is radically different from covariational techniques as we do not deduce causal relations

DESIGNING RESEARCH IN THE SOCIAL SCIENCES

from the manipulation or approximation of an experimental design, but aim to directly observe and report the unfolding of causal processes.

On this common ground, there exist a wide range of operational definitions of 'causal mechanism' (Hedström and Swedberg, 1998). For instance, some authors start from the basic assumption that the only governing regularities in social reality are those involving individual agency, and that consequently there exist no macro-level mechanisms. Others argue that mechanisms consist of processes whereby structures constrain and at the same time enable agency, and whereby agents can modify or maintain structures. In our view, the simpler notion of mechanism refers to the pathway or process by which an effect is produced (Gerring, 2007a). The ambition of the mechanistic approach is indeed to find the 'building blocks' of 'middle-range' theories and then to reconstruct the sequences of causal processes in order to respond to the 'how' question. Therefore, we should concentrate on the study of mechanisms, especially when we want to discover the process underlying the relationship between a cause and its effect in order to develop a causal explanation of a particular event (Ahn et al., 1995). It is worth adding that the study of causal mechanisms is frequently considered as a second step in deeper causal analysis after the application of other methods such as comparative case studies or statistical comparisons that have identified covariational evidence of a causal relation.

The most prominent method for the empirical application of this perspective in the social sciences is called 'process tracing'. The idea of process tracing is to identify and cut down the 'causal chain' that connects independent and dependent variables and to examine each sequence in detail. We must start behaving like detectives, collecting small pieces of evidence and looking for traces of a hypothesized causal mechanism within the context of each particular case (George and Bennett, 2005). Then the strategy for causal analysis involves the identification of recurrent evidence of the process that connects the cause to its effect. In other words, we have to find the 'smoking gun' by breaking causal sequences in a systematic way until each micro-linkage is self-evident and the whole chain leads coherently from the primary cause A to its final effect Z. For instance, process tracing studies were employed to investigate the influence of non-governmental organizations (NGOs) in international environmental negotiations, in order to establish how and under what conditions NGOs matter. To this end, evidence was collected of the process whereby NGO participation in international environmental negotiations shapes political outcomes, in order to produce a causal chain linking NGOs' transmission of information, actors' utilization of information, and the effects of that information (Betsill and Corell, 2001). Then this first step can be decomposed further by investigating the occurrence of communication, reception of communication, behaviour modification, and so on. In this way, it was possible to retrace the process through which Greenpeace was eventually able to influence the Gerber Corporation and stop the use of genetically modified ingredients in baby food.

Process tracing was frequently criticized for its rather vague quality standards and criteria for operationalization. More recently, however, the methodological sophistication of this technique has been strengthened with the help of the application of Bayesian logic (Bennett, 2008). Bayesian logic, in brief, relies on knowledge of prior events to estimate the probability of future events. Process tracing and Bayesian analysis are considered similar in many respects. Both are attentive to seeking alternative explanations, to gathering diverse sources and kinds of evidence, and to recognizing potential subjectivist biases in collected data. Therefore, the two approaches agree that the probative value of evidence may vary according to prior expectations about competing theories. Thus, for both approaches it is crucial to accumulate diverse kinds of evidence as regards the confirmation or refutation of the hypotheses under consideration. Finally, both approaches proceed through the confrontation of confirmative evidence for some hypotheses and the discarding of hypothesized explanations that proved implausible. Process tracing and Bayesian analysis differ as regards the formalization of the analytical procedure, which is quite inductive in process tracing but requires more specifications in Bayesian analysis about the definition of prior beliefs, the probabilities of hypotheses being true, and their updating after collecting empirical evidence. They also differ in that process tracing is more oriented towards hypothesis generation, whereas the Bayesian approach is more appropriate for hypothesis testing. This comparison also reveals the limits of process tracing pertaining to the risk of an infinite regression to the primary cause, the limited generalization of findings given the necessarily small number of cases, and the lack of a precise and systematic formulation of the analytical procedure.

Set-relations analysis

The third strategy of causal analysis in empirical research corresponds to the configurational study of set relations, in the form of sufficient and necessary conditions for the outcomes investigated. This approach is extensively discussed in Chapter 6. The underlying logic of causal analysis is comparative but neither covariational nor process-oriented, and thus has distinctive advantages and limitations. The operationalization of the famous Kantian 'democratic peace' hypothesis offers an illustration of this approach. According to this hypothesis, 'democracies do not go to war against each other'. A first research design could seek to confirm or refute the existence of a statistically significant difference between pairs of democratic countries and pairs in which at least one country is a non-democracy. However, given the extremely high number of negative cases (for example, non-wartime periods), this difference is expected to be very low. A second research design could be used to assess whether pairs of democratic countries are significantly associated with peaceful coexistence. But many alternative paths leading to peace exist. The research design that correctly operationalizes the Kantian proposition is a third one, which empirically verifies whether the presence of a democratic dyad systematically leads to peaceful coexistence, or, in other words, whether democracy is sufficient for peaceful coexistence.

In fact, some types of causal relation are better understood as subset relations, and not as symmetrical relationships (Ragin, 2008). Statistics and covariational qualitative techniques assume symmetry by design. When covariational reasoning is used to test for a positive connection between a cause and an effect, it tests equally for a negative connection between the cause and the effect. In contrast, the study of set relations allows us to unpack information that is pooled and conflated in correlations, so as to uncover a particular type of causal connection that is overlooked in traditional comparative analyses. For example, if some theory predicts that shareholder-value-oriented firms have short-term profitability targets that hinder their industrial sustainability in the long run, the related hypothesis is essentially asymmetrical, that is, that shareholder-oriented firms are a subset of non-sustainable ones. This statement is not contradicted by the fact that many non-sustainable firms are not shareholder-oriented. They might be non-sustainable for other reasons, such as structural market transformations, economic crisis, or simple mismanagement. Yet the symmetrical version of the argument, which would be taken for granted when one applies covariational methods (that shareholder-oriented firms are not sustainable, and non-shareholder-oriented firms are sustainable), would reframe the expected causal connection in an unintended manner, which produces imprecise and even erroneous results.

A crucial feature of set-relation analysis is that causation is better understood by focusing on how factors combine rather than compete to create the outcome. To this end, a 'configurational approach' is adopted to conceive of each case as a combination of causal conditions leading to the outcome investigated (Ragin, 2008). When conditions together explain the outcome, they are referred to as 'causal recipes'. This perspective is particularly helpful for case-oriented research that requires cases to be studied holistically, that is, by fully accounting for the causes of a certain effect, as opposed to variable-oriented research, which focuses on the net effect of supposedly independent variables. Therefore, the key issue is not which variable has the strongest effect but how different conditions combine and how many combinations are capable of generating the same outcome. Afterwards, it is possible to specify the context that enables or disables the occurrence of specific causes. For instance, to explain the outbreak of mass protest in Latin American countries, the researcher may study the combined effect of the severity of austerity measures imposed by the International Monetary Fund, the concentration of poor people in urban slums, the perceived corruption of government, and previous experiences of mobilization.

When causation is understood in terms of subset relations, it must be operationalized in an appropriate manner, as explained in detail in Chapter 6. Following Ragin, there are two basic procedures for dedicated qualitative comparative analysis (QCA). The first is the test of necessity: the examination of whether instances of the effect Z represent a subset of a specific cause A, that is, when the presence of the effect Z always implies the condition A. The second is the analysis of sufficiency: the identification of the combinations of causal conditions A, B, C that constitute a subset of the effect Z, that is, when the conditions A, B, C always imply the presence of Z. Subset relations allow researchers to study complex patterns of causation – conjunctural causation, that is, where a combination of conditions is required to produce the effect, and multiple causation, defined as a situation in which the effect may follow from several different conditions or combinations of causal conditions. The application of this technique made it possible, for instance, to show that there exist two causal paths leading to firms' co-determination through employee representation in the board of directors: a Scandinavian one and an Austrian–German–Dutch one. Both require strong union coordination and consensus-based political systems to integrate labour into political compromises; but, while in Scandinavia the strength of the Left favoured compromises that led not only to co-determination but also to greater transparency in corporate governance and investor protection, in the Germanic case the presence of powerful concentrated owners allowed them to build protective measures against outside investors and employee representatives (Jackson, 2005).

In another example, Epstein et al. (2008) use fuzzy-set QCA to explore the determinants of poor employment performance in low-end private-sector services in 14 countries between 1979 and 1995. Their research goal was to explore the diversity of the causal configurations leading to the outcome, by assessing the sufficiency of multiple pathways via the logic of set-theoretic relations. The outcome was the change in employment rates. The authors measured change in absolute terms: the employment rate in 1995 minus the employment rate in 1979. The causal conditions were (a) low earnings inequality, (b) high wage increases, (c) high payroll and consumption taxes, (d) high employment protection regulations, (e) high

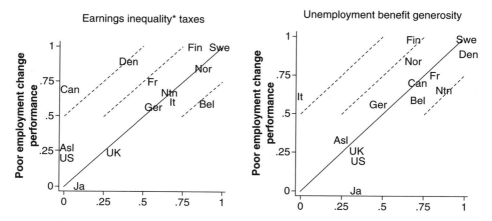

Figure 3.1 Poor employment change performance by causal configurations

Source: Epstein et al. (2008)

unemployment benefit generosity, and (f) high public employment. Different models were tested with different specifications. In the end, the authors discovered five pathways leading to the outcome with satisfactory consistency and coverage scores. The two plots in Figure 3.1 present the last two of these pathways. These plots must be interpreted in terms of perfect causal sufficiency if every case were located above the main diagonal. The scatterplot also shows which cases are covered by the solutions. The first of these two solutions points to a fairly simple explanation: a combination of low earnings inequality and high payroll and consumption taxes was a sufficient condition for generating poor low-end private-sector service employment performance. The other causal configuration consists of a single causal factor: high unemployment benefit generosity. Therefore, it appears that different combination of variables can lead to the outcome, a result that would have hardly become visible with an analytical technique focusing on the average net effect of variables on the explanandum.

In conclusion, some disadvantages of QCA can be mentioned as well. This technique is not suitable for the in-depth study of processes, as it focuses on the synchronic impact of some conditions A, B, C on the effect Z. For the same reason, its extension to time series and panel data is very limited. Moreover, the analytical procedure implies a specific research design, in line with the analysis of necessary and sufficient conditions, which is not entirely compatible with other analytical techniques that focus on the net effect of independent variables (Schneider and Wagemann, 2010).

Towards a unified view of causal analysis

This chapter has reviewed conceptual approaches to, and the main empirical strategies of, causal analysis. There are several such approaches and strategies, and we should adapt them to our research goals and research questions. It is therefore reasonable to have a pluralistic vision of research design in the social sciences. At the same time it is important to implement each strategy in a way that fits the research questions, theory, methodology and data analysis, and to evaluate its quality by reference to shared standards (Brady et al., 2006).

It is not merely hard but impossible to reach a final, unique agreement about the foundations of causal analysis. Even the more common and apparently general characterization of such analysis ('a cause raises the probability of an event') risks overlooking important phenomena, such as INUS conditions, which do not raise individually the probability of the occurrence of an event. In this sense, we can consider, pragmatically, that different conceptions of causation can coexist without contradicting one another and can even be fruitfully combined as in the case of quasi-experimental research. At the theoretical level, Gerring's suggestion of a 'criterial framework' for causal arguments offers an elegant way out. Causal propositions may follow different goals, but they should be judged with reference to a shared and more or less uniform set of formal properties: specification, precision, breadth, boundedness, completeness, parsimony, differentiation, priority, independence, contingency, mechanism, analytic utility, intelligibility, relevance, innovation and comparison (Gerring, 2001). At this stage, it is not important to know exactly what these criteria involve, but it should be recognized that causal analyses can be appreciated and evaluated through an external standard to distinguish a 'good' causal proposition from a weak or uninteresting one, following a conventionalist definition of causation ('what causation is used for'), rather than a functionalist ('what causation does') or an essentialist ('what causation is') definition.

At the methodological level, an intense debate is taking place about the usefulness and compatibility of different research traditions. On the one hand, Brady et al. (2006) suggest that so-called data-set (or quantitative) observations and causal-process (or qualitative) observations are both important for causal analysis with the purpose of hypothesis testing, and should be combined because quantitative and qualitative tools can complement one another to offer more analytical power. On the other hand, Beck (2010) considers this endeavour as either banal or unfeasible, because the two types of data could just be marginally accommodated but not 'adjoined' in a meaningful way. From Beck's perspective, only statistical analysis based on 'rectangular data sets' and, to a lesser extent, qualitative research that adopts quantitative standards are useful for proper causal analysis. It is impossible to tackle here all the points of this rather technical debate. However, it is interesting to note that even in disciplines that are considered the archetypical prototype of 'hard' science and an inspiring paradigm for conventional 'quantitative' thinking in social sciences, a 'non-covariational' conception of causation has been widely accepted for quite some time. For example, as reported by Brady et al. (2006), in the mid-twentieth century the discovery of microwave background radiation provided 'smoking gun' support for the 'big bang' theory, and suddenly changed the discipline of astronomy. This type of radiation constitutes in fact an expected but still unobserved marker of the effects of the big bang, by supporting the hypothesis that the universe is not infinitely old and it is not in a steady state. In this case, the logic of causal analysis is not unlike an in-depth case study. Even physicists do not limit their research to measuring the average impact of an independent variable on a dependent variable by using a large-N data set. Rather, they refine their theories progressively by cutting down causal sequences until they develop an experiment that seeks the ultimate necessary condition for validating the theory.

Different research strategies are compatible, and even very common, in the 'extreme' case of physics. Therefore, it is reasonable to believe that methodological pluralism is useful for improving causal analysis also in the social sciences. The failure to recognize this variety, both from the quantitative and from the qualitative sides, is harmful, and would lead the social sciences to look like 'an odd anthropological sect that imagines, theorizes, and measures a world that is not there, and spends its time predicting the unpredictable, rather than being a progressive intellectual discipline' (Blyth, 2006). Hopefully, much contemporary empirical research in the social sciences has already gone beyond the 'cultural' divide between 'qualitativists' and 'quantitativists' so that this distinction makes less and less sense. More or less implicitly or explicitly, social scientists tend to think in an integrated way about data analysis. Qualitative and quantitative techniques are frequently combined. What is more, the methodological boundaries are becoming increasingly indistinct. Would you consider the systematic analysis of 80 face-to-face interviews (a not so uncommon number for PhD dissertations) with a package such as NVivo or ATLAS.ti to follow a quantitative or a qualitative research design? Last but not least, some recent analytical techniques aim to transcend this divide and cannot be classified as 'qualitative' or 'quantitative' once and for all: examples are social network analysis, comparative configurational methods such as qualitative comparative analysis, and formal modelling.

However, the different methodological techniques must share similar standards to be fruitfully combined. Adcock and Collier (2001) mention four crucial issues: the validity of measurement; the distinction between measurement and conceptual disputes; the generality of research strategies; and the assessment of validation procedures. The criteria for evaluating the various overarching goals of valid causal analyses and for appraising the basic trade-offs in selecting the appropriate research tools are discussed throughout the remainder of this book. Specific research strategies will be presented with reference to a number of central issues for empirical research in the social sciences: the application of the potential-outcomes framework for causal inference (Chapter 4), the study of temporality (Chapter 5), the investigation of heterogeneity (Chapter 6), and the operationalization of interdependence (Chapter 7).

Before concluding, it is worth mentioning that recent advances in social science methodology demonstrate that different methods can and should be not only juxtaposed but also integrated in a coherent theoretical and empirical analytical framework. For instance, it is possible to combine cross-case and within-case methods to compensate each individual method's inherent weaknesses (Kuehn and Rohlfing, 2009). The first step, normally involving regression analysis or qualitative comparative analysis, is used to detect regularities and variation at the cross-case level. The second step involves a case study of the causal process to trace the connection between the cause A and its effect Z. Nested analysis is a promising operationalization of multi-method research, where case study and statistical analysis produce a synergetic added value not by emphasizing the reduction of causal analysis to a common logic, but rather by making the most of the distinctive complementarities in the two research methodologies. Statistical analyses inform case selection, provide direction for additional case studies, and can be used to systematically test hypotheses generated from a small number of cases. Case studies can be used to assess the accuracy of macro-level relationships between variables, to generate new research questions from outliers and deviant cases, and to improve measurement techniques (Lieberman, 2005).

Table 3.2 summarizes some of the key insights of the chapter. Strategies for causal analysis are presented with their implications and trade-offs. Experiments, comparative case studies, statistical analysis, process analysis and set-relations analysis are thus discussed and compared in terms of their underlying conceptual approaches, assumptions, types of data, logics of causal analysis, analytical techniques, research aims, advantages and disadvantages.

Table 3.2 Strategies for causal analysis with their implications and trade-offs

	Experiments	Comparative case studies	Statistical analysis	Process analysis	Set-relations analysis
Approach(es)	Probabilistic, counterfactual, manipulative	Regularity, partially manipulative	Probabilistic, partially counterfactual	Regularity	Regularity, partially counterfactual
Assumptions	Causation can be deduced from the difference between treated and control groups	Case selection approximates an experimental design	Statistical manipulation approximates an experimental design	Causation can be observed almost *in vivo* by breaking causal sequences into self-evident linkages	Causation is multiple and conjunctural, and can be examined with necessary and sufficient conditions
Data	Experimental or quasi-experimental	Observational	Observational	Observational	Observational
Logic of causal analysis	Covariation	Covariation	Covariation	Mechanismic	Subset analysis
Analytical techniques	Selection, randomization, matching	Most similar systems design and most dissimilar systems design	Regression	Narratives, analytical games	Boolean algebra (crisp-set QCA) or fuzzy-set theory (fuzzy-set QCA)
Aim	Isolate the effect of the treatment	Account for particular cases	Estimate the effect of independent variables	Retrace the connection between variables	Find different combinations of explanatory variables
Advantages	Reliable, permits causal inference	Simple, easily applicable	Varied range of robust analytical techniques	Depth and precision	Exploration of diversity and discovery
Disadvantages	Not always feasible in the social sciences for practical and ethical reasons	Ceteris paribus is an unlikely situation	Requires suitable data which are relatively rare in the social sciences (quality and quantity)	Risk of ad hoc explanation, limited generalization	Rigid, mostly synchronic and sometimes difficult to interpret

Checklist

- There are four main approaches to causal analysis: regularity, probabilistic, counterfactual and manipulative.
- Inference is the ultimate goal of causal analysis, but fully inferential causal analysis is quite exceptional in the social sciences.
- Different strategies for causal analysis in empirical research exist, which combine insights from the four approaches, in accordance with different research goals and types of data.
- Experiments, comparative case studies and statistical analysis are based on a covariational logic of inference.
- Process analysis aims at observing the unfolding of causal processes almost 'in vivo'.
- Set-relations analysis focuses on direct connections among variables in terms of sufficiency and necessity.
- Methodological pluralism is indispensable for causal analysis appropriate to diverse research goals, and at the same time a unified framework for causation with shared standards is pragmatically possible.

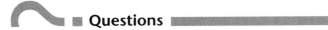 ## Questions

1 To what extent did Hume and Mill share a similar conception of causation?
2 Explain why experiments, comparative case studies and statistical analysis can be considered as comparative methods.
3 What is the difference between causal analysis and causal inference?
4 Can we identify and examine causal mechanisms at the macro level?
5 Take one of your preferred pieces of empirical research. Try to transform a correlational hypothesis into set-theoretic terms. Which are the advantages and disadvantages?

Further reading

Brady, H.E. and Collier, D. (eds) (2004) *Rethinking Social Inquiry. Diverse Tools, Shared Standards.* Lanham, MD: Rowman and Littlefield. Excellent collection that pushed forward the research agenda about methodological pluralism.

Goertz, G. (2006) *Social Science Concepts: A User's Guide.* Princeton, NJ: Princeton University Press. Innovative book about the conceptual foundations of social science theories and research design.

King, G., Keohane, R.O. and Verba, S. (1994) *Designing Social Inquiry: Scientific Inference in Qualitative Research.* Princeton, NJ: Princeton University Press. Seminal book on research design, advocating more rigorous and systematic research in 'qualitative' studies from a 'quantitative' perspective.

Mackie, J.L. (1974) *The Cement of the Universe: A Study of Causation.* Oxford: Clarendon Press. Classic philosophical and methodological treatment of causal complexity.

FOUR

Statistical research designs for causal inference

Introduction

In Chapter 3 we discussed the different ways in which the social sciences conceptualize causation and argued that there is no single way in which causal relationships can be defined and analysed empirically. In this chapter, we focus on a specific set of approaches to constructing research designs for causal analysis, namely, one based on the potential-outcomes framework developed in statistics. As discussed in Chapter 3, this perspective is both probabilistic and counterfactual. It is probabilistic because it does not assume that the presence of a given cause leads invariably to a given effect, and it is counterfactual because it involves the comparison of actual configurations with hypothetical alternatives that are not observed in reality. In essence, this approach underscores the necessity to rely on comparable groups in order to achieve valid causal inferences. An important implication is that the *design* of a study is of paramount importance. The way in which the data are produced is the critical step of the research, while the actual data analysis, while obviously important, plays a secondary role. However, a convincing design requires research questions to be broken down to manageable pieces. Thus, the big trade-off in this perspective is between reliable inferences (that is, conclusions based on empirical evidence) on very specific causal relationships on the one hand, and their broader context and complexity (and, possibly, theoretical relevance) on the other hand.

The chapter first distinguishes between two general perspectives on causality, namely, one that places the *causes* of effects in the foreground, and another that is more interested in the *effects* of causes. We then introduce the potential-outcomes framework before discussing several research designs for causal inference, notably various types of experiments and quasi-experiments. This is followed by a discussion of the implications for research design, and the conclusion summarizes the main points.

Causes of effects and effects of causes

To understand the specificities of statistical research designs for causal inference, it is useful to consider a general difference between quantitative and qualitative approaches to causal analysis. While quantitative approaches typically focus on the 'effects of causes', qualitative approaches usually examine the 'causes of effects' (Mahoney and Goertz, 2006). An equivalent distinction is that between 'forward' and 'reverse' causal inference: forward causal inference asks 'What might happen if we do X?' while reverse causal inference asks 'What causes Y?' (Gelman, 2011). The difference between the two approaches overlaps in part with that characterizing 'variable-oriented research' on the one hand and 'case-oriented research' on the other (Ragin, 1987: 34–68; see also Chapter 3, this volume). Obviously, both are legitimate and fruitful perspectives in the social sciences, each with its own trade-offs. Moreover, it would be wrong to draw a sharp distinction between qualitative and quantitative research. As we will see throughout this chapter, although statistical research designs for causal inference necessarily rely on quantitative techniques (otherwise they would not be 'statistical'), qualitative information and substantive knowledge are an important precondition for meaningful analyses and are often an integral component of experiments and quasi-experiments.

For instance, consider the case of women's quotas in parliamentary elections. Figure 4.1 compares the percentage of women in parliament in 69 countries with and 84 countries without quotas (Tripp and Kang, 2008). Each dot represents a country, and Finland, Sweden, France and the Netherlands are highlighted. Horizontal lines represent the average percentage of women in parliament in each group. From an effects-of-causes perspective, we would investigate the consequences of quotas on female representation. That is, the starting point is the presumed cause (quotas), and the aim is to measure its causal connection with the presumed effect (for example, the percentage of women in parliament). The fact that, on average, countries with quotas have more women in parliament than those without quotas suggests that quotas might be conducive to better female representation. On the other hand, from a causes-of-effects perspective we would begin with the outcome and trace our way back to the possible causes. For instance, we could ask why two relatively similar countries such as Finland and the Netherlands have similar shares of women in parliament (about 37 per cent), although only the Netherlands has gender quotas. We could also ask

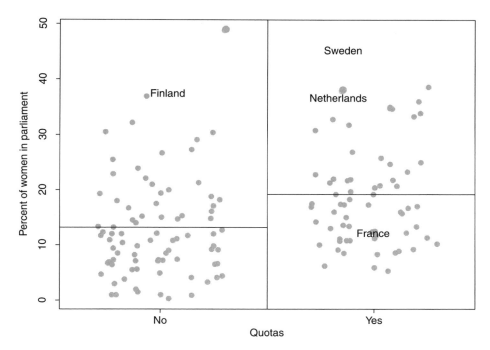

Figure 4.1 Percentage of women in parliament in 69 countries with and 84 countries without quotas. Each dot represents a country. Horizontal lines represent the average percentage of women in parliament in each group

Source: based on Tripp and Kang (2008)

why, in Sweden, there are almost four times as many women in parliament as in France (45.3 per cent compared to 12.2 per cent), given that both countries have introduced quotas. The first perspective would be likely to produce a single estimate of the causal effect, while the second would probably give an extensive account of the numerous factors influencing female representation and explain the cases holistically, that is, in all their complexity. However, significant qualitative knowledge is also required in the former, both for constructing an appropriate research design and for interpreting the finding correctly.

Statistical research designs embrace the effect-of-causes approach. As Gelman (2011) argues, 'What causes Y?' is often the question that motivates the analysis in the first place. However, attempting to answer the question directly leads inevitably to a proliferation of hypotheses, most of which are actually likely to have *some* validity. Thus, the risk is that the analysis becomes intractable. This is the problem of overdetermination, or the fact that there are always a myriad of factors contributing in some way to a specific outcome. As we discuss in Chapter 6, there are methods that allow us to address this issue from a case-oriented perspective, that is, within a causes-of-effects approach. However, statistical designs reframe the question in terms of the effects of causes. They break the question down, identify a particularly interesting factor, and ask what consequences it has on the outcome of interest. An implication of this strategy is that multiple analyses are needed to uncover complex causal paths, because each analysis can examine only one at a time. Or, as Gelman (2011) puts it, in this perspective we are trying to learn about a specific causal path within a more complex causal structure, but not about the causal structure itself. Thus, statistical designs prioritize the reliability of very specific causal estimates at the expense of the broader context in which they operate and possibly even of the connection with the original (theoretical and/ or empirical) problem, which must be redefined in order to make it fit within the strict requirements of the analytical design.

The potential-outcomes framework

The potential-outcomes framework, also known as the counterfactual model, pre-supposes a dichotomous treatment (D_i), such as (to continue our example from the previous section) the presence or absence of women's quotas. If $D_i = 1$, then country i has quotas for the representation of women in parliament, while if $D_i = 0$, then it does not. Further, the framework assumes that there are two potential outcomes for each unit i, Y_{1i} and Y_{0i}. The outcomes are associated with the two possible values of the treatment. In our example, Y_{1i} is the percentage of women in parliament in country i in the presence of quotas, while Y_{0i} is that percentage if the same country i does not have quotas. Formally, we can represent this idea as follows:

$$Y_i = \begin{cases} Y_{1i} \; if \, D_i = 1 \\ Y_{0i} \; if \, D_i = 0 \end{cases}$$

Notice that both outcomes refer to the same unit. But, of course, it is impossible that, in our example, the same country both does and does not have quotas. This is why the two outcomes are called 'potential'; only one is realized and can be observed, while the other is its logical counterpart, which exists only in the realm of ideas. However, conceptually, both are necessary for the definition of a causal effect. If we were able to observe, for the same country i, the percentage of women both with and without quotas, then we could compute the causal effect for that country simply as the difference between the two outcomes:

$$Y_{1i} - Y_{0i}$$

On this basis, and always on the assumption that both outcomes can be observed (which, in fact, is not possible), we can define two other quantities. The first is the average treatment effect (ATE), which, as the name indicates, is the average effect of the treatment for all units (for instance, the average effect of quotas in all countries):

$$\text{ATE} = \frac{1}{n} \sum_{i=1}^{n} (Y_{1i} - Y_{0i})$$

That is, the ATE is defined as the average difference between the two potential outcomes in all countries. The second quantity is the average treatment effect on the treated (ATT), that is, the effect of the treatment averaged only over units that actually receive the treatment (for instance, the average effect of quotas in countries with quotas):

$$\text{ATT} = \frac{1}{\sum_{i=1}^{n} D_i} \sum_{i=1}^{n} D_i (Y_{1i} - Y_{0i})$$

That is, we make the same computation as for the ATE, but only for the subset of countries with quotas (those for which $D_i = 1$). Countries without quotas ($D_i = 0$) are disregarded.

These definitions rely on a critical assumption, namely, the so-called stable unit treatment value assumption (SUTVA) (Morgan and Winship, 2007: 37–40). This has two components. First, the treatment must be the same for all units. While the *effect* of the treatment can vary across units (if it did not, we would not need to compute averages for the ATE and ATT), the treatment itself must be equivalent in all units. In our example, this assumption is in fact violated because there are several types of quotas, namely, compulsory or voluntary party quotas, reserved lists, and women-only lists (Tripp and Kang, 2008: 347). By collapsing them in a simple 'quotas versus no quotas' dichotomy, we assume that each of these instruments has the same consequences for female representation, which is unlikely to be the case. However, this assumption is necessary in the potential-outcomes framework. Second, the outcomes in one unit must be independent of the treatment status in other units. In other words, the percentage of women in a given country must be unrelated to whether or not other countries have quotas. This assumption should be met in our example, but it is easy to imagine other situations in which it does not hold, for instance when the treatment has network effects or other types of externalities. The interdependencies discussed in Chapter 7 are good cases in point.

As noted above, these definitions of treatment effects are purely theoretical. In reality, we cannot observe the same unit both with and without the treatment. This is known as the 'fundamental problem of causal inference' (Holland, 1986), and it is what makes causal inference so difficult in practice. The nature of the problem is summarized in Table 4.1. In reality we can observe two outcomes, namely, in our example, the percentage of women in parliament in the presence of quotas given that there are actually quotas, and the percentage in the absence of quotas given that there are actually no quotas. However, to compute the quantities defined above, we would need also the two corresponding counterfactual outcomes, namely, the percentage of women in parliament in the absence of quotas in countries that actually have quotas, and the percentage in the presence of quotas in countries that actually have quotas. To illustrate more intuitively, take the case of France. Because this country has women's quotas, we are here in the top-left corner of Table 4.1. To compute the causal effect of quotas in France, we should take the difference between the observed percentage of women in parliament (12.2 per cent) and the value that we would observe if France had no quotas, that is, the value of the top-right corner of Table 4.1. The same logic applies to countries that have no quotas, namely, those in the bottom-right corner, which would need to be compared with their counterfactuals in the bottom-left corner.

Table 4.1 The fundamental problem of causal inference (based on Morgan and Winship, 2007: 35)

	(% women if quotas) Y_{1i}	(% women if no quotas) Y_{0i}
(Quotas) $D_i = 1$	$Y_{1i} \mid D_i = 1$ (Observable)	$Y_{1i} \mid D_i = 0$ (Counterfactual)
(No quotas) $D_i = 0$	$Y_{0i} \mid D_i = 1$ (Counterfactual)	$Y_{0i} \mid D_i = 0$ (Observable)

What if we compute the difference between the two quantities we can actually observe? As we have seen in Figure 4.1, countries with quotas have, on average, more women in parliament (19.2 per cent) than those without (13.2 per cent). It turns out that this observed difference in averages is equal to the ATT (one of our quantities of interest), plus a selection bias (Angrist and Pischke, 2009: 14). In our example, the selection bias corresponds to the average difference between the percentage of women in parliament without quotas in countries that actually have quotas (a counterfactual) and the percentage without quotas in countries that actually do not have them (which is observable). The former group includes countries such as France, Germany, and Sweden, while the latter includes countries such as Ghana, Syria, and Vietnam. In fact, Table 4.2 shows that the two groups differ systematically in a number of ways. Countries with quotas tend to be wealthier, more democratic, and more likely to have a proportional system of electoral representation. Although the difference is only borderline significant, women in countries with quotas also tend to be more educated. All these factors are likely to be associated with a higher share of women in parliament even in the absence of quotas. This is what 'selection bias' means in this context. Countries are not assigned quotas randomly; they self-select into this policy. Therefore, countries with and countries without quotas differ in a number of ways and the two groups are not well comparable.

Table 4.2 Countries with and countries without quotas are quite different (calculations based on Tripp and Kang, 2008)

	Quotas	No quotas	Difference	Significance level
GDP/cap (log)	7.96	7.11	0.85	0.001
Women's education	47.82	46.22	1.61	0.096
Democracy	2.55	2.04	0.52	0.000
Electoral system	0.57	0.29	0.28	0.000

In sum, within the potential-outcomes framework, causal effects are clearly defined but cannot be directly computed in practice because the required counterfactuals are unobservable. However, researchers can rely on several methods to estimate them. We turn to these in the next section.

Methods

Regression

Regression analysis is:

> [a]n extension of correlation analysis, which makes predictions about the value of a dependent variable using data about one or more independent variables. A key parameter estimated in a regression analysis is the magnitude of change in the dependent variable associated with a unit change in an independent variable. This parameter is referred to as the slope or the regression coefficient. (Brady and Collier, 2004: 303)

In most quantitative studies, the default research design applies this technique to observational data, that is, information that was not generated by a process controlled by the researcher. The data set used by Tripp and Kang (2008) is a typical example. By contrast, experimental data are those produced under the supervision of the researcher. To continue with our example, a bivariate regression (that is, including just one explanatory variable) of the share of women in parliament on quotas indicates that countries with quotas have on average about 6 per cent more women in parliament than countries without quotas, and that the difference is statistically highly significant.[1] This difference corresponds exactly to what is shown in Figure 4.1. An obvious problem with this analysis is that it fails to control for the differences that exist across countries beyond the presence of quotas, such as those shown in Table 4.2. In other words, the bivariate regression neglects the selection bias problem. A multivariate regression (that is, including several explanatory variables) can mitigate it, to a certain extent. If we include the variables listed in Table 4.2, quotas remain significantly associated with female representation, but the size of the effect is reduced by half in comparison with the bivariate regression. That is, with per capita gross domestic product (GDP), women's education, democracy, and the type of electoral system controlled for, countries with quotas have on average only about 3.2 per cent more women in parliament than countries without quotas.[2] The inclusion of control variables is known also as 'covariate adjustment', which means that the analysis adjusts the estimate of the causal effect for those covariates (that is, variables) that can be taken into account.

Under some conditions, regression can yield unbiased estimates of causal effects (Morgan and Winship, 2007: 136–42). These conditions, however, are quite restrictive and generally unlikely to be met in practice.

First, there must be no omitted variables in the analysis. That is, in our example, all factors influencing the percentage of women in parliament besides quotas must be measured and included in the regression. Obviously, no analysis can ever fulfil this requirement perfectly, which means that only rarely can the causal estimates produced by regression analysis be credibly considered unbiased.

Second, the functional relationship between the control variables and the outcome must be fully and correctly specified. This means, for instance, that any non-linearities in the relationship between say, per capita GDP and women's representation (for instance, the correlation is stronger at lower levels of per capita GDP), as well as any interactions (for instance, the correlation between women's

---

[1] % women = 13.18 (1.03) + 6.02 (1.53) × quotas. OLS estimates, standard errors in parentheses.

[2] % women = −1.67 (5.68) + 3.2 (1.55) × quotas + 6.02 × electoral system + 0.11 (1.16) × democracy + 0.11 (0.14) × women's education + 1.18 (0.59) × GDP/cap (log). OLS estimates, standard errors in parentheses.

education and representation depends on the level of per capita GDP) must be explicitly and correctly modelled. This quickly becomes intractable with even just a handful of variables, a problem that is known as the 'curse of dimensionality'. This requirement stems from the fact that, in most practical situations, the treatment and control groups are quite different; in other words, the covariates are not balanced between them. In fact, this is the case in our example, as shown in Table 4.2. Therefore, the analysis needs to make assumptions in order to extrapolate the comparison between countries with and without quotas for specific combinations of control variables. The problem can be alleviated by a method called 'matching' (Ho et al., 2007), which attempts to make the treated and control groups more similar by removing 'incomparable' cases. One can, for instance, compute the probability that a unit receives the treatment (the 'propensity score') and then find, for each treated unit, an untreated unit with a very similar propensity score. If this procedure is successful (which depends on the characteristics of the data set), then a better balance between the two groups is achieved (that is, they are more comparable) and the analysis becomes less dependent on the specific assumptions made by the regression model. However, matching improves comparability only with respect to variables that can actually be observed. Thus, the first condition (no omitted variables) remains a big problem.

Experiments

As we have seen, two main practical problems arise when the potential-outcomes approach is implemented empirically. First, selection bias is ubiquitous, which means that the comparability of the treatment and control groups is usually limited. Second, while regression can in principle solve this problem, omitted variables and the 'curse of dimensionality' will in most cases lead to biased estimates of causal effects. The appeal of the experimental approach is that it is much more effective in ensuring that treated and control units are in fact comparable. This occurs through 'randomization', that is, random assignment of treatment to the units. Specifically, what defines experiments is that randomization is undertaken by researchers themselves. With randomization, systematic differences between the two groups can occur only by chance and, if the number of units is sufficiently large, with a very low probability. Moreover, the procedure works for both observable and unobservable characteristics, such that omitted variables are no longer a problem. Because randomization is so powerful, the data can in principle be analysed with simple techniques, and the difference in means for the outcome between treatment and control groups (or, equivalently, the coefficient of a bivariate regression) can be interpreted as the ATE as well as the ATT. A common problem is that units are not selected randomly from the population, such that it is not possible to generalize the estimates straightforwardly beyond the sample.

However, the estimates are still valid for the units that were part of the experiment. It should be emphasized that, of course, randomization is not perfect and there are several ways in which it can go wrong. For instance, it is possible that not all the units that are assigned to the treatment are actually treated or, conversely, that some control units become exposed to it ('non-compliance'); it is also possible that, for one reason or another, outcomes cannot be observed for some units ('attrition') (Gerber and Green, 2008). However, experiments have an unparalleled capacity to uncover causal relationships and are widely considered the 'gold standard' in this respect.

In our women's quotas example, an experiment would imply that quotas are attributed to countries randomly. As a consequence, and in contrast to what we have seen in Table 4.2, the groups of countries with and without quotas would be very similar, if not exactly identical, in all characteristics that could potentially affect women's representation, including those that cannot be observed. Therefore, the average difference in the percentages of women in parliament between the two groups could in principle be interpreted as the causal effect of quotas. The example shows the advantages of the experimental approach, but also an obvious drawback in the social sciences. In many, if not most, cases, randomization cannot be implemented for a number of practical and ethical reasons. For instance, imposing a dictatorship on a random subset of democracies (to see the consequences on economic growth, for example) is impossible in practice and, even if it were feasible, would be unethical. Given these problems, it is not surprising that experiments are not the first method that comes to mind when one thinks of social science research. At the same time, in recent years they have been used with increasing frequency and success and have become a mainstream tool for social scientists (Druckman et al., 2006). We can distinguish among three broad types, namely, laboratory, survey and field experiments, which we discuss in the following subsections.

Laboratory experiments

Laboratory experiments are 'experiments where the subjects are recruited to a common location, the experiment is largely conducted at that location, and the researcher controls almost all aspects in that location, *except* for subjects' behavior' (Morton and Williams, 2008: 346; emphasis in original). They are what first comes to mind when we hear the word 'experiment,' namely, a relatively small group of people, not necessarily representative of the broader population (for example, students), following precise instructions to perform a set of abstract tasks.

Despite their stylized nature, laboratory experiments can help to uncover important causal relationships. For example, Correll (2004) was interested in how cultural beliefs about gender differences in ability affect career choices through the self-assessment of performance. If it is commonly accepted in society that, say, men are better than women at mathematics, then the theory is that, at equal levels of objective skills, men will evaluate their competence more highly than women do. Consequently, men will be more inclined than women to pursue a career in a field where maths is important, thus reproducing existing gender imbalances. To estimate the causal effect of cultural frames, Correll (2004) set up an experiment in which about 80 undergraduate students were asked to perform a test purportedly designed to develop a new examination for graduate school admission. The test had no right or wrong answers (but was perceived as credible) and all subjects were given the same score, that is, the same objective assessment of their skills. By contrast, their cultural expectations (that is, the treatment) were manipulated by assigning subjects randomly to two groups. The treated group was told that males tend to perform better at the task, while the control group was informed that there are usually no gender differences in this context. After completing the test and receiving the (fake) scores, subjects were asked to provide a self-assessment of their performance and to answer questions about how likely they would be to pursue a career requiring high levels of the skills that were purportedly tested. In line with the theoretical expectations, the analysis showed that, under the treatment condition, females' self-assessment was lower than males', and that males' assessment under the treatment was higher than under the control condition. Further, these biased self-assessments were related to potential career plans.

A second example is Dunning and Harrison (2010), which studied how cross-cutting cleavages moderate the political saliency of ethnicity. The theory is that ethnic differences play a more important role in politics if citizens speaking a given language, for instance, belong to a different religion and are poorer than those speaking other languages. If, however, the different cleavages (linguistic, religious, economic) are not superposed in this way, then it is expected that language is less relevant as a determinant of political behaviour. Dunning and Harrison (2010) studied this argument in the case of Mali, a highly ethnically diverse country, by focusing on 'cousinage', which is a form of identity and social bonds connected with groups of patronymics (surnames) but distinct from ethnicity. The 824 subjects of the experiments, recruited in Mali's capital city, were shown videotaped political speeches by a purported political independent considering being a candidate for deputy in the National Assembly. Subjects were asked to evaluate the candidate on a number of dimensions. The treatment was the politician's last name, which subjects could readily associate with both ethnicity and cousinage ties. This set-up yielded four combinations of subjects' and politician's ethnicity and cousinage, namely, same ethnicity/cousins, same ethnicity/not cousins, different ethnicity/cousins, and different ethnicity/not cousins. Additionally, in the control group the politician's name was not given. In line with theoretical expectations, the candidate was evaluated best by the subjects when they shared both ethnicity and cousinage and worst in the opposite scenario. Additionally, cousinage compensated for ethnicity: the candidate was evaluated similarly when subjects and candidate were from the same ethnic group but without cousinage ties and when they were from a different ethnic group but with cousinage ties.

In order to produce valid results, laboratory experiments must consider an extensive list of potential problems, such as the nature of experimental manipulations, location, artificiality, subjects' selection and motivation, and ethical concerns (for a thorough discussion, see Morton and Williams, 2010). Furthermore, they are vulnerable to the objection that, while their internal validity may be strong (that is, their results are valid within the context of the experiment), their conclusions cannot be generalized to the 'real world'. We return to this point in the conclusion.

Survey experiments

Survey experiments randomly assign the respondents of a survey to control and treatment conditions through the manipulation of the form or placement of questions (Gaines et al., 2007: 3–4). Because many survey experiments use samples that are representative of the population, they promise to achieve both internal and external validity, the first through randomization, and the second through representativeness (Barabas and Jerit, 2010: 226). These potential qualities, in combination with increasingly easy and cheap access to survey resources, have made survey experiments more popular among social scientists in recent years.

For example, Hainmueller and Hiscox (2010) examined attitudes towards immigration. They asked whether, as predicted by the labour market competition model, people tend to oppose immigrants with a skills level similar to their own, who would be perceived as a more direct threat in the competition for jobs. The experiment was embedded in a survey completed by 1,601 respondents in the United States, who were randomly divided into two groups. Those in the treatment group were asked whether they agreed that the USA should accept more highly skilled immigrants from other countries. The question asked in the control group was identical except that 'highly skilled' was replaced with 'low-skilled'. The authors were able to confirm that randomization worked well because the distributions of respondents' characteristics in the two groups were statistically indistinguishable. The main finding of the analysis is that, contrary to theory, both low-skilled and highly skilled respondents prefer highly skilled immigrants, which suggests that non-economic concerns are very important to explaining attitudes towards immigration.

Another example is Linos (2011), who studied cross-national interdependencies (one of the topics of Chapter 7) in the field of family policy with an experiment in which 1,291 Americans were asked whether they agreed that the United States should increase taxes to finance paid maternity leave. Respondents were assigned randomly either to a control group, in which the question was formulated neutrally, or to one of four treatment groups. In the first and second treatment groups, respondents were informed that the proposed policy was already in place in Canada or in most Western countries, respectively. In the third, respondents learned that the policy was recommended by the United Nations. Finally, in the fourth the policy was endorsed by 'American family policy experts'. The results show that, while in the control group only 20 per cent of respondents supported increasing taxes to pay for maternity leave, the share jumped to about 40 per cent in the treatment groups referring to Canada or other Western countries. Interestingly, the effect of foreign models was comparable to that of American experts, while that of the UN was even slightly higher. Thus, foreign experiences seemed to play a significant role in shaping public opinion on family policy, which could be an important channel through which policies spread cross-nationally.

Researchers employing survey experiments face a distinct set of issues (Gaines et al., 2007; Barabas and Jerit, 2010). The treatment can be problematic in several ways. It is typically administered as a single exposure to an artificially intense stimulus, while in reality people may be exposed to it to varying degrees, at several points in time, and in combination with other factors. Moreover, exposure to the real-world version of the treatment prior to the survey can bias the results. Also, survey experiments usually measure the immediate effects of the treatment, but it would be important to know how long they last. In short, even if the sample is representative, external validity can be compromised if the treatment itself lacks representativeness.

Field experiments

Field experiments 'are experiments where the researcher's intervention takes place in an environment where the researcher has only limited control beyond the intervention conducted' (Morton and Williams, 2008: 346). The central characteristic of experiments (randomized treatment assignment) is preserved but takes place in the 'real world', which complicates its implementation in various ways. Field experiments are well established particularly in the study of political behaviour and the political economy of development, but they have also caught on in other sub-fields. Because of the logistical requirements, which often involve prolonged stays in the area where the experiments take place and contacts with a large number of local actors, researchers gain detailed knowledge of their cases, comparable to that of typical qualitative fieldwork. Thus, the qualitative–quantitative distinction is not very meaningful here.

For instance, Olken (2010) studied a classic question of democratic theory, namely, the comparative advantages of direct democracy and representation. The field experiment randomized the political process through which infrastructure projects were selected in 49 Indonesian villages. About 53 per cent of the villages were randomly assigned to a direct democratic process in which all adults eligible to vote in national elections could express their preference. In the remaining villages the standard process was followed. Project selection took place in small meetings open to the public but, in fact, were attended by a limited number of members of the local elite (such as government officials and representatives of various groups). On average, about 20 times as many people participated in the referenda as in the meetings. The randomization produced treatment and control groups that were statistically indistinguishable with respect to both village characteristics (such as ethnic and religious fragmentation, distance to sub-district capital, population) and individual characteristics (education, gender, age, occupation). The results of the experiment showed that the same projects were selected under both decision-making processes, which suggests that representation does not lead to outcomes that are biased in favour of the elite's preferences. However, villagers were significantly more satisfied with the decisions when they were taken through referenda. Thus, it seems that the main effect of direct democracy is to increase the legitimacy of decisions, but not necessarily to shift their content closer to the population's preferences.

Another field experiment attempted to uncover the effects of political advertising on voters' preferences by randomizing radio and television advertisements, for a total value of about $2 million, during the 2006 re-election campaign of Texas governor Rick Perry (Gerber et al., 2011). The study randomized both the starting date and the volume of advertisements across 20 media markets in Texas, but not stations or programmes. The outcome, that is, voters' evaluation of the candidate, was measured using large daily polls. Results showed a strong short-term effect of the advertisements. The maximum advertisements volume was associated with an increase of almost five percentage points in the candidate's vote share during the week in which the advertisements were aired. However, this effect vanished as soon as a week afterwards. Thus, the results suggest that political advertising does make a difference, but this difference evaporates quite quickly.

In addition to problems common to all experiments (such as external validity), field experiments present some specific challenges (Humphreys and Weinstein, 2009: 373–6). Given that many interesting variables cannot be randomized because of practical constraints, only a relatively small subset of questions can be investigated with this method. A possible solution is to focus on smaller units (for example, municipalities instead of countries), but this will reduce the external validity of the analysis. Because field experiments take place in real time and in real settings, many factors are not under the control of researchers and can therefore contaminate the findings. A common problem is spillovers, or the fact that intervention in one unit may affect outcomes in other units. As discussed above, this violates the SUTVA assumption of the potential-outcomes framework. The logistics of field experiments also constrains their size and reduces the precision of the estimates, which is a problem especially if the effects are small. Finally, because they operate in real contexts, field experiments also raise certain ethical concerns.

Quasi-experiments

Quasi-experiments are observational studies (that is, they use data that were not generated by a process controlled by the researcher) in which, thanks to circumstances outside the researcher's control, random treatment assignment is approximated to a certain extent. That is, although the assignment of units to treatment or to control status is not determined by the researchers but by naturally occurring social and political processes, some features of the procedures make it credible to assume that it is 'as if at random'. As Dunning (2008) argues, the plausibility of this assumption is variable and the burden of proof must be on the researcher. Thus, it is useful to situate quasi-experiments on a continuum with standard observational studies at one end and classical randomized experiments at the other. Making the case convincingly usually requires detailed knowledge of the context of the quasi-experiment. Moreover, the data are seldom readily available. Their acquisition often necessitates archival work or other procedures typically associated with qualitative studies. This demonstrates again that the distinction between quantitative and qualitative approaches is not very relevant.

Quasi-experiments can take different forms. We discuss three: natural experiments, discontinuity designs, and instrumental variables.

Natural experiments

In natural experiments, the 'as if at random' component comes from some social, economic, and/or political process that separates two groups cleanly on a theoretically relevant dimension. That is, although the quasi-randomization occurs without the researcher's intervention, it produces well-defined treatment and control groups.

For instance, Hyde (2007) studied the effects of international election monitoring on electoral fraud with data from the 2003 presidential election in Armenia, using polling stations as units of analysis. The outcome variable was the share of votes of incumbent President Kocharian, who was widely believed to have orchestrated extensive fraud operations. Poll stations in the treatment group were those visited by international observers, while those in the control group were not inspected by the monitors. To measure the treatment status of poll stations, Hyde (2007) relied on the list of assigned polling stations produced by the organization in charge of monitoring the elections, the Office for Democratic Institutions and Human Rights of the Organization for Security and Co-operation in Europe (OSCE/ODIHR). The validity of the natural experiment rests upon the assumption that international observers were assigned to polling stations in a way that approximates random assignment, and Hyde (2007) discussed in detail why this assumption was plausible in this case. The OSCE/ODIHR staff completed the lists arbitrarily, only on the basis of logistical considerations and with no knowledge of the socio-economic and political characteristics of the polling stations. The analysis showed that the incumbent presidents received significantly more votes (between 2 and 4 per cent) in stations that were not monitored than in those that were visited by observers, which suggests that this control mechanism has an impact on the extent of electoral fraud.

In another study, Bhavnani (2009) exploited an actual randomization, albeit one which he did not design, to investigate the long-term effects of quotas on female representation, that is, their consequences after they are withdrawn. A policy initiative in India reserved a certain number of seats for women in local elections, which were chosen randomly for one legislature. The goal of this selection procedure was not to allow an evaluation of the policy (though this was a welcome side product), but rather to make it as fair as possible by ensuring that men would be excluded from certain seats only temporarily, and without biases towards specific seats. Reserved and unreserved seats were statistically indistinguishable on many relevant dimensions, which suggests that the randomization is likely to have worked. The analysis of elections in 1997 and 2002 showed that quotas had an effect on female representation not only during the election in which they were enforced, which must be true if the policy is implemented properly, but also in the next election, after they were no longer in force. A comparison of districts that were open both in 1997 and in 2002 with those that were reserved in 1997 but open again in 2002 shows that the percentage of female winners was significantly higher in the latter districts (21.6 per cent compared to 3.7 per cent). This indicates that the effects of quotas extend beyond their duration, possibly by introducing new female candidates into politics and by changing the perceptions of voters and parties.

Natural experiments are appealing because they feature randomization in a real-world setting without the direct involvement of the researcher. However, because researchers have no control over them, and because good natural experiments are rare, they often originate in the availability of a convenient configuration instead of in a previously defined research question. In this sense, they tend to be method-driven rather than problem-driven. Nonetheless, this is not necessarily problematic and the examples that we have just seen prove that natural experiments can be used to investigate important questions.

Discontinuity designs

Similar to natural experiments, discontinuity designs exploit sources of quasi-randomization originating in social and political processes. In contrast to natural experiments, they rely on sharp jumps, or 'discontinuities', in a continuous variable. The cut-off point determines whether a unit is exposed to the treatment or not, the idea being that treatment assignment is 'as if at random' for units on either side of it. Elections are a typical example of such discontinuities because it is quite reasonable to assume that, in narrow elections, the outcome is due in large part to chance. While candidates who win by a landslide are likely to be very different from those who receive only a handful of votes, candidates on either side of the election threshold are probably similar in many respects.

Using these ideas, Eggers and Hainmueller (2009) compared the wealth at death of narrow winners and losers in British national elections and found that successful Conservative Party candidates died with about £546,000, compared with about £298,000 for candidates from the same party who were not elected. By contrast, the difference was much smaller for Labour Party candidates, suggesting that the material benefits of serving in Parliament differ across political parties. Gerber and Hopkins (2011) also relied on the random component of elections, but to examine the effects of partisanship on public policy at the local level. The comparison of 134 elections in 59 large American cities revealed that in most policy areas changes in public spending were very similar regardless of whether a Republican or a Democrat narrowly won. The one exception was policing expenditures, which were higher under successful Republican candidates. These findings suggest that partisan effects are small at the local level.

Lalive and Zweimüller (2009) exploited a different type of discontinuity, namely, the date at which a longer period of parental leave entered into force in Austria, to estimate the effects of this policy on mothers' further childbearing and careers. Mothers giving birth after 30 June 1990 were able to benefit from paid leave of 2 years instead of 1 year under the policy in force until that date. Because of this sharp cut-off, the duration of the parental leave can be considered to be randomly assigned to mothers giving birth shortly before or after 30 June. Indeed, the two groups were indistinguishable on many observed socio-economic characteristics such as age and work history and profile. The comparison of the two groups showed that longer parental leave causes women to have more additional children. It also reduces their employment and earnings, but only in the short term.

Sharp cut-offs, such as those found in elections and other settings, generally offer quite convincing sources of quasi-randomization, even though researchers should carefully check whether actors are aware of the discontinuity and exploit it, as in the case of income tax thresholds (Green et al., 2009: 401). However, it is important to note that the causal effects estimated with this method apply only at the threshold and cannot be extrapolated to all units. Because, usually, only relatively few observations are sufficiently close to the threshold, the results produced by regression discontinuity designs apply to a specific subsample, which limits their external validity. Moreover, there are trade-offs but no clear guidelines regarding the width of the window around the threshold (Green et al., 2009). A larger window (and, thus, more observations) makes estimates more precise but potentially biased by unobserved factors, while a smaller window reduces the bias but reduces the number of observations and, thus, the precision of the estimates.

Instrumental variables

Instrumental variables are factors that can be used to replace treatment variables for which the 'as if at random' assumption does not hold (Sovey and Green, 2010). They have to meet three crucial assumptions. The first is relatively innocuous and states that the instrument and the treatment are correlated, after relevant covariates are controlled for. The second and third assumptions are usually much more problematic. The 'exclusion restriction' means that the instrument affects outcomes exclusively through its correlation with the treatment, that is, it has no direct effect on the outcomes, while the 'ignorability assumption' requires that the instrument is 'as if at random'. Thus, good instruments are those produced by some sort of quasi-experiment. Concretely, the estimation proceeds in two stages. In the first, the treatment variable is regressed on the instrument and the results are used to compute expected values for the treatment. In the second stage, these values replace the treatment in the main regression.

In a famous study, Acemoglu et al. (2001) addressed the effects of institutions on economic development. A simple regression of development on institutions is likely to be inappropriate (even with many control variables), for two reasons. First, the causal relationship can arguably go both ways: better institutions cause higher economic development, but higher economic development can also cause better institutions. Second, similar to the example of women's quotas discussed above, it is likely that countries with different degrees of economic development are different on many other dimensions as well. To circumvent these problems, Acemoglu et al. (2001) employed mortality rates of European settlers (proxied by those of soldiers, bishops, and sailors) as an instrument for current institutions. The argument is that European powers set up different types of institutions depending on their ability to settle. If a region was hospitable, then European-style institutions were constructed with an emphasis on property rights and checks against government power, while if it was not hospitable, colonizers set up 'extractive states' for the purpose of transferring as many resources as possible from the colony. The analysis shows a strong association between current institutions, instrumented by settler mortality, and economic development, which corroborates the argument that a causal relationship is at play rather than a mere correlation. An important caveat is the plausibility of the exclusion restriction, that is, the possibility that the effect of settler mortality on economic development could work through something other than institutions. For instance, the mortality rates of colonizers could be related to current diseases, which may have had an impact on development. In this case, institutions would not be part of the causal chain. However, the authors argue convincingly that the causes of European deaths in the colonies (mainly malaria and yellow fever) were not likely to be connected with economic development because the indigenous populations had developed immunities against these diseases.

In another application, election-day rainfall was used as instrument for turnout to estimate its effects on electoral outcomes in the United States (Hansford and Gomez, 2010). In effect, many studies have suggested that higher turnout is beneficial to leftist parties (or Democrats in the United States), but the problem is that many factors are likely to influence both the decision to vote and the vote itself at the same time. By contrast, the weather on election day is likely to affect the choice to go to the polling booth, but not the preference expressed in the vote.[3] Moreover, rainfall on a specific day can probably be considered an 'as if at random' event. The analysis was able to confirm that higher turnout does indeed cause a higher vote share for Democratic candidates.

Finally, in a study already discussed in Chapter 3, Kern and Hainmueller (2009) studied the effects of West German television on public support for the East German communist regime, using a survey of East German teenagers. The survey included information for both the dependent (regime support) and treatment (exposure to West German television) variables. Because it is highly likely that people who watch a lot of West German programmes have different predispositions towards the communist regime in the first place, the treatment cannot be considered 'as if at random'. However, while West German television reception was generally possible in East Germany, it was blocked in some regions (especially near Dresden) because of their topography. As long as living in Dresden *per se* was not directly related to regime support and that region was generally comparable with the rest of the country, living in Dresden can be used as an instrument for television exposure. The analysis showed that, quite counter-intuitively, West

---

[3]But recall the Italian expression 'Piove, governo ladro'.

German television caused greater support for the East German regime, possibly because East German citizens consumed it primarily for entertainment and not as a source of information.

Like the other approaches, instrumental variables come with their own set of problems (Sovey and Green, 2010). In fact, the list of potential issues is even longer because, in addition to the need to find a suitable 'quasi-experiment', the instrument must fit within the model that is used in the estimation in a very specific way. Also, the results must be interpreted carefully because the causal effects estimates apply to a particular subset of units and are known as 'local average treatment effects'. In sum, if the right conditions are fulfilled, instrumental variables are a valuable tool, but in practice their application is quite tricky.

Lessons for research design

If we take the statistical approach to causal inference seriously, the consequences for research design are wide-ranging. The main lesson is that the design is the most important part of the research because it is at this stage that the possibility of credibly identifying causal effects can be influenced. In fact, in the ideal-typical case of a 'perfect' research design, that is, an experiment that is designed and implemented flawlessly, the analysis stage becomes almost trivial because it suffices to compare mean outcomes in the treatment and control groups. The sophistication of the methods used in the analysis must increase with imperfections in the research design in order to correct them *ex post*.

To illustrate, consider again the example of women's quotas and female representation in parliament (Tripp and Kang, 2008). The research design adopted by the authors, which is typical of cross-national quantitative studies, was simply to collect data on as many countries as possible for the dependent variable (percentage of women in parliament), treatment variable (quotas), and control variables (countries' background characteristics). Here ends the design stage and begins the analysis, which, to produce credible causal estimates, needs to fix the basic problem that countries with and countries without quotas are not really comparable. As discussed above, standard regression tools and newer matching methods can help, but only up to a point. The fundamental problem is that they can adjust for the factors that we do observe, but not for those that we do not, which are virtually always an issue. Thus, *ex post* fixes are bound to be imperfect.

By contrast, the statistical approach to causal inference aims to fix things *ex ante* by constructing or finding suitable treatment and control groups in advance of the analysis. As we have seen, this goal can be achieved with different means. First, we can design our own experiments in the lab or in the field, or base them on surveys. That is, the treatment can be randomized by the researcher in an artificial setting, in the real world, or via the questions asked in a survey. Second, we can try to find constellations in which randomization is approximated without the direct intervention of the researcher. Natural experiments, discontinuity designs, and suitable instrumental variables are three options. In all these cases, the most traction for causal inferences is gained through the way the comparison between treatment and control groups is configured, not through the specific techniques used to analyse the data. The key benefit is that, if randomization is implemented properly or is approximated sufficiently in a real-world setting, it produces groups that are comparable not only for their observed but also for their unobserved characteristics. This is a major advantage for the validity of causal inferences.

Thus, the quality of the research design is of the essence. The exacting requirement of a plausible 'as if at random' assumption implies that downloading pre-packaged data sets and letting the computer do the counting is not enough, no matter how sophisticated the techniques. More creative solutions are required, and few will involve broad cross-national comparisons, for the simple reason that broad international comparisons are likely to be, well, incomparable. In fact, none of the examples discussed in this chapter compared countries. Instead, they focused on specific within-country variations and used original data, often assembled with great effort. Unfortunately, there are no clear guidelines for identifying promising comparisons. The criteria that the research design must meet are clear, but discovering the right configuration in practice is an art more than a science.

We emphasize that, in many ways, statistical research designs for causal inference transcend the usual qualitative–quantitative distinctions. Obviously, they have strong quantitative components because they rely on statistical techniques to estimate causal effects. However, they also require significant qualitative work and substantive knowledge to identify the most promising cases, to collect hard-to-access data through archival work or other qualitative procedures, and generally to construct a meaningful study. In some cases, such as field experiments, researchers are actually involved in fieldwork comparable to that of many traditional qualitative studies. Thus, these research designs do not fit well within a simple quantitative–qualitative typology. The limits of such distinctions are a general theme of this book.

As with all approaches, statistical research designs for causal inference must face trade-offs. The most important trade-off is that between validity and relevance. A common criticism of this approach is that it leads to a focus on small, tractable questions at the expense of big problems that are harder to study. It is undeniable that research in this tradition prioritizes internal over external validity. At the same time, the former is arguably a prerequisite for the latter. In other words, it does not make much sense to generalize findings that are not credible. Moreover, as Angrist and Pischke (2010) argue, external validity, or generalization, remains an important goal that can be achieved through the cumulation of well-designed but necessarily narrow studies. Finally, the examples discussed in this chapter studied problems such as the political salience of ethnicity, attitudes towards immigration, the consequences of direct democracy in comparison to representation, and the foreign influences of support for autocratic rule. These are all 'big' questions and, even though each study individually did not provide definitive answers, they did supply convincing evidence on the causal effects in a specific setting. Other studies should try to replicate them in other contexts. If they are successful, then the external validity and generalizability of the findings will be strengthened.

Conclusion

Figure 4.2 summarizes the main points of this chapter. We can classify statistical research designs for causal inference along two dimensions. First, is the treatment assigned randomly, and, if so, how? Second, to what extent are the treated and control units comparable?

In the standard regression approach, supplemented or not by matching, there is no randomization and, typically, self-selection into the treatment. For instance, the same variables that explain why countries adopt women's quotas

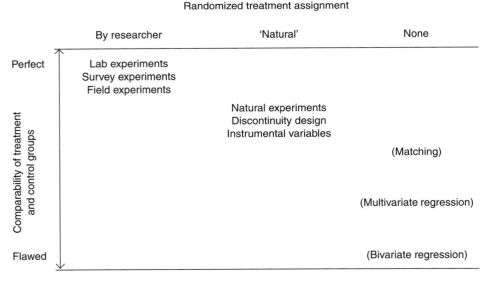

Figure 4.2 A classification of statistical research designs for causal inference. Matching and regression are in parentheses because, strictly speaking, they are estimation techniques and not research designs

DESIGNING RESEARCH IN THE SOCIAL SCIENCES

(the treatment) are likely to influence female representation in parliament (the outcome). The problem is bigger if these variables are not included in the analysis (bivariate regression) than if they are (multivariate regression), and matching can mitigate the problem further. However, there is no way around the fact that the adjustment can be made only for those variables that can be observed, but not for those that are unobserved. Therefore, the comparability of the treatment and control groups (countries with and countries without quotas) and, consequently, the validity of causal inferences will be relatively limited.

By contrast, in experiments the treatment is randomized by researchers themselves and, in principle, the treatment and control units will be highly comparable. Experiments can take place in the lab, in the field, and within surveys. Quasi-experiments can credibly make the assumption that the treatment is assigned 'as if at random' because of a particular process occurring in the real world, without the researcher's intervention. The comparability of the treatment and control groups will in principle be quite high, significantly better than in the standard regression approach, but somewhat worse than in experiments. The validity of the causal inferences will vary accordingly.

In this context, an important trade-off is that between complexity or realism of the research question and reliability of the causal estimates. To achieve the latter, statistical research designs narrow down complex theoretical and/or empirical questions to smaller, tractable questions. These research designs can produce valid estimates of causal relationships, but many different analyses are necessary to give the full picture of a complex phenomenon. By contrast, other research designs discussed in this book put the emphasis on a holistic view of causal processes, but at the cost of validity.

To conclude, the statistical approach emphasizes the importance of research design for valid causal inferences. The primary concern is the construction of comparable treatment and control groups. This will be difficult with standard cross-national data sets. Instead, researchers should produce their own experiments or look for configurations in the real world that can approximate them, which requires considerable qualitative knowledge and not just the mastery of quantitative techniques.

Checklist

- The key for causal inference is the construction or identification of appropriate treatment and control groups.
- Random assignment of treatment to the units ('randomization') is the gold standard for causal inference because it is the best way to make sure that the treatment and control groups are comparable.

- We speak of experiments when researchers themselves undertake the randomization. We can distinguish between laboratory, survey and field experiments.
- We speak of quasi-experiments when randomization is approximated due to circumstances outside the researchers' control. Natural experiments and discontinuity designs belong to this category.
- A successful experiment or quasi-experiment requires not just the application of quantitative techniques, but also significant qualitative knowledge.

 ## ■ Questions ■

1 Read closely five articles making causal arguments in your field of study. To what extent do they correspond to a 'causes-of-effects' or 'effects-of-causes' perspective?
2 For each of the five articles, reframe the causal claims using the potential-outcomes framework and construct the equivalent of Table 4.1.
3 Read five articles making causal arguments using standard regression methods. To what extent can the findings actually be interpreted causally?
4 Think of a specific research question. What would be the ideal experiment to test the causal argument? Now try to develop a research design that can approximate it as much as possible in practice.
5 Read closely five of the articles cited as examples in this chapter (or other articles of your choice) and assess them with respect to the trade-off between the validity of the causal inference and the relevance or importance of the findings.

■■ Further reading ■

Angrist, J.D. and Pischke, J. (2009) *Mostly Harmless Econometrics: An Empiricist Companion.* Princeton, NJ: Princeton University Press. A relatively non-technical introductory text written by economists.

Angrist, J.D. and Pischke, J. (2010) The credibility revolution in empirical economics: how better research design is taking the con out of econometrics. *Journal of Economic Perspectives*, 24 (2): 3–30. A non-technical summary of the book by the same authors.

Morgan, S.L. and Winship, C. (2007) *Counterfactuals and Causal Inference. Methods and Principles for Social Research.* Cambridge: Cambridge University Press. A relatively technical introductory text written by sociologists.

Morton, R.B. and Williams, K.C. (2010). *Experimental Political Science and the Study of Causality: From Nature to the Lab.* Cambridge: Cambridge University Press. A relatively technical introductory text written by political scientists.

FIVE

Temporality

Introduction

This chapter introduces the research strategies for the study of temporality in the social sciences. Temporality is a foundational concept for causal analysis because causal relationships unfold over time – and become observable only after a certain lapse of time. Moreover, time can be considered as an objective empirical dimension along which information can be gathered and observations made. In this sense, temporality can be studied in different ways, which can also be combined, for instance through historical case studies, descriptive statistics, simulations of artificial societies or the analysis of sequences of career paths. The chapter starts with research goals, such as the examination of the historical trend of macro-variables and the quantification of the impact of time-related factors on individual-level variables. It then presents and discusses the research designs that are suitable for these research goals.

We may be interested in different time-related variables, pursuing different research goals and following different analytical techniques. For instance, psychologists may want to study the effect of psychological therapies and treatments on the duration of depressive episodes; economists may want to assess abnormal fluctuations in stock market returns and possibly make predictions on future variations of stock prices; lawyers may try to explain the variation in the duration of civil and criminal trials in different jurisdictions; sociologists may seek to compare the family–career balance of a cohort of respondents over time; political scientists may want to interpret the persistence of social welfare policies in advanced democracies in a context of economic globalization; and so forth. The chapter presents the main strategies for operationalizing the time dimension and time-related variables in empirical research. As will be shown, each strategy corresponds to certain specific research goals and analytical techniques. It is thus possible to examine the time span of social phenomena with historical or simulative methods. The description and analysis of a tendency make it possible to characterize the overall trend of macro-phenomena or point out the presence of unexpected deviations and anomalies in a tendency. Levels and stocks represent entities in which variables can be aggregated to account for different operationalizations of quantities when examined over time. Time-related variables may also refer to the explanatory power of non-commutative sequencing. In this sense, the temporal ordering of events or processes is expected to have a crucial impact on outcomes. Furthermore, the notion of timing refers to the causes and effects of transitions from one social state to another, and can be used to study the consequences of specific events over time. Finally, the concept of path dependence permits us to make sense of the tension between change and stability of actors and structures in the social world.

Different conceptualizations of time

The notion of time has different meanings in the social sciences. Three broad conceptualizations exist. First, following Elias's (1992) definition, the meaning of time varies historically in different societies, in relation with the organization of work and the shared values of the members of the community. Therefore, the notion of time derives from the framework constituted by groups of people to order and delimit the observed continuum of natural and social changes. Elias showed how this framework tended to become more extensive and sophisticated with the process of civilization. In primitive societies, people said: 'we are cold'. At a later stage, the concept of 'winter' emerged. Finally, a universal calendar categorized 'winter' as a certain season even in temperate countries. In the context of globalization, the symbolic dimension of time is becoming more homogeneous and increasingly universal. Following a similar argument, Bauman (2000) interprets time as a relatively recent category of thought and one of the defining characteristics of modernity. The beginning of the modern era is associated with a progressive emancipation of the notion of time from the notion of space, following human progress and technical development, leading to a processable and dynamic perception of society instead of the static and immutable vision that was prevalent in the pre-modern agrarian social order.

From another perspective, time is appreciated through a subjective psychological dimension (Zakay, 1990). For instance, in time-estimation experiments, participants are asked to delimitate, produce, reproduce or compare the duration of a certain standard interval in order to assess the 'over- or underestimation of the standard', the 'relative speed of the internal and external clocks' and 'the relative magnitude of the subjective and objective temporal units'. Subjective time is measured, on the one hand, through the individual cognitive capacity to keep track of units of time for prospective judgements. On the other hand, it is assessed through a process, which is used for retrospective and relative judgements, wherein duration is based on the differential priority of events. This standpoint is particularly pertinent when the perception of time is used to explain certain types of individual behaviour such as decision-making under stress, the attention of children in the classroom, and the shopping preferences of customers (Hornik, 1984).

Finally, time can be conceived of as an objective empirical dimension along which to gather information and to make observations (Bartolini, 1993). In this sense, the term 'time' is preferred to that of 'history', because the former is conceptually more precise and less problematical in its array of significations. In the rest of this chapter we endorse this position to conceive of time-related factors as variables to be explained and included in explanatory models.

Before engaging in the discussion of the different research strategies for the study of time in the social sciences, it is useful to briefly specify which unit of analysis does matter. The first unit of analysis refers to the investigation of historical events rather than contemporary social phenomena. This way, the idea of 'time' is simply operationalized as 'the past'. The study of the past requires a number of tools that are typical of historiography, such as archival sources, archaeological evidence or different types of secondary literature (Bloch, 1992). However, these techniques for data collection are employed for practical reasons, such as the obvious impossibility of conducting survey inquiries, interviews and direct observations of past events; but they do not configure specific research designs for data analysis. The second type of unit of analysis pertains to the study of particular periods, which implies the periodization of historical phenomena, that is, the descriptive categorization of time into meaningful blocks of social events (Besserman, 1996). The criteria of periodization are rather unstable and the classifications are often debated, but the aim of periodization is always to identify a number of relatively constant and homogeneous sets of contextual conditions, to define the boundaries and date phenomena such as 'the Roman Empire'; 'the Middle Ages', 'the French Revolution'. Again, this is mostly a descriptive task that does not require a specific research design. The third perspective is more analytical and focuses on time as (another) dimension of variation, along with synchronic variations. This view typically implies the comparison of two or more points in time (Bartolini, 1993). In some cases, temporal variations (from year to year, from week to week, and so on) can be considered even more important than spatial variations concerning differences between countries and between regions, or differences among individuals of target samples, groups or populations, especially for explaining phenomena such as cyclical economic variations, social attitudes and political behaviour. This last perspective – time as a dimension of variation – is the most pertinent for the following discussion, which presents the different ways of operationalizing and assessing the time dimension in social science empirical research.

Research goals and research designs

Different research designs can be fruitfully employed to pursue different research goals related to the study of temporality in the social sciences, corresponding to specific techniques of data analysis. They are presented in the following subsections and discussed comprehensively at the end of the chapter.

Time span

To begin with, social scientists are frequently interested in the study of time span, sometimes called 'duration', that is, time periods or, more precisely, the amount of time from when something starts to when it ends. The early approaches to time span adopt functional and teleological perspectives. In this sense, for instance, the Marxian conception of history assumes as implicit explanatory factor the dialectical progress of history itself, towards a final stage that is seen as inevitable.

The macro-historical empirical perspectives of the second half of the twentieth century are more explicit about the causal relevance of time span. To begin with, we can mention the so-called macro-history of the *longue durée*. This school of thought relies on the study of the past on very large scales, to make sense of structural social processes: in other words, social processes become visible only when many centuries of historical development are considered:

> The way to study history is to view it as a long duration, as what I have called the *longue durée*. It is not the only way, but it is one which by itself can pose all the great problems of social structures, past and present. It is the only language binding history to the present, creating one indivisible whole. (Braudel, 1958)

A typical example is the explanation of the development of Western civilization in the Mediterranean following the long-term development of commerce. Eventful history takes the reverse approach to time span, focusing on localized, crucial events – important human actions through time – that explain structural change (Sewell, 1996). Finally, long-term and short-term approaches have been reconciled using Wallerstein's (1987) world systems theory related to the unfolding of long-term events in connection with the position and relationships among nation states within a capitalist system, and following Tilly's

(2006) approach, which analyses the transformative role of sequences of crisis over long periods of time. Macro-historical perspectives usually adopt interpretive historical methods to make sense of time span, or comparative historical analysis to locate the 'macro-causes' of phenomena under study (Mahoney and Rueschemeyer, 2003).

More recently, simulative models of artificial societies have operationalized the notion of time span even more explicitly and in a very different manner. Simulations are computer-based models of the macro-consequences of local interactions of actors within artificial societies. The most common simulative procedure relates to the development of agent-based models, reporting the interactions of the members of a population whose characteristics and range of behaviours are defined by the researcher, according to certain rules concerning the shape and units of actors' utility functions, the process by which they make decisions, and the ways they are interdependent (Benoit, 2001). This computational methodology allows the analyst to create, analyse and experiment with artificial worlds populated by agents that interact in 'non-trivial ways' over time (Epstein and Axtell, 1996). The standard research design for actor-based models is as follows. The first step is the identification of the purpose of the analysis, that is, the questions the model is intended to answer. Then the researcher analyses the system under study by detecting the components and their interactions, using relevant data sources. Then the model is applied to conduct a series of experiments by systematically varying parameters and assumptions over different time spans. Finally, the robustness of the model and its results are tested by using sensitivity analysis and other techniques. The research design scheme for agent modelling is summarized as follows (adapted from Macal and North, 2010):

1 Identify the agents and develop and implement a theory of agent behaviour.
2 Identify the relationships among agents and develop and implement a theory of agent interaction.
3 Obtain agent-related data.
4 Validate agents' behaviour models and the model as a whole.
5 Run the model for different time spans and analyse the output.
6 Link the micro-scale behaviours of the agents to the macro-scale behaviours of the system.

As an example, we can refer to Axelrod's (1997) seminal work, *The Complexity of Cooperation*. The key research question was about the structural conditions for the emergence of cooperative attitudes among 'egoistic' agents in a world without central authority. In other words, the research goal was to identify the most effective strategies for reaching cooperation in non-zero-sum games where there is a unilateral incentive to defect, as in the prisoner's dilemma (see below for a discussion of game theory). Axelrod was able to show that cooperative strategies outperform non-cooperative strategies and lead to evolutionary cooperative equilibria, which cannot be 'overrun' by actors with non-cooperative strategies. Axelrod illustrated his point with the trench warfare on the western front in World War I, when front-line soldiers often refrained from shooting to kill so long as the soldiers on the other side reciprocated the restraint. According to this argument, the conditions for cooperation do not require rationality, the exchange of information or commitments, trust, altruism or a central authority. Instead, for cooperation to emerge a durable relationship is necessary, that is, an indefinite or unknown time span of the interaction. This means that the probability of the 'next encounter' between the same two individuals must be big enough to make defection an unprofitable strategy. In this model, cooperation appears in the population in the first place within small clusters and subsists when actors are able to extend their clusters and protect them from outsiders with the help of 'discriminating structures', in such a way that the overall level of cooperation tends to increase. Following Axelrod, actors' strategic rationality can be (very) bounded: these agents can come to cooperate with each other through trial-and-error processes, learning, the possibility of mutual rewards, and imitation of successful players.

Simulation can be very informative and useful in generating new hypotheses. However, there appears to be a strong trade-off between their internal and external validity. The persistent problem of simulative approaches to time span is their interpretation for social dynamics in the real world. On the one hand, the implicit underlying assumptions of agent-based models implement a methodologically individualist view of the social world, which usually omits, or downplays, the role of institutions and other social structures, and which assumes unrealistic homogenizing assumptions about interacting agents. Therefore, the explanatory power of such models is highly contingent. On the other hand, agent-based models are difficult to validate empirically. How can we verify that the mechanisms isolated by the model resemble those operating in the real world? This operation requires the progressive refinement of the model by reducing the number of parameters and by reducing the space between the possible 'worlds' that are explored (Windrum et al., 2007). However, the final step of validation always implies the direct or indirect comparison of the model with empirically observable evidence.

Tendency

The notion of tendency refers to the examination of prevailing movements in a given direction over time and implies the predisposition of phenomena to proceed in a particular way. The study of tendency permits the characterization of the overall trend of macro-phenomena or points to the presence of deviations and anomalies in particular trends. Measures of time tendency are useful for making sense of historical developments, scattered by different types of time points, such as days of the week, times of the month, or times of year.

Descriptive statistics are used to illustrate the historical tendency of variables such as production and consumption trends, population patterns, technological dynamism, urbanization, and industrial development. Political economists have highlighted sustained long-term aggregate economic growth and the recurrent fluctuations around this growth path, often referred to as business cycles. For instance, it is interesting to examine the growth rate experienced by the US economy in the long run and the consequences of this tendency. Real per capita GDP in the USA grew from $3,340 in 1870 to $33,330 in 2000 (in 1996 dollars), corresponding to a growth rate of 1.8 per cent per year, which gave the USA the second-highest level of per capita GDP in the world in 2000 (Barro and Sala-i-Martin, 2004). Another example is the so-called modernization theory, which postulates a linkage between economic development and democracy. Lipset's (1959, 1963) well-known argument is that economic development increases wealth and, concomitantly, enhances education, communication, and in turn equality, which is associated with the presence of a large, moderate middle-class supporting democracy. Przeworski and Limongi (1997) proposed amending the classic version of modernization theory by introducing a conceptual distinction between an endogenous and an exogenous theory of democratization. The endogenous explanation follows the modernization logic: through a gradual process of differentiation and specialization of social and political structures, economic development increases the probability that autocratic countries will undergo a transition to democracy. According to the exogenous theory, in contrast, democracy is established independently of economic development, but once in place it is more likely to survive in developed countries. More recently, Welzel and Inglehart (2003) have identified a 'post-modernist' tendency towards an increase in personal life satisfaction, political satisfaction, interpersonal trust and support, producing a 'coherent syndrome' of socioeconomic development, rising emancipatory values and democratization (Figure 5.1).

Two crucial issues need to be tackled when designing research studies that investigate the tendency of variables of interest. On the one hand, changes in the long run must be distinguished from cyclical shifts due, for example, to socioeconomic factors. On the other hand, standard techniques such as regression analysis can be misleading when applied to series with variable trends, because of the presence of so-called stochastic movements, that is, components of time series that do not contain any systematic movements and thus cannot be represented by deterministic functions of time (Stock and Watson, 1988). The econometrics of trends and cycles provides solutions to these problems, with the help of structural time-series models (Harvey, 1997). The aim of structural time-series models is to break down the linearity of regressions and to make the analysis more flexible by letting the level and slope parameters change over time. These parameters are assumed to follow 'random walks' leading to a stochastic trend in which the level and slope are allowed to evolve over time. Other components can be added to the model – in particular, cycles and seasonal components. With this method, the parameters of trend evolution are estimated by maximum likelihood. The whole model is therefore handled within a unified statistical framework that has a direct interpretation. It can be thought of simply as a regression model in which the explanatory variables are functions of time and the parameters are time-varying.

Another interesting analytical perspective that can be applied to the study of trends is the analysis of anomalies with event studies. Here the aim is not to control and overcome the deceptive effect of trends and cycles, but to study precisely the effect of peculiar or unexpected events on trends and cycles, such as the effect of a managerial decision or a regulatory change on the value of firms in the stock exchange. The underlying assumption is that the effect of an important event will be reflected in contextual variables, such as the prices of securities. In finance, this methodology has been applied to mergers between companies, to acquisitions, to the issue of new equity and to earnings announcements, in order to measure the impact of changes in the regulatory environment and to assess damages in case liability studies (Schwert, 1981). The procedure for an event study can be summarized as follows (MacKinlay, 1997). The initial task is to define the event of interest and identify the period over which the researcher can hypothetically observe the effects of the event, for instance the security prices of the firms involved in this event. This 'event window' must be larger than the specific period of interest, so that the periods surrounding the event can be examined. Then, to avoid any bias, the researcher must define the criteria for including the objects investigated (such as firms) in the analysis. The key point is to measure the abnormal return in order to appraise the event's impact. In this case, the abnormal return is the actual return over the event window minus the normal return of the firm. The normal return is defined as the expected return without conditioning on the occurring event. To estimate normal returns, the researcher needs a 'normal performance' model, whose simpler form is derived from a calculation based on the period prior to the event window. Afterwards, the abnormal returns can be estimated. The last point is the testing framework for the abnormal returns, regarding the techniques for aggregating the individual abnormal returns, by paying attention, when only few observations are included, to whether the empirical results are critically influenced by a few important cases, such as the performance of one or two big firms (Figure 5.2).

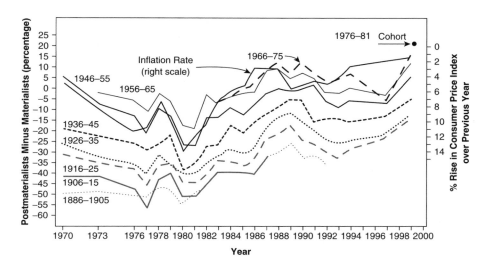

Figure 5.1 Trends

Source: Inglehart (1997)

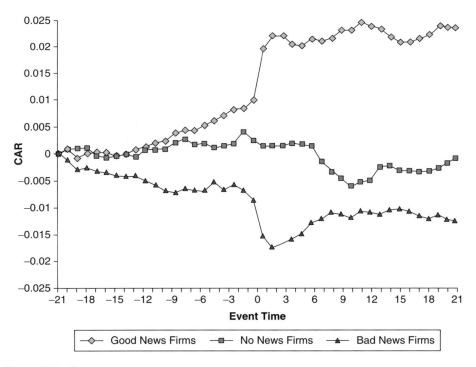

Figure 5.2 Events

Source: MacKinlay (1997)

Levels and stocks

The notions of levels and stocks are very common in the social sciences. As such, the analysis of levels and stocks requires not a specific research design but rather a conceptual clarification. A level variable captures the differences in degree, while a stock variable is measured at a specific point in time, but represents a quantity that has been accumulated. In public finance, for example, the national budget primary deficit is defined as the difference between what the government spends and the revenue it receives from all types of taxes, net of transfer payments, during a particular year, and the total deficit is the primary deficit plus interest payments. The deficit thus measures a positive or negative level. In contrast, the national debt reflects the accumulation of yearly deficits. So each year's deficit is added to the existing debt, producing a stock variable.

The difference between levels and stocks has interesting implications for the study of other types of social phenomena representing entities in which variables can be aggregated to account for different operationalizations of quantities when examined over time. This point can be exemplified by the discussion about the link between economic growth and the level of democracy, which has been extensively investigated. In theory, three competing positions exist. The first argument is that democracy has no observable implications for growth. The proponents of this view argue that variables other than political regimes matter for economic growth, and policies that favour growth can be promoted independently of the regime. These studies generally rely on quite restrictive definitions of democracy (for example, free elections). The second position underscores the fact that democracy has moderate negative (or zero) direct effects on growth, and/or has varied indirect positive effects, so that the overall effect of democracy on growth is expected to be (moderately) negative (Barro, 1996, 1999). Finally, a non-linear relationship is suggested, whereby an increase in democracy may enhance short-term growth at low levels of democracy but reduce short-term growth when higher levels of political freedom have been attained (Sirowy and Inkeles, 1990). Yet the empirical results remain inconclusive. Indeed, according to an extensive review article of 84 published studies of democracy and growth (Doucouliagos and Ulubaşoğlu, 2008), 15 per cent of the regression estimates of this link are negative and statistically significant, 21 per cent are negative and statistically insignificant, 37 per cent are positive and statistically insignificant, and 27 per cent are positive and statistically significant.

Gerring et al. (2005) have studied the connection between regime type and economic growth using an explanatory variable operationalized as a stock. They propose a historical examination of the effect of democracy on growth. They assume that if democracy matters for growth today, this effect stems not from its level but from the stock of democracy. In this sense, democracy is treated not as an immediate cause but as a long-term determinant of growth. The institutional effect of democracy is expected to be cumulative and to unfold over long periods of time. When measured as a stock variable, democracy appears to have a strong positive relationship to growth performance regardless of the specifications of the model. It is worth adding that, to correctly model these complex phenomena, Minier (1998) suggests restricting the comparison to similar countries instead of comparing all existing cases. For instance, the trajectory of Portugal should be compared not with the patterns of democratization in Ecuador or Peru, but with comparable initially high-income countries also exhibiting high growth rates, such as Greece and Spain. Using this approach, she has been able to show that changes towards increased democracy produce faster growth than in similar countries that did not experience democratization.

Sequences

We are also often interested in the study of sequential processes. A sequence is an ordered list of events. Unlike in a set, in a sequence the ordering matters. In formal terms, finite sequences are sometimes known as 'strings' and infinite sequences as 'streams'. The key issue of the empirical analysis of sequences is the dependence of an interval-measured sequence upon its own past (Abbott, 1995). In the rest of this section we focus on identifying the nature of the phenomenon represented by the sequence of observations.

Time-series analysis is the most straightforward way to examine sequences. The key insight is that, rather than treating the dynamic properties of data as problems that must be corrected statistically, time-series analysis allows the researcher to model these dynamics explicitly. The crucial point of this type of research design is how to deal with variables that are autocorrelated, that is, related with themselves over time. In fact, when the value of a variable at time t is related to its value at $t + 1$, the assumptions of standard regression models regarding the independence of observations are untenable (Pevehouse and Brozek, 2008). A rewarding way of dealing with this problem is with vector autoregressions (VARs), which allow us to model time dynamics among a set of endogenous variables (Brandt and Williams, 2007. A VAR is an econometric model used to capture the evolution of, and the interdependencies between, multiple time series. All the variables in a VAR are treated symmetrically by including for each variable an equation explaining its evolution based on its own lags and the lags of all the other variables in the model, and in which explanatory variables are also dependent variables. Very few assumed restrictions are used. Brandt and Williams (2007) indeed present VAR as a generalization of other approaches, which should be used specifically when the precise structure of the relationships among the variables is unknown, as is frequently the case with real-world data. Intuitively, the procedure for implementing VAR is as follows. The researcher starts with a number of time series that are expected to be interrelated (Pevehouse and Brozek, 2008). Several models are estimated in order to assess which specifications provide the best fit to the data. Hypothesis testing is quite complicated as it is not possible to interpret coefficients directly. The procedure thus involves the application of 'simulated shocks' to a variable of interest in order to detect its influence on the values of other variables in the system. Then variance decomposition allows the researcher to determine the influence of each variable in the system of equations. An interesting illustration of this approach is Goldstein and Pevehouse's (1997) study of the cooperative patterns in the Bosnian conflict in the early 1990s. The authors studied the reactions of armed forces to previous internal and external military interventions. From their empirical analysis it appeared that hostility from US and NATO forces caused the Serbs to adopt more cooperative behaviour towards the Bosnians, and that Serb forces were more responsive to American actions than to European ones (see Figure 5.3).

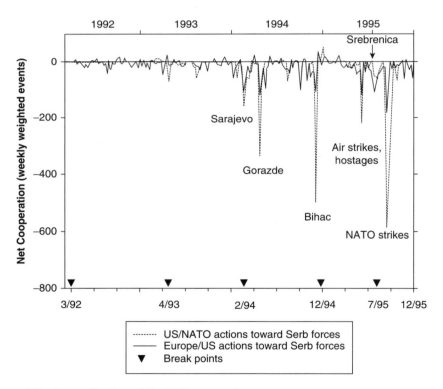

Figure 5.3 An application of the VAR approach

Source: Goldstein and Pevehouse (1997)

The concept of sequence is even more explicit in the methodology of optimal matching. Optimal matching is a method of sequence analysis used to assess the similarity of ordered arrays of items that usually represent a time-ordered sequence of social states or events experienced by individuals. The objective is to identify typologies of sequences empirically. Optimal matching is especially used to study multifaceted professional careers such as job-changing, promotion, and unemployment periods. The core procedure has two steps (Chan, 1995). First, given a set of sequences, the distance between each pair of sequences is calculated with an iterative minimization procedure. This gives the researcher a distance matrix for all the sequences. Second, it is possible to apply classical tools such as cluster analysis to the distance matrix to determine whether the sequences correspond to distinct career ideal types. Any typology, if found, can be used as an independent or dependent variable in further research. As an illustration, Abbott and Hrycak (1990) studied the resemblance among career patterns of musicians active in Germany in the eighteenth century. These careers show progressions and sectoral mobility in a context where very few top positions were available in music establishments. The application of optimal matching makes it possible to highlight the existence of three typical careers: organist careers, careers in the court and careers in church spheres. Furthermore, each career appeared to be dominated by a single type of job. For instance, the typical career in the court was 15 years as a court instrumentalist, with no other career service. At the same time, there is no evidence of a systematic drift from insecure to more secure church jobs. It also appears that the spheres were strictly separated, with certain notable exceptions such as J.S. Bach.

VAR models and sequence analysis are very powerful techniques. The main problem is that they require a considerable amount of quality data scattered over different points in time, which is relatively rare in the social sciences. They are therefore plagued by a classical trade-off concerning the restrictiveness of the conditions of application of the proposed methods: that is, these powerful techniques can be applied only to a small number of 'real world' problems. It is worth mentioning that temporal qualitative comparative analysis (TQCA) offers an alternative way to make sense of sequences, by introducing the idea of 'non-commutativity' of historical configurations into standard qualitative comparative analysis (Caren and Panofsky, 2005). QCA and fuzzy-set QCA, while highlighting the 'multiple and conjunctural' nature of causation (see Chapter 6), are unfit to capture the sequential unfolding of events producing historical paths of causation. TQCA involves the possibility of sequencing the causal conditions related to each case. To begin with, TQCA requires the researcher to know the sequence in which events unfolded: the researcher must specify which factors 'always come first', 'always come last', 'always come in a specific order', and whether the conditions could come in any order. This procedure will greatly expand the number of possible configurations, and therefore reinforce the problem of 'limited diversity' (Ragin, 2008), but it is possible to place theoretical restrictions to limit the number of configurations and reduce the set to a manageable size, and find the most parsimonious solution to the QCA equation representing the causal process. TQCA as such is only applicable to crisp-set QCA. However, following Caren and Panofsky, the inclusion of temporality in fuzzy-set analysis is possible with a workaround, that is, by defining one or more fuzzy sets that account for some quality of time. For example, we can add a condition to assess the membership of different countries in the set of 'quick economic growth after democratization'.

What is more, the methodology of process tracing allows us to study sequences from a case-based qualitative perspective. As anticipated in Chapter 4, process tracing involves studying sequences of pieces of evidence that contribute to supporting or overturning alternative explanatory hypotheses (Bennett, 2010). Process tracing is a sequence-based approach that examines mechanisms operating at an analytical level below that of a more encompassing theory (Checkel, 2007). It identifies a step-by-step causal chain that links independent and dependent variables. Therefore, the sequence of interest concerns the hypothesized causal mechanisms, which are temporally and/or logically consequential. Following Collier (2011):

> process tracing can make decisive contributions to diverse research objectives, including: (a) identifying novel political and social phenomena and systematically describing them; (b) evaluating prior explanatory hypotheses, discovering new hypotheses, and assessing these new causal claims; (c) gaining insight into causal mechanisms; and (d) providing an alternative means – compared with conventional regression analysis and inference based on statistical models – of addressing challenging problems such as reciprocal causation, spuriousness, and selection bias.

Empirically, process tracing can be applied to data collected in different ways, namely to documentary research and interviews. This method has been applied to different areas, for instance in educational research, in order to study the moment-by-moment thinking of students as they interact with textual materials in private study settings (Marland et al., 1992).

Finally, another alternative way to make sense of the order of events is through the game-theoretic study of strategic decisions. The notion of sequence is indeed crucial for game theory, that is, the analysis of interactive decision-making based on anticipations of the choices of other 'players' who play the 'game'. A famous application of this approach is the Cuban missile crisis, which started with a Soviet attempt in October 1962 to install in Cuba ballistic missiles equipped with nuclear weapons that were able to strike the United States, and could have triggered a third world war. The US objective was the immediate removal of Soviet missiles, and US policy-makers seriously considered two strategies to achieve this end: a naval blockade and a tactical air strike (Dixit and Skeath, 1999). Game theory models the ways in which strategic interactions among supposedly rational agents – such as political decision-makers – produce outcomes based on the preferences of those agents, whereas, at the end of the day, the outcomes in question might have been intended by none of the agents. Most games have a sequential component, entailing strategic situations in which there is an order of play. This reflects the view that most real-life games do not terminate after the players make their initial strategy choices. Therefore, the researcher will posit that participants in sequential games use a particular type of interactive thinking about how their current actions will influence future actions, both for their rivals and for themselves. In the Cuban missile crisis case, US President John F. Kennedy and his crisis cabinet considered that an early strike could have had unpredictable consequences and decided instead to deploy a naval quarantine around the waters of Cuba and to announce that any missile launch from Cuba would be considered as an act of war against the United States. This was a demonstration of the credibility of American resolve. At this point, the Soviets were compelled to make their move under considerable threat. Given that a nuclear escalation was a very undesirable option, First Secretary Nikita Khrushchev wanted a solution that would preserve his reputation in the Soviet Union. He was able to propose the removal of the missiles based on a guarantee that the US would not attack Cuba. At the same time, Kennedy offered to dismantle US missiles in Turkey. After further negotiations, this agreement was considered relatively satisfactory by both parties and eventually led to a solution of the crisis. In this example, the strategy was quite clearly determined by taking into account the sequence of past and predicted future moves of both players.

Analysis of sequential games also provides additional information on game strategies, for instance when it is to a player's advantage to move first and when it is better to move second (Dixit and Skeath, 1999). Simple sequential games presuppose that the game is played once; while permitting sequential moves and countermoves by the players within a game after they make their initial strategy choices, they do not assume that the game is repeated. Repeated play, in contrast, allows players to make threats, which are rendered credible by being enforceable in later games. By retaining the previous rules of sequential play in individual games, but permitting the games themselves to be repeated, one can analyse both the stability of outcomes in repeated play and the effectiveness of threats. Therefore, for instance, outcomes that are unstable in the single play of a sequential game may be rendered stable when the game is repeated, because players – anticipating its recurrence – change their rationality calculations (Brams, 2003). Finally, in dynamic, multi-stage games involving incomplete information, the existing situation of uncertainty (about the preferences of other players) leads to additional interesting strategic possibilities. For instance, uncertainty about the pay-offs of other players is modelled as a game in which players are uncertain about which node of the game they are located on. This procedure involves the use of a fictitious player who randomly selects players' types from a known probability distribution (McCarty and Meirowitz, 2007). Of course, one of the main problems of game theory is related to the assumptions about the pay-offs that actors involved in games will attribute to their moves and those of their opponents. As for simulations, we face a trade-off between internal and external validity which can be resolved only by combining formal-deductive models with empirical research based on 'real world' data.

Timing

Sometimes we are interested in the study of timing, that is, in the examination of the spacing of events in time. This perspective is pertinent to the study of certain particular phenomena, which imply a change of social state or a transition from one social state to another, such as the adoption of certain kinds of public policies, changes in job or employment status, partnership records which include the start and end dates of co-residential relationships, the onset of and recovery from mental disorders, and the experience of stressful and pleasant life events. Event history analysis is used in the social sciences to study these changes and transitions. This way, for instance, it is possible to determine at what time periods the event of interest is likely to occur, and to establish why some individuals experience the event earlier than others or do not experience the event of interest at all during the study period.

Following Box-Steffensmeier and Jones (2004), the starting point of event history analysis is the modelling of the duration of some social process. The research design operationalizes the duration until the occurrence of the event of interest, where the duration is measured from the time at which an individual becomes exposed to the 'risk' of experiencing the investigated event. The event history approach presupposes that the duration spent in one social state is related to the probability of experiencing some event, or, more precisely, that the duration spent in one social state affects the probability that some entity will make a transition to another social state (Box-Steffensmeier and Jones, 2004). Hence, basic event history data consist of the length of time a unit spends in a state before experiencing an event, and an indicator denoting whether or not the observation has already transited from its previous social state. It is important for the researcher to have a theoretically sound reason for hypothesizing when a social process for an observation can begin. This involves the notion of being 'at risk'. Observations at risk are simply the sample of units that begin a social process; this way, they become 'at risk' of experiencing the event. In so-called discrete-time models, the units are at risk of experiencing the event at predefined times.

Continuous-time models, in contrast, presuppose that an event can occur at any point in time. In either formulation, once the event is experienced, the unit exits the 'risk set', so that, at each observation period, the risk set progressively becomes smaller until no units are at risk as each has experienced the event or is right-censored (that is, the unit 'survived' until the final time considered in our study, and we have no subsequent information).

An example is useful to illustrate this approach (Kenny et al., 2006). Consider a study of 200 couples who are followed for 10 years after marriage. For each couple it was possible to determine whether or not they broke up, and, if they did, when the break-up occurred. For instance, if a couple broke up during the fifth year of marriage in the middle of the year, their score would be 4.5. Then time 0 must be defined, in order to establish the 'risk set'. In this example, it is defined as the day of marriage. Afterwards, it is possible to establish the percentage of couples who have broken up after each year of marriage. In an empirical application cited by Kenny et al. (2006), it was found that 93 per cent remain together after 1 year and 55 per cent after 10 years. The analyst can then plot the decreasing percentage of couples who have not broken up for each of the 10 years of the study with a so-called cumulative survival function. After modelling this function, it becomes possible to try to understand the factors that increase or decrease the survival rate. For break-up, we might ask the following questions. Are couples who marry younger at greater risk of break-up? Are gay and lesbian couples more or less likely to break up than heterosexual couples? If a baby is born, is there an increase or a decrease in the risk of break-up? An important variant of this technique, which is also used for diffusion studies, is so-called dyadic event history analysis, that is, when the units of analysis are not individuals but relationships that involve two actors, as discussed in Chapter 7.

Path dependence

To conclude the discussion of temporality, the notion of 'path dependence' can be cited as very important for conceptualizing social phenomena that are embedded in the temporal processes that shape their development, implying positive or negative feedback effects (Thelen, 1999). In particular, the study of path dependence makes it possible to highlight the relevance of past arrangements and historical legacies in structuring individual and collective behaviour. Path dependence is usually operationalized with the idea of 'increasing returns', that is, processes where the probability of further steps along the path increases with each move along that path. Increasing returns processes are based on the assumption that the relative benefits of the current activity compared with other possible options increase over time, producing self-reinforcing processes (Pierson, 2000). To illustrate the logic underlying increasing returns, Pierson takes an example of a large box with two balls, one black and the other red. If there is a rule according to which, when removing one ball, we have to return it to the box accompanied by an additional ball of the same colour, and if we repeat this process until the box fills up, then we have a process with positive feedbacks. The distribution of coloured balls is at first entirely determined by chance, but then each step along a path increases the 'attractiveness' of this path. A famous real-world example of path dependence relates to the diffusion of the so-called QWERTY standard, the most common modern-day keyboard layout. This layout is today considered suboptimal for electronic keyboards as it was designed to prevent jams while typing at speed on mechanical typewriters. And yet it is still used for computer keyboards and mobile devices because the cost of switching to any alternative option has grown exponentially over time.

Two additional elements connected to the notion of increasing returns can be mentioned. First, not only does the probability of further steps along the same path increase with each move along that path but also early events – 'critical junctures' involving the past choice of a particular path – are more important than later ones. If we think again of the box with black and red balls, it is evident that the first draws have stronger effects on the final outcome, that is, on the shape of the distribution. In contrast, later draws have a marginal effect on the distribution, which will eventually settle down to an equilibrium. In practice, critical junctures are major events that establish certain directions of change and close other alternatives (Kelemen and Capoccia, 2007). Lipset and Rokkan formulated their well-known hypothesis that in advanced industrialized countries the party systems of the 1960s still reflect the cleavage structures of the 1920s, that is, the cleavages existing at the time when the modern parties were established. That period constitutes a critical juncture producing long-term effects on the structuration of political representation, party systems and voting behaviour.

Second, as one of the trade-offs connected to the concept of path dependence, it is important to avoid considering that 'if all you have is a hammer, everything looks like a nail'. The concept of 'drift' (for example, policy drift, regulatory drift) indicates the fact that substantial change for individuals and groups may occur even in the case of path dependence, when there is a growing mismatch between their demands on the system in place and the capacity of the system to meet those demands. An example is the literature on the retrenchment of social welfare, which may happen even without explicit cuts in social benefits (Hacker, 2004). In fact, existing policies supplying structural benefits may be insufficiently adapted to evolving social needs and cover a declining portion of the risks that citizens face. This phenomenon occurs when new risks and social demands emerge from structural transformations of society and economy and are not covered by existing policies. This is typically the case with population ageing, the entry of women into labour markets, the increased instability of family structures, and the rise of young temporary workers.

In terms of research design, the study of path dependence usually relies on historical explanations that stress chains of causal mechanisms and contextual variables, using historical case studies, small-N comparison, and analytical narratives. To begin with, historical case studies seek to identify the causes of particular, singular outcomes (Mahoney et al., 2009). The study of path dependence is said to involve a type of causal complexity that is best examined with the 'thick' analysis that is typical of case studies, in order to operationalize the possibility that more than one path has been taken, to account for the contingency of any causal story, to examine the closure of some causal paths over time, and to highlight the constraints on the selected path (Bennett and Elman, 2006a). This perspective implies within-case analysis for identifying causal mechanisms through qualitative process analysis and typological theorizing. For example, if one hypothesizes that a high level of economic development is sufficient for the survival of democracy, then process analysis can be used to explore the mechanisms through which high levels of economic development generate democratic stability over time, such as the development of a large middle class with moderate political attitudes.

Small-N comparisons make it possible to engage with the question of path dependence through another approach. Systematic case comparisons can address path-dependent explanations by codifying complex narrative structures with a detailed analysis of historical cases, which is suitable for the study of rare events, so facilitating the search for omitted variables and allowing for the study of interaction effects within few cases (Bennett and Elman, 2006b). The notions of causal order and duration are crucial. For example, in the field of comparative-historical analysis, researchers commonly argue that a given variable may have different effects depending on its timing or duration. In fact, early events that are characterized by relative 'openness' and 'contingency' are particularly relevant to the study of path-dependent sequences. Moreover, researchers may use counterfactual analysis in evaluating the argument that the selection of a particular event from a menu of possible events has a decisive long-run impact. The counterfactual assumption is that if an alternative event had been selected at this early stage, the sequence of events would not have unfolded or would have done so in a very different manner. Finally, a 'conjunctural' analysis considers specifically the intersection point of two or more separately determined sequences. For example, in Moore's (1966) classic study, one major explanation involves a series of events leading to the development of commercial agriculture in developed countries (Mahoney, 2004).

Finally, analytical narratives represent an effort to combine historical and comparative research with rational choice models, by insisting on the combination of deep knowledge of the case and the use of a theoretically formalized model. This approach represents one attempt to improve explanations of unique events and outcomes and to unravel particular puzzles, while at the same time addressing broader questions of the past and the present time. The notion of path dependence is a primary element of the analysis because institutions constrain and facilitate action while also having a formative effect on individuals and their preferences.

Path dependence is incorporated in an analytical view derived from the theory of games. The main assumption is that actors' choices are coordinated, regularized, stabilized, and patterned because they are made in equilibrium. From this starting point, the key questions become how any particular equilibrium emerged in a world of multiple equilibria and why it changes (Levi, 2004). It is important to identify the criteria for reducing the number of variables and selecting the relevant explanations within the vast amount of material presented by historical and case research so as to reconstruct a coherent, explicitly formalized, plausible model to be presented in narrative form (Levi, 2002). For instance, Weingast focused on the balance rule, or the equal representation of the North and the South of the United States, provided by the federal institutions, and the compromise over the admission of slave states, in explaining American ante-bellum political stability, while also showing how its breakdown was a critical factor in precipitating the civil war (Bates et al., 1998).

Conclusion

The purpose of this chapter has been to present the most common research strategies for the study of temporality. In social science research, time can be conceived of as an objective empirical dimension along which to gather information and to make observations. This perspective focuses on time as an important dimension of variation, along with synchronic variations, which requires the comparison of two or more points in time. In our research projects we may want to focus on different aspects of the time dimension as we pursue different research goals and use different analytical techniques following different types of research designs. To begin with, it is possible to examine the time span of social phenomena with historical or simulative methods. This approach can be used, for instance, to study how cooperative attitudes among individuals can emerge without central authority. Then the analysis of tendency makes it possible to characterize the overall trend of macro-phenomena or point out the presence of unexpected deviations and anomalies within a trend. For instance, the tendency of variables may relate to production and consumption trends, population patterns, technological dynamism, urbanization, and industrial development. Levels and stocks represent entities in which variables can be aggregated to account for different operationalizations of quantities when examined over time. Time-related variables may also refer to the explanatory power of sequencing, that is, the ordering of events. In this case, typical analytical techniques are time-series analysis, optimal matching, temporal qualitative comparative analysis, process tracing and game theory. In this sense, the temporal ordering of events or processes is expected to have a crucial impact on outcomes. Furthermore, the notion of timing refers to the causes and effects of transitions from one social state to another, and can be used to study the consequences of specific events over time, for which the standard methodology is event study. Finally, the concept of path dependence permits us to make sense of the tension between change and stability of actors and structures in the social world, with qualitative case studies and analytical narratives. The main features are represented in Table 5.1.

Table 5.1 Summary of research designs for the study of temporality

Research focus	Analytical technique	Main research goal
Time span	Functionalist historical analysis	Present a teleological development
	Macro-historical analysis	Operationalize very long temporality
	Simulation of agent-based models	Study the outcomes emerging from complex interactions
Tendency	Descriptive statistics	Describe general trends
	Econometrics of trends and cycles	Account for stochastic movements and control for the deceptive effect of trends
	Event studies	Study the consequences of anomalies in trends
Levels	Standard regression etc.	Operationalize differences in degree
Stocks	Standard regression etc.	Operationalize differences in accumulated quantities
Sequences	Time series	Deal with variables that are related to themselves over time
	Optimal matching	Identify typologies of sequences empirically
	Temporal Qualitative Comparative Analysis	Examine non-commutative configurations of conditions
	Process tracing	Trace the causal process in a series of intermediate steps, until each connection becomes 'self-evident'
	Strategic games	Model dynamic and repeated interactions
Timing	Event-history analysis	Study the transition from one social state to another
Path dependence	Case studies	Investigate the mechanisms of continuity and change
	Small-N comparisons	Highlight contextual patterns
	Analytical narratives	Study actor-based macro-outcomes

Checklist

- Causal relations typically unfold over time.
- Time can be conceived of as an objective empirical dimension along which to gather information and to make observations.
- Different research designs can be fruitfully employed to pursue different research goals related to the study of temporality in the social sciences. They correspond to specific techniques for data analysis.
- Time span and tendency are usually examined with statistical methods.
- The study of sequence and timing permit the application of many different quantitative and qualitative techniques.
- Path dependence is very important for conceptualizing social phenomena that are embedded in the temporal processes.

Questions

1 Think about possible applications of subjectivist and objectivist conceptions of time.
2 Which method would you apply to estimate the trend of petrol consumption in Italy in the period from 1945 to 2010 and generate forecasts for 24 months?
3 What is the difference between event studies and event history analysis?
4 Which specific conception of time can be studied with game theory, and how?
5 Under what conditions can we qualify a phenomenon as path-dependent?

Further reading

Abbott, A. (2001) *Time Matters: On Theory and Method*. Chicago: University of Chicago Press. Reference book for sequence analysis.

Box-Steffensmeier, J.M. and Jones, B.S. (1997) Time is of the essence: Event history models in political science. American Journal of Political Science, 41 (4), 1414–61. Introduction to event history analysis.

Pevehouse, J.C. and Brozek, J.D. (2008) Time-series analysis. In J.M. Box-Steffensmeier, H.E. Brady and D. Collier (eds), *The Oxford Handbook of Political Methodology*. Oxford: Oxford University Press. Clear and concise introduction to the methodology of time series analysis.

Pierson, P. (2004) *Politics in Time: History, Institutions, and Social Analysis*. Princeton, NJ: Princeton University Press. The reference book for the empirical analysis of path dependence, applied to the development of a wide range of social processes.

SIX

Heterogeneity

Introduction

Sometimes we do not pay attention to the homogeneous effect of independent variables, to the verification of regular patterns of behaviour, or to the search for general principles. Instead, we may be interested in the fact that social phenomena present dissimilar features, behave differently from each other and constitute diverse classes of things. To qualify this variety, the words 'heterogeneity' and 'diversity' are quite interchangeable. It is worth noting that 'heterogeneity' tends to stress the presence of unrelated parts or elements (such as a fruitcake that contains cake, cherries and walnuts), while 'diversity' signifies the state or quality of being different or distinct (in this sense, a fruitcake has different properties from a cheesecake) (Little, 1991). Why should we be interested in heterogeneity? Focusing on regularities presupposes the application of homogenizing assumptions to the observed entities. However, in many cases social phenomena are deeply heterogeneous at many levels of scale. We may be interested precisely in exploring these levels to make sense of this heterogeneity.

A first form of heterogeneity can be discovered across individuals or social groups. Individuals vary in their socio-economic status, motives, ideational frameworks, emotions and behaviour. Individuals may also act for a variety of motives at the same time and shift their motives over time. Similarly, social groups can display different degrees of internal and external heterogeneity as regards their composition, function, role and resources. Second is the heterogeneity of causal relations. Social phenomena are commonly the result of a combination of conditions that is highly contingent. Revolutions may be caused by peasant support for revolt, the breakdown of state institutions and the existence of a harsh system of land tenure, all coming together at a moment in time. The explanations of social phenomena are also frequently equifinal – that is, different sets of factors may explain the same outcome. For instance, the effective management of firms can be accomplished through very different strategies – the stable placement of products or services in a clearly defined segment of the market, or continued product development and market development in different segments. Third, heterogeneity can concern the particular cases that are examined. In fact, some 'special' feature may be discovered within the categories of things and events that are investigated, such as students, organizations, cities, religions, democracies, and social movements. For instance, most countries ratified the Kyoto Protocol for the control of carbon emissions, but the largest economy in the world, the United States, did not. Therefore, in discussions of the effectiveness of global governance in the realm of climate change, this special case would deserve special attention.

The aim of this chapter is to introduce the reader to research strategies for examining these different forms of heterogeneity. In line with research goals, different methods and techniques exist for grouping variables and for the examination of the variation between and among samples. Then complex causation can be operationalized with innovative configurational methods, that is, with dedicated qualitative comparative analysis (QCA). The investigation of special cases concludes the chapter. But first it is useful to engage in the conceptualization of heterogeneity.

Heterogeneity in kind and in degree

When undertaking social science research and especially when a research study aims to examine the heterogeneity of social phenomena, it is crucial to avoid certain conceptual mistakes, which have been anticipated in Chapter 2 (Sartori, 1991). To begin with, not being able to distinguish between differences in kind and differences in degree will lead us to draw the wrong conclusions from our empirical analysis. According to Sartori's famous example, this problem, called 'degreeism', occurs when one cannot distinguish between a cat and a dog, and speaks of different degrees of 'cat-dogs'. This way, no hypotheses about the characteristics of different classes of objects can be confidently validated, and much explanatory power is lost. Sartori's discussion of 'concept stretching' is likewise pertinent for the study of heterogeneity. This refers to the trade-off between the 'intension' and the 'extension' of conceptual categories – and to the related need to find a suitable balance between them. Intension relates to the number of properties of a concept, while extension is the number of cases to which the concept can be applied. Excessive intension will lead overly precise categories to be inapplicable for comparative research beyond a specific case. On the other hand, excessively extended categories will include almost everything in the related concept, thus eliminating their heuristic validity.

Differences in kind and differences in degrees must be analytically separated when designing a research project for the study of heterogeneity. They can, however, be combined in the conduct of empirical research, in order to enhance analytical leverage. Differences in kind are usually connected to 'qualitative' variations, which indicate whether a social phenomenon does or does not exhibit the characteristic of interest (such as being a democratic or an authoritarian regime); differences in degree refer to 'quantitative' variations between categories that fall in the interval between two extreme states (for example, the range between a minimal and a full democracy) (Ragin, 2000). Heterogeneity in kind presupposes the discussion of thresholds, typologies and categories, in line with the insights expressed in Chapter 2, in order to study the conformity of cases to analytical constructs and ideal types (Kvist, 2006). Heterogeneity in degree requires us to measure and situate ordinal and continuous variables on scales along a continuum between the two extremes.

To illustrate the point, we can take the example of a classical topic of comparative politics, namely, the construction of a typology of political regime types. One may argue that there is a qualitative difference between democracies and authoritarian regimes. This means that there is a threshold below which a regime cannot be considered democratic, or, in other terms, we identify some properties that are necessary for considering a regime democratic: typically, free elections. At the same time, democracy may vary in its level. Some regimes may be more democratic than others. Thus, regimes can be classified as democracies or non-democracies. Then, in a second step, a further set of criteria can be applied to those regimes deemed democratic to establish what makes democracy more democratic. The concept of democracy must be precise enough to provide meaningful information by including sufficient dimensions: electoral competition, the rule of law, freedom of expression, and so on. But it must also be broad enough to permit comparisons by 'travelling' across countries. For instance, a definition of democracy based on the experience of a single country would be too narrow for comparative research.

Measuring differences

Differences in kind are assessed by nominal measurement, with items assigned to groups or categories; examples are gender, ethnic background, political affiliation, and major subject taken in college.

Differences in degree are assessed by ordinal, interval or ratio measurement. Ordinal measurement produces a rank ordering of units; examples are graded attitude towards the death penalty, and movie ratings. In an interval measurement the distance between numbers or units on the scale is equal; examples are temperature, academic grade average, and verbal aptitude score. In a ratio measurement there is also a meaningful zero point; examples are weight, income, reaction time, and family size.

The study of heterogeneity

Different forms of heterogeneity can be examined empirically with different research designs and analytical techniques. First, the methods for grouping variables and cases and the methods for examining the variation between and among samples are presented. Then configurational comparative methods are introduced for the study of complex causation. Finally, the principles for examining different types of special cases are discussed.

Finding groups: Factor analysis and related techniques

The heterogeneity of social phenomena can be operationalized, explored and managed by looking for groups of cases and groups of variables in the available data. The potential research questions to be investigated are numerous. For example, marketing researchers are usually very interested in finding groups in data. Market segmentation research aims to identify groups of entities (people, markets, organizations) that share certain common characteristics (shopping attitudes, purchase propensies, media habits, and so forth) in order to develop a better understanding of sellers' and consumers' behaviour. This type of analysis is also employed in the development of potential new product opportunities by grouping brands and products to determine the larger market structure and to identify entities that may become interchangeable in test market studies. Finally, the analysis of groups can be used as a data reduction technique to develop aggregates of data which are more general and more easily managed than individual observations (Punj and Stewart, 1983).

Factor analysis (FA) is the most common analytical technique to examine the heterogeneity among observed variables. The main applications of factor-analytic techniques are to reduce the number of variables, to discover and explore the structure in the relationships between variables, to classify variables, and to test whether a specified set of constructs is influencing results in a predicted way with so-called confirmatory factor analysis (Harrington, 2008). FA searches for potential joint variations in response to a lower number of unobserved variables called factors. It is possible, for example, that variations in three or four observed variables mainly reflect the variations in a single unobserved variable, or in a reduced number of unobserved variables. So a small set of variables (if possible, uncorrelated) can be obtained from a large set of variables (most of which are correlated to each other), in order to create indices with variables that actually measure the same concept. In short, FA allows us to group together variables that seem to explain the same variance. In statistical terms, the observed variables are modelled as linear combinations of the potential factors, plus error terms. The common factor model (CFM) is the standard analytical technique for FA (Field, 2009). This model posits that each observed variable is influenced partially by underlying common factors and partially by underlying unique factors. The strength of the link between each factor and each measure varies, such that a given factor influences some measures more than others. Then the analysis is executed by examining the pattern of correlations between the observed measures. Measures that are highly correlated (either positively or negatively) are considered to be influenced by the same factors, while those that are relatively uncorrelated are probably influenced by different factors. Principal component analysis (PCA) is a statistical technique closely related to the CFM, but is used when variables are expected to be highly correlated. It reveals which variables are 'loaded' on a factor, which represents a classification axis. Then the principal component matrix can be 'rotated' to improve interpretation, so as to maximize the loading of variables to each factor.

Next, *cluster analysis* has a similar aim except that it is used when, rather than trying to group together *variables*, we are interested in grouping *cases* (Kaufman and Rousseeuw, 1990). In a sense, the underlying logic is quite the reverse of that of factor analysis: rather than forming groups of variables based on the measurement of these variables, cluster analysis aims to group the observations based on their measurement on several variables. The statistical units will be combined in order to minimize the 'logical distance' within each group and to maximize it between groups. The 'logical distance' is quantified by coefficients of similarity and dissimilarity between these unities. Most of the methods for grouping similar cases work in a hierarchical way. All cases are first treated as an initial cluster. Then cases are merged following a procedure specific to the method chosen. Therefore, at the beginning there are as many clusters as cases, and at the end one big cluster containing all cases. We have to decide to cut the clustering tree at a meaningful point in order to identify 'intermediary' relevant clusters of cases with high similarity. Therefore, the fundamental point is the definition of a measure of similarity or distance between objects. The other key point is the rule under which the groups are formed. Generally, measures of distance are appropriate for quantitative data, while measures of association are used for qualitative data. The simplest clustering method is single linkage, based on the correlations of Euclidean distances between pairs of cases (Field, 2009).

As an example, let us a look at a cross-national research project on students' motivations (Krebs et al., 2000). In this study, German and Slovenian students were given a questionnaire containing questions related to motivational aspects:

power motivation, job motivation, job aspiration, self-esteem, gender role stereo-types, and so forth. Factor analysis was used to uncover the dimensional structure within achievement motivation items, while application of cluster analysis made it possible to establish a typology of groups of respondents characterized by a spe-cial achievement motivation profile. Factor analysis made it possible to identify three motivational profiles: 'work orientation' (representing an effort dimension, the desire to work hard and to do a good job), 'mastery' (a preference for diffi-cult, challenging tasks and for meeting internally prescribed standards of perfor-mance), and 'competitiveness' (the enjoyment of interpersonal competition and the desire to win and do better than others). Afterwards, cluster analysis was used to find achievement motivation types. It revealed two types with a distinctive strong profile: the low-motivation type, represented by men and women equally, and the strong-motivation type, over-represented by men.

Finally, *correspondence analysis* (CA) is an exploratory descriptive technique designed to analyse tables containing some measure of correspondence between rows and columns. The results provide information about the structure of categor-ical variables included in the table, similarly to the aforementioned techniques, but in a manner that is appropriate for this type of data. The most common kind of table of this type is the standardized two-way frequency cross-tabulation of frequencies. This is a very simple method but it can offer some useful descriptive information.

Multiple correspondence analysis (MCA) is an extension of correspondence analysis that aims to analyse the 'multi-way' pattern of relationships of several categorical dependent variables. As such, it can also be seen as a generalization of principal component analysis when the variables to be analysed are categorical instead of quantitative (Greenacre and Blasius, 2006). MCA is obtained by apply-ing a standard CA to an indicator matrix. Each nominal variable comprises several levels, and each of these levels is coded as a binary variable. For example, gender is one nominal variable with two levels. The pattern for a male observation will then be 0–1 and for a female observation 1–0. The complete data table is thus composed of binary columns with one column taking the value '1' per nominal variable. MCA can also accommodate quantitative variables by recoding them as binary variables with multiple levels. A classic example that helped popular-ize MCA is the sociological analysis presented in the book *Distinction* (Bourdieu, 1984). The author used MCAs to provide a detailed illustration of his thesis that the determinants of taste, cultural discrimination and choice lie in the posses-sion of two forms of capital, economic and cultural, with subgroupings defined by seniority and the related mode of acquisition. The analysis of categorical data produces visual representations of the relationships between the row categories and the column categories in the same space (Robson and Sanders, 2009). For instance, Figure 6.1 is a simplified diagram from *Distinction* showing a double

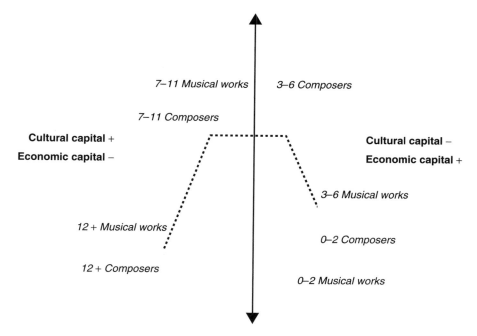

Figure 6.1 Petit-bourgeois (French) tastes

Source: adapted from Bourdieu (1984)

structure of opposition within the middle class: the opposition between those respondents capable of identifying composers, works of music, and so on, and those respondents with limited knowledge and the most 'common' preferences, and the opposition between the 'class fractions' that possess the least and the most cultural capital in relation to their educational qualifications.

In conclusion, factor analysis and related techniques are powerful methods to group data, make sense of data heterogeneity and find latent variables. However, these techniques group data in ways that are not always obvious or plausible, and sometimes the structure that appears in the data seems to show systematic patterns and yet be random. Another disadvantage is that there is no standard method to decide how many factors to keep after the analysis. The main trade-off is therefore that between the precision of the categorization and the meaningfulness of the distinction among the categories.

The analysis of variance

The *analysis of variance* (ANOVA) introduces a more explicit explanatory perspective to the study of heterogeneity as presented so far. It represents a set of statistical techniques that can be used after (or instead of) factor analysis and related techniques, that is, when the explanatory variables are nominal, to discriminate between groups of individuals, collective actors, places, things, and so forth. ANOVA makes it possible to investigate further the heterogeneity of social phenomena by decomposing the variability in the dependent variable among the different factors, and allows us to evaluate the difference between sets of scores. More precisely, ANOVA seeks to compare the internal variability in two or more sets of data with the variability between them. The aim is to examine the characteristics of the groups that determine the distinction between the observed phenomena, according to the following principle: if the populations really have the same mean, what is the chance that random sampling would result in the means observed in this experiment? Therefore, the assumption underlying ANOVA is that the variance in a given number of groups can be decomposed into within-group variance and between-group variance. The null hypothesis typically states that the observed differences between groups are due to chance alone.

ANOVA is frequently applied, for example, in the study of medications. Experimenters may want to test different formulations of a pain-relief medicine, and randomly assign volunteers to different drug formulations. In this case, ANOVA is used to determine whether groups of volunteers may be in some way significantly different from each other. When between-group variance contributes significantly to the total variance, then the phenomenon is found to be related to characteristics of each group, in this case to the different treatments. Conversely, when within-group variance contributes significantly to the total variance, then the phenomenon is considered as homogeneously related to characteristics of all groups. In other words, the logic of the comparison is based on the idea that when the internal variability within groups is higher than the variability between groups, then the only difference between these groups is probably the result of internal variability (Gamst et al., 2008).

The *multivariate analysis of variance* (MANOVA) is an extension of univariate ANOVA techniques. The major distinction is that in ANOVA we evaluate mean differences on a single dependent variable, whereas in MANOVA, mean differences on two or more dependent variables simultaneously are evaluated. As noted by Bray and Maxwell (1985), although ANOVA and MANOVA are frequently associated with experimental studies involving a manipulation introduced by the experimenter, both techniques are in fact appropriate whenever the research question involves a comparison of mean scores. Like ANOVA, MANOVA is usually conducted as a two-step process. The first step is to test the overall hypothesis of no differences in the means for the different groups. If this test is significant, the second step is to conduct tests to explain group differences. A recent variant of this approach is to rely on confidence intervals rather than tests of significance. MANOVA can be used, for example, when a psychologist wants to investigate how children educated in Catholic schools differ from children educated in state schools on a number of tests that measure their reading, mathematics, and moral reasoning skills (Grice and Iwasaki, 2009). The psychologist can examine how the two groups differ on a linear combination of the three measures. Then it is possible to investigate Grice and Iwasaki's (2009) hypothesis that children in Catholic schools may score higher on moral reasoning skills relative to reading and maths, or higher or lower on maths relative to reading, than do children in state schools. It is apparent that this type of research question inherently presupposes the application of multivariate analytical techniques because they look for simultaneous and interrelated effects among the variables of interest.

A simple example of ANOVA is a comparative study on the quality, significance and levels of university education in some Canadian provinces (Mason, 2011). The goal of this exploratory study is to establish whether significant differences exist across the provinces. Random samples of degree holders were collected using the geographic units of census subdivisions, including cities, towns and municipalities. Procedures are tested on two separate criteria: the number of people with at least one university degree, and the number of degree holders per capita. The analysis focuses on the differences in these criteria between the means of the different samples. ANOVA is used to determine whether any differences among these means are greater than would be expected by chance. According to the results, differences in the numbers of degrees between provinces are not significant. Therefore, there is no point in examining the first criterion further. The analysis on the second criterion revealed a significant difference between provinces in the number of people per capita with at least one degree. Examining the provinces of British Columbia, Newfoundland and Ontario more closely, following the pairwise comparison of means, the researcher realized that British Columbia and Newfoundland did indeed have similar numbers of people per capita holding at least one degree, but a significant difference existed in the number of people with at least one degree per capita between British Columbia and Ontario. The pairwise calculations between Newfoundland and Ontario also demonstrated a significant difference between those two provinces in the number of degree holders per capita, with Ontario having more. These findings are confirmed when they are compared with the confidence intervals for each province. The source of this variability is considered to be related to financial resources, since Ontario spends more money per student on education than any other province and has one of the lowest student–teacher ratios. Other possible explanatory factors include access to a university and the socio-economic structure. For instance, Ontario has more universities than any other province, while Newfoundland has only one and British Columbia few. British Columbia has an extensive network of community colleges, but very few universities to serve its population. Finally, people living in British Columbia and Newfoundland may be more likely to attend a technical school rather than a university due to the distinct industrial structures and job markets of those provinces.

Set-theoretic analysis of necessary and sufficient conditions

It is possible to address the heterogeneity of social phenomena from a radically different perspective, namely *causal heterogeneity*. This type of heterogeneity relates to the idea that causation may be more complex than is normally understood in comparative research, while displaying systematic cross-case patterns. Causation may be multiple, involving the possibility of equifinal solutions, that is, the manifestation of causal heterogeneity through different causal paths that lead to the same outcome (Bennett and Elman, 2006b). For example, pairs of countries may be at peace with each other because they are both democratic or, alternatively, because they maintain close economic ties. Causation can also be conjunctural: each causal path can comprise a combination of individually necessary causal factors. Conjunctural causation rejects the traditional principle of causal 'additivity', assuming instead that several causes can and should be combined for the expected outcome to occur. So conditions are no longer considered as 'independent' variables with an unconditional 'net' effect on the 'dependent' variable. Also, the 'uniformity' of causal effects is rejected: a given condition may, when combined with others, lead sometimes to the positive outcome, and sometimes, when differently combined, to the negative outcome (Berg-Schlosser et al., 2009). Multiple and conjunctural explanations can also go together. For example, antisocial behaviour in children may be explained by ineffective parental practices combined with school failure and rejection by peers, or by a punitive school discipline environment combined with genetic factors.

Dedicated qualitative comparative analysis provides powerful tools for the analysis of such causal complexity. QCA facilitates a form of counterfactual analysis that is grounded in case-oriented research practices. Following Ragin (2008), QCA makes it possible to unpack causal arguments from the 'symmetrical' character they display in traditional qualitative or quantitative covariational analysis, where information is pooled and conflated in a two-way relationship of the type 'the more, the more and the less, the less'. Instead, an asymmetric view of causation facilitates an interpretation of causal relationships in which causes may be necessary but not sufficient or sufficient but not necessary for the investigated outcome. It is worth adding that QCA is ideal for (but not limited to) small- to intermediate-N research (say, 5–50 cases). This corresponds to a range where there are too many cases for 'thick' qualitative analysis but too few cases for most conventional statistical techniques.

QCA is explicitly 'diversity-oriented' (Ragin, 2000) in so far as it requires familiarity and in-depth knowledge of cases, while being focused on the discovery of different combinations of cross-case patterns and permitting the examination of singular cases. In fact, QCA's examination of cross-case patterns respects the diversity of cases and their heterogeneity with regard to different causally relevant conditions by conceiving of cases as configurations, that is, combinations of conditions leading to a given outcome (Rihoux and Lobe, 2009). Furthermore, when a given combination of conditions explains only a few cases, or even only one single case, the corresponding solution is not a priori considered as less relevant or less important than other combinations of conditions that would account for more cases, because each case matters in most applications of QCA: even 'outliers' and 'deviant cases' (Rihoux and Ragin, 2008). The analytical focus of QCA is not on the average size of the net effect of independent variables on a dependent variable, but on the diversity of causal patterns leading to the outcome of interest. This crucial feature of QCA points to an existing trade-off when choosing QCA, that is, between the study of how variables compete to produce an effect and the study of how conditions combine to create the outcome.

As anticipated in Chapter 3, many complex causal relations that are relevant for the analysis of social phenomena are at best described in terms of necessity and sufficiency. To make these insights operational, QCA relies on the analysis of set-theoretic relations. Necessity means that the outcome is a subset of the causal conditions, while sufficiency exists when the causal condition is a subset of the outcome (see Figure 6.2). It is also possible to study more complex patterns, as those determined by INUS conditions – causal conditions that are insufficient but necessary parts of causal recipes which are themselves unnecessary but sufficient – related to specific combinations of causal conditions that form a subset of the cases with the outcome. These combinations of causal conditions are substantially relevant both for 'case-oriented' and 'variable-oriented' research, because independent variables that exert partial mean effects in well-specified statistical models could in fact be INUS causes – insufficient but necessary parts of a causal combination that is unnecessary but sufficient for the result (Mahoney, 2008). Following Ragin (2000), this complex form of causation is (implicitly) very common in so-called case-oriented research, as it refers to a frequent state of affairs in the 'real world'. For instance, consider the classical example, 'a short circuit caused the fire' (Mackie, 1965). This does not imply that a short circuit was necessary for the occurrence of fire (as a fire could have been caused by a cigarette butt). Nor does it imply that the short circuit was sufficient for the ensuing fire (as without the presence of flammable material the fire would not have occurred). However, we can consider that the short circuit was as an indispensable, and 'non-trivial', member of a set of conditions that was sufficient for explaining the occurrence of the fire. The non-trivialness of a sufficient condition means that this condition forms a relatively large subset of the outcome. The most trivial sufficient condition is one that never occurs; consequently, the most trivial necessary condition is one that is always present (Goertz, 2006a). Furthermore, SUIN conditions are sufficient but unnecessary parts of a combination that is insufficient but necessary for the result. In this case, the constitutive attributes of a necessary cause are treated as causes themselves. For example, if the presence of a non-democracy is necessary for war, then lower-level constitutive properties of non-democracies, such as the absence of regular elections, are also considered necessary for this outcome.

Figure 6.2 illustrates the set-theoretic logic underlying sufficiency and necessity. Using the example of Skocpol's famous argument about social revolution, peasant autonomy in a context of landlord vulnerability is a sufficient condition for the outcome of peasant revolt, a causal relation that is empirically verified when the former is a subset of the latter condition (Goertz, 2006b). To follow Ragin's (2000) example, having an advanced degree can be considered a necessary condition of a professional career when this outcome represents a subset of the causal condition.

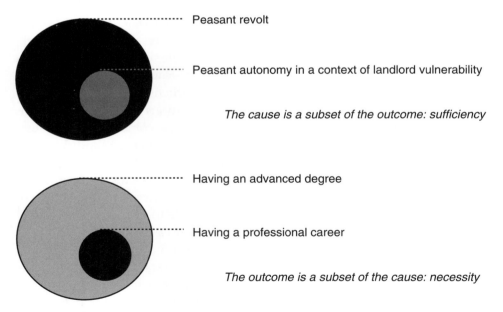

Peasant revolt

Peasant autonomy in a context of landlord vulnerability

The cause is a subset of the outcome: sufficiency

Having an advanced degree

Having a professional career

The outcome is a subset of the cause: necessity

Figure 6.2 Necessary and sufficient conditions

In short, the procedure for standard QCA analysis is as follows. In so-called crisp-set QCA (csQCA), we start by considering the presence/absence of cases in all of the logically possible combinations of a given set of causal conditions and then we use Boolean algebra to analyse the varied connections between causal combinations and the outcome. According to Boolean algebra used in dichotomous csQCA, a case is either in or out of a set, with 1 indicating the presence and 0 the absence of the condition. Fuzzy-set QCA (fsQCA) is a generalization of QCA, where each case is examined in terms of its degree of membership in different combinations of causally relevant conditions. When fuzzy-set theory is used, the membership in sets can be partial, with membership ranging from 1 indicating full membership to 0 indicating non-membership (Ragin, 2000). In formal terms, a fuzzy set is a 'class of objects with a continuum of grades of memberships', characterized by 'a membership function that assigns to each object a grade of membership between zero and one' (Zadeh, 1965). Variables can be 'purposefully calibrated' in fuzzy sets to indicate their degree of membership. To use Ragin's example, an east European country might have a membership score of 0.68 in the (fuzzy) set of 'rich countries' ranging from 0 to 1, whereas this attribute (richness) can be less easily translated in mere dichotomous terms.

Then the fuzzy subset relation is assessed using the fuzzy set algebra implemented in software packages such as fsQCA. The crucial point is the principle that cases should be viewed in terms of configurations of causally relevant conditions. To represent combinations of conditions, we use an analytic device known as a truth table, which lists all the logically possible configurations representing combinations of selected conditions and sorts cases according to the observed combinations. Also listed in the truth table is an outcome value for each combination of causal conditions. The aim of fsQCA is to derive a logical statement describing the different combinations of conditions linked to an outcome, as summarized in the truth table (Ragin, 2006a). The first analytical step after coding data and arranging them in the truth table is to discover all causal conditions (that is, 'independent variables') with membership scores that are consistently greater than or equal to outcome ('dependent variable') membership scores, in order to determine the possible necessary conditions. The second step is to examine the sufficient conditions by comparing membership scores in the outcome with the scores of all possible combinations of conditions. Then 'consistency' and 'coverage' can be assessed, respectively indicating the quality of the connection, that is, how closely the subset relation is approximated (the degree to which the cases sharing a given combination of conditions agree in displaying the outcome), and the empirical relevance of consistent subsets, that is, the proportion of cases following a specific path and composing the solution (Ragin, 2006b). Consistency and coverage are 'descriptive measures for evaluating the strength of the empirical support for arguments specifying set-theoretic connections' (Ragin, 2008). The procedure for calculating consistency, implemented in the fuzzy-truth table algorithm of the fs/QCA software, is as follows. First, the consistent cases are differentiated from the inconsistent ones when their membership score in the causal condition is less than or equal to membership in the outcome; then the sum of the consistent membership scores in a (combination of) causal condition(s) divided by the sum of all membership scores in the (combination of) causal condition(s) produces the final measure of set-theoretic consistency. This measure can be further refined with credit for near misses and penalties for scores that greatly exceed their mark. Then the set-theoretic measurement of coverage corresponds to the number of cases that display the outcome following a specific path divided by the total number of instances of the outcome in crisp-set analysis; and, similarly, to the proportion of the sum of the membership scores in the outcome in the case of fuzzy-set analysis. The different solutions offered by the fs/QCA software should be interpreted with the help of these pieces of information.

A (simplified) fuzzy-set analysis can help clarify the procedure. The argument will be illustrated with an example using real data on independent regulatory agencies (IRAs) (Gilardi, 2005, 2008). Gilardi examined and successfully tested the determinants of IRAs' formal independence from politicians with multiple regression analysis. According to a first hypothesis, governments delegate powers to independent agencies in order to increase the credibility of their policies, so that higher formal independence is expected in sectors where credibility pressures are higher (that is, in utility regulation) than in other sectors. According to a second hypothesis, political uncertainty may explain formal independence, since the risk for governments of being replaced by coalitions with different preferences provides incentives to grant agencies more independence in order to make it more difficult for future policy-makers to change current government's policies. Finally, the institutional context is deemed to play a crucial mediating role pertaining to the number of veto players, which are expected to represent the functional equivalent of delegation, being thus negatively related to the level of independence of formally independent regulators. The last version of the data set can be reanalysed with fuzzy-set QCA concerning IRAs in 17 European countries and seven sectors, with the exclusion of some cases where there is no IRA and very few missing data (Greece), for a total number of cases of exactly 100. This subsection presents a simplified fuzzy-set analysis of Gilardi's argument, using utilities versus other sectors (utilities), many veto players (fsvps) and high replacement risk (fsrr) as explanatory conditions, and high formal independence as the outcome (fsindep). The 'utilities' variable is dichotomous in nature and hence does not require any manipulation. The calibration procedure of the remaining three variables was informed by theoretical considerations and based on three quantitative measures: the maximum, the minimum and the average value. Given this information, the benchmarks used for veto players are situated at 4.0 (full membership in the set), 1.0 (full out) and 2.5 (crossover point of maximal ambiguity); those for replacement rate are 0.5 (full in), 0.0 (full out) and 0.25 (crossover point); and those for formal independence are 0.8 (full in), 0.0 (full out) and 0.4 (crossover point).

Table 6.1 Truth table

Configuration	Condition fsvps	Condition fsrr	Condition utilities	Number of cases	Outcome fsindep	Consistency
1	0	0	0	37	0	0.60
2	1	1	0	17	0	0.65
3	0	0	1	14	1	0.94
4	1	0	0	9	0	0.64
5	1	1	1	8	1	0.93
6	0	1	0	7	1	0.83
7	0	1	1	4	1	0.98
8	1	0	1	4	0	0.78

Table 6.1 summarizes all logically possible configurations. For instance, the second row displays 17 cases that populate the combination 110 $\rightarrow$ 0. This corresponds to the combination of the causal conditions veto players, replacement rate and the absence of utilities. The outcome of formal independence is labelled 0, as the consistency of this combination is below the predetermined consistency score (usually 0.8) displayed in the last column. The third row present 14 cases with the configuration 0 0 1$\rightarrow$ 1. Therefore, the absence of veto players combined with a low replacement rate and the presence of utilities corresponds to high formal independence. The fuzzy-set algorithm simplifies the existing configurations to the minimal formulas. The results of the fuzzy-set analysis are very much in line with Gilardi's argument while also allowing us to fine-tune previous findings. They can be summarized with the following solution:

$$\text{utilities* ~ fsvps + fsrr* ~ fsvps + utilities*fsrr} \rightarrow \text{fsindep.}$$

Three consistent and empirically relevant paths lead to high formal independence. The two first combinations, utilities*~ fsvps and fsrr* ~ fsvps, which can be summarized with the expression ~ fsvps*(fsrr + utilities), show that governments grant high independence to regulatory agencies when they have incentives, due to high political uncertainty or high credibility requirements, and can make decisions because of the absence of veto players; while according to the third combination, utilities*fsrr, they also do so when functional pressures are extremely high.

We conclude this subsection with a summary of the QCA procedure:

1 Focus on cases
   - Substantial knowledge
   - Theoretically and empirically informed
2 A set of binary variables (crisp-set QCA) or variables calibrated in sets (fuzzy-set QCA)
   - Some explanatory conditions
   - One outcome
3 All configurations represented in a 'truth table'
4 Check for necessary conditions
5 Logical minimization of the formula that is sufficient for the outcome
6 Discuss consistency and coverage
7 Interpretation of results

The analysis of 'special' cases

Case-oriented qualitative approaches can help the examination of the heterogeneity of social phenomena by focusing on 'special' events and instances. Case studies are widely used in the social sciences, and their distinctive contribution is broadly acknowledged (Byrne and Ragin, 2009). The basic logic of the case study approach is to observe one or a few cases intensively, instead of observing many cases superficially (Gerring, 2007b). The unit of analysis to be investigated can be an individual, a social group (family, ethnic group, religious group, and so on), an organization (public sector organization, firm), a territorial unity (nation state, region, city), or an event (election). Case studies as a research strategy are especially suitable when the 'how' question is being posed, when we have little control over events and we want to illustrate the full complexity of social phenomena (Yin, 2003). In addition, they are appropriate for theory development and hypothesis formation, according to a logic of discovery (George and Bennett, 2005). To this end, the main characteristics of the case study approach include a focus on contextual conditions, the examination of the interrelationships that compose a specific entity, and the analysis of the connection between the contextual factors and the entity being studied. The trade-off typically related to case study research is the apparent lack of generalizability of in-depth research studies. The purpose of this subsection is to show how informed case selection of special cases can nevertheless enhance analytical leverage and make it possible to extend the insights derived from case studies to a larger number of cases.

The term 'special case study' refers neither to studies that investigate 'a bounded unit in an attempt to elucidate a single outcome occurring within that unit' (Gerring, 2006) nor to case analysis 'relying on the same sort of covariational evidence utilized in non-case study research' (Gerring, 2004). We mean, rather, an intensive study of a case representing a particular type of outcome in a broader population of cases and where the objective is to discover something about this population. Special cases are frequently disregarded in macro-quantitative research as they are treated as noise, as 'part of the error term', or at best as abnormal and unimportant deviations determined by hazard or undetermined conditions. In contrast, case study research that is oriented more explicitly towards the analysis of heterogeneity considers special cases as particularly interesting for theory development and further empirical research. The most important stage of designing 'special case studies' is the selection of some peculiarity of their outcomes with reference to the universe of available cases. How can we select special cases from a larger universe for close inspection and intensive analysis? Random sampling is not a viable approach when only a small number of cases are to be selected. Furthermore, this design explicitly requires taking into account the occurrence of the outcome of interest on the dependent variable. Hence attention should be paid to purposive modes of sampling. As noted by Mahoney and Goertz (2006), this case selection practice is appropriate when the research goal is to explain particular outcomes, and when in-depth familiarity with each case is required. Different types of special cases exist and their distinct contribution to the analysis of heterogeneity should be recognized, in so far as each of them facilitates a different strategy for case analysis. The discussion presented below relies mainly on the landmark work of Seawright and Gerring (2008) on this topic.

The simpler special-case design operationalizes the so-called *typical case*. The typical case exemplifies a theoretically sound, empirically stable relationship. It may be considered a representative case of a cross-case relationship. The typical case is well explained by an existing theoretical model, and so is the best choice for further and deeper examination of the phenomenon of interest. In particular, we can confidently apply a 'process tracing' procedure to this case in order to explore the causal mechanisms at work. The main aim, therefore, is to deepen our knowledge of a well-recognized causal relation. As such, the in-depth study of a typical case is also the natural second step of a mixed-method 'nested' analytical strategy, after the discovery of a robust relation among the variables of interest (Lieberman, 2005). The underlying logic of this type of case study can be exemplified by the Kantian 'democratic peace' argument mentioned in Chapter 3. According to this hypothesis, democratic countries never go to war with one other because it is expected that a majority of the people, and their representatives, would never choose to go to war unless in self-defence. Therefore, in this context a typical case for this theory is represented by instances of peaceful coexistence between two classic democratic countries, precisely as would be expected.

The selection of an *extreme case* implies the analysis of instances that display extreme values on the independent or dependent variables. Extreme values are those observations that lie unusually far away from the mean of the investigated distribution. The crucial property of this type of special case is its relative rareness, not its positive or negative value. In fact, when most cases are positive along a given dimension, then a negative case constitutes an extreme case, and when most cases are negative, then a positive case constitutes an extreme case. Extreme cases can also provide more general information about the phenomena under investigation. We are interested in the reasons for this rareness, which could facilitate refining the underlying theory or conceptualization and open up new research questions. With regard to the democratic peace argument, an extreme case to be studied intensively would be a very peaceful dictatorship. It would be extreme in the sense of displaying unusually high levels of 'peacefulness'.

The *deviant case* procedure focuses on unusual cases that can be especially problematic or, conversely, especially good in a more closely defined sense (Flyvbjerg, 2006). These cases have a surprising value in terms of some general understanding of a topic, whether a specific theory or common sense. Thus, they are helpful for the study of theoretical anomalies that are poorly explained. Whereas the extreme case method selects cases by reference to their relative position in a given distribution, the deviant case method focuses on cases that are considered anomalous by reference to some general model of causal relations. Of course, the latter may well be a subset of the former. According to Seawright and Gerring (2008), the important point is that since deviance can be assessed only in relation to the general theoretical model, the relative deviance of a case will change when the general model is altered. In our example, an aggressive attitude on the part of a (quasi-)democratic country towards other (quasi-)democracies would be a deviant case that could challenge the democratic peace theory.

The study of an *influential case* follows a different, pragmatically oriented logic. The aim of this procedure is to examine cases that could substantially influence findings on a larger cross-case theory. Therefore, the starting point is the identification of the cases fitting the model that (might) affect the overall set of findings for the whole population. This way, it becomes possible to check the assumptions behind the model of causal relations and to assess the magnitude of potential shortcomings such as the presence of missing variables. Influential cases are substantially important and hence particularly relevant for results. From a case study perspective, the role in armed conflicts of a country as important as the United States can be considered as an influential case, whose behaviour has extremely relevant consequences for the whole population of democratic countries.

Finally, *crucial cases* deserve a detailed discussion, as they probably represent the most powerful special case method. Eckstein (1975) famously described the crucial case as one 'that must closely fit a theory if one is to have confidence in the theory's validity, or, conversely, must not fit equally well any rule contrary to that proposed', thus permitting logical deductions of the type 'if this is (not) valid for this case, then it applies to all (no) cases' (Flyvbjerg, 2006). Consequently, information from crucial cases is central to the confirmation or disconfirmation of a theoretical prediction. Accordingly, two types of crucial case exist, that is, 'most likely' and least likely' cases (Gerring, 2007a). The most likely case is disconfirmatory, in the sense that it targets a case that, on all dimensions except the variable of theoretical interest, is predicted to display a certain outcome and yet does not. In our example, this would be the case of a conflict involving two long-standing established democracies. The least likely case is confirmatory, in so far as on all dimensions except the variable of theoretical interest, this case is predicted not to display a certain outcome and yet does so: for instance, when peaceful coexistence persists between two democratic countries despite reasons to engage in a conflict (such as territorial disputes).

To follow Gerring, the logic of a least likely research design may be briefly summarized as follows. Since the confirmation of a theory is related to the greater probability of a hypothesis being true than false, then the 'stranger' the theoretical prediction, in comparison with what we would normally expect, the greater the degree of confirmation that the test will give. A strong theory is thus confirmed by the extraordinary fit between the prediction and a set of facts found in a single case, and the corresponding lack of fit between all other theories and this set of facts. Therefore, it is assumed that when we identify a causal relation in an unlikely setting, (say) the positive effect of some institutions on the cooperative behaviour of people in deeply divided societies, the variable of interest should have an even more positive effect in more propitious settings – for example, in homogeneous, cohesive societies.

On the other hand, the most likely case makes it possible to challenge an existing theory, in line with the idea that it is easier to disconfirm an inference than to confirm the same inference. In fact, when a theoretical expectation is factually disconfirmed even in a very likely setting for expecting positive outcomes, then we can straightforwardly conclude that the underlying theory requires careful reconsideration. For example, it was thought that a homogeneous society was a necessary condition for long-standing political stability. In this context, the path-breaking work of Lijphart, initially focused on the Netherlands, a peaceful country with deep cultural cleavages, made it possible to refute that old theory with a single case study, which was later reinforced and confirmed by other case studies (notably Switzerland) and, afterwards, by systematic comparative research (Gerring, 2004).

Let us summarize the example of special case studies applied to the Kantian democratic peace argument (adapted from Seawright and Gerring, 2008):

Type of special case	Analytical logic	Goal	Example
Typical case	It exemplifies a stable relationship.	It is useful to explore the underlying causal mechanisms.	The peaceful coexistence between two democratic countries.
Extreme case	It displays extreme values in a distribution.	It allows us to refine or reconceptualize a theory.	A very peaceful dictatorship.
Deviant case	It displays unusual values with reference to theoretical expectations.	It addresses the anomalies of general models.	The aggressive attitude of a (quasi-)democratic country towards other (quasi-)democracies.
Influential case	It displays unusual values with reference to theoretical expectations.	It addresses the anomalies of general models.	The aggressive attitude of a (quasi-)democratic country towards other (quasi-)democracies.
Crucial (or critical) case	It is (not) predicted to produce an outcome and yet does not (does) do so.	Most likely: it makes it possible to disconfirm/challenge a theory. Least likely: it makes it possible to confirm/corroborate a theory.	A conflict involving two long-standing established democracies, or peace between two democratic countries despite reasons to engage in a conflict.

Special cases can be studied with a variety of methods: for instance, qualitative comparisons of a handful of cases based on face-to-face interviews or focus groups, single-outcome studies relying on official documents and secondary literature, and historical case studies informed by archival sources. However, the technique that most directly fits with the heuristic aims of studying a special case is probably ethnographic research. Ethnographic research is the systematic study of a particular phenomenon, based upon extensive fieldwork in one or more selected locales (Riemer, 2009). In turn, fieldwork can be defined as a form of inquiry that requires us to be immersed personally in the ongoing social activities of some individual or group (Wolcott, 1995). The main aim of ethnography is to explore localized social systems in order to understand the 'study hosts' from their own system of meaning (Whitehead, 2005). As a consequence, the ethnographer adopts an interpretative and reflexive epistemological position and focuses on observable 'socio-cultural' practices, processes and contexts, for the purposes of description and extension of social theory. Classical ethnography implied the total immersion of the researcher in the field setting 24 hours a day over an extended period of time. For instance, Margaret Mead spent the year 1925 in Samoa living with the inhabitants to answer the questions 'are the disturbances which vex our adolescents due to the nature of adolescence itself or to the civilization? Under different conditions does adolescence present a different picture?' In modern research, for example about educational institutions or work settings, this full immersion is not always necessary. Nevertheless, spending a considerable time with the subjects of our study remains important. As an illustration, Claire Hall was physically located in Oftel (the regulator for the UK telecommunications industries) for two years and spent four days a week observing, interviewing, questioning, reading and functioning as a participant observer in Oftel's work (Hall et al., 2000). Her fieldwork allowed her to produce an in-depth inside study of one of the new utility regulators in the UK, so as to understand regulation from the viewpoint of the civil servants under observation, but also to locate observed patterns within a general theoretical framework about organizational practices.

Conclusion

This chapter has focused on the analysis of heterogeneity. The purpose of the chapter was to introduce the main research strategies for examining different forms of heterogeneity in social phenomena (summarized in Table 6.2). A first form of heterogeneity regards differences across individuals or social groups. Individuals vary in their socio-economic status, motives, ideational frameworks, emotions and behaviour. Individuals may also act from a variety of motives at the same time and shift their motives over time. Similarly, social groups can display different degrees of internal and external heterogeneity with regard to their composition, function, role and resources. This type of heterogeneity can be operationalized, explored and potentially reduced by looking for groups in the data at hand by means of factor analysis and related techniques. The analysis of variance permits a further step, that is, to examine the characteristics of the groups that determine the distinction between the observed phenomena. The second form of heterogeneity concerns causal relations. Standard analytical techniques overlook complex causation that may affect some phenomena. Causation may indeed be multiple: different causal paths may explain the same outcome. Causation can also be conjunctural: each causal path can comprise a combination of relevant causal factors. Qualitative comparative analysis is the analytical technique that makes these insights operational, relying on set-theoretical reasoning to decompose symmetrical causal relations and to analyse necessary and sufficient conditions. Its main purpose is no longer to estimate the net effect of supposedly independence variables, but to show the different ways in which explanatory conditions combine to form the outcome of interest. Third, heterogeneity can be found in cases that deserve to be examined in detail. Their 'special' features offer analytical leverage for discovering something about the larger population represented by the observed case. The study of special case relies on explicit criteria for case selection to enhance the analytical leverage of in-depth research, and allows us to generalize our findings to some extent.

Table 6.2 Research designs for the study of heterogeneity/diversity

Research focus	Analytical technique	Goals
Groups	Factor analysis and related techniques	Form groups by assessing the heterogeneity of cases and variables
Variance	ANOVA	Determine the variability of the dependent variable across different groups
Set-theoretic analysis	QCA, fsQCA	Discover and explore the heterogeneity of complex causal patterns
Special cases	Purposely selected case studies	Address peculiar events and instances to corroborate or refine broader arguments

Checklist

- Researchers may be interested in the heterogeneity of social phenomena, rather than the homogeneous effect of independent variables, the verification of regular patterns of behaviour, or the search for general principles.
- In many cases social phenomena are deeply heterogeneous at many levels of scale.
- A first form of heterogeneity can be discovered across and within individuals or social groups.
- A second form is the heterogeneity of causal relations, to be analysed with 'diversity-oriented' methods such as qualitative comparative analysis.
- Third, the examination of special cases allows us to discover something about a larger population through the analysis of particular types of outcomes.

Questions

1 In which real-world cases can the study of social heterogeneity be more interesting than the investigation of homogeneous causal effects?
2 Compare the aims of factor analysis and ANOVA and explain how they differ.

3   How can we operationalize the examination of necessary and sufficient conditions in empirical comparative research?
4   What type of information is contained in a truth table?
5   Try to develop a special case study design for the examination of a topic of your choice that is traditionally addressed by means of statistical analysis.

Further reading

Bray, J.H. and Maxwell, S.E. (1985) *Multivariate Analysis of Variance*. Beverly Hills, CA: Sage Publications. Key reference for methods for the analysis of variance.

Gerring, J. (2007) *Case Study Research: Principles and Practices*. Cambridge: Cambridge University Press. Reference book on the methodology of qualitative case study research.

Kaufman, L. and Rousseeuw, P.J. (1990) *Finding Groups in Data: An Introduction to Cluster Analysis*. New York: Wiley. Rigorous and readable introduction to cluster analysis and related techniques.

Little, D. (1991) *Varieties of Social Explanation*. Boulder, CO: Westview Press. Insightful introduction to the philosophy of social science with an emphasis on the varieties of social processes and forms of explanation in the social sciences.

Rihoux, B. and Ragin, C. (2008) *Configurational Comparative Analysis*. Thousand Oaks, CA: Sage Publications. Excellent volume providing a gentle introduction to qualitative comparative analysis.

SEVEN

Interdependence

Introduction

Interdependence is one of the defining features of the social world and is apparent in many social science sub-fields and research questions. Methods textbooks often treat it as a difficulty for empirical analyses under the label 'Galton's problem' because of Sir Francis Galton's famous comment at an anthropology conference at the end of the nineteenth century (Tylor, 1889: 270):

> It was extremely desirable, for the sake of those who may wish to study the evidence for Dr. Tylor's conclusions, that full information should be given as to the degree in which the customs of the tribes and races which are compared together are independent. It might be, that some of the tribes had derived them from a common source, so that they were duplicates of the same original.

Thus, Galton argued that the lack of independence of the units complicated comparative analyses. In their influential discussion of the comparative method, Przeworski and Teune (1970: 52) reformulated the issue as follows: 'how many independent events can we observe? If the similarity within a group of systems is a result of diffusion, there is only one independent observation.' However, interdependence is more than a source of methodological problems. It is an interesting subject of study in its own right. Indeed, many important literatures in the social sciences have examined the nature, sources and consequences of interdependence among individuals, groups, organizations, states and many other units.

This chapter first gives an overview of some of the most important research questions, with a focus on interdependence, such as institutional isomorphism, social influence, international conflict, democratic dominoes, transnational networks, policy diffusion and transfer, and federalism as policy laboratory. It then discusses the methods that can be employed to study these phenomena, namely, social network analysis, spatial regression, dyadic analysis and qualitative approaches.

The study of interdependence in the social sciences

Interdependence is a classic question in social science, which has been studied from several, often overlapping, perspectives. Rogers' (2003) classic book, first published in 1962 and now in its fifth edition, reviews the literature from a communication perspective and with numerous applied examples in many different areas, such as typewriter and computer keyboard types, hybrid corn, miracle rice, kindergartens, stop AIDS campaigns, electric cars, fax and internet, modern mathematics, cell phones, and needle-exchange programmes.

In sociology, a classic concept is institutional isomorphism, that is, the tendency of organizations to become more alike in conforming with their institutional environment. DiMaggio and Powell (1983) distinguished three types of isomorphism. First, coercive isomorphism denotes compliance with external constraints. The revision of financial reporting practices by large American companies following a change in regulatory requirements is a case in point (Mezias, 1990). Second, mimetic isomorphism means that organizations tend to adopt the practices prevalent in their peer group as a response to uncertainty about the effectiveness of different alternatives. For instance, Fligstein (1985) studied the spread of the multi-divisional form (a particular type of organization) among large American firms during the period 1919–79 and found that firms were more likely to adopt this type of structure if other firms in the industry also did so. Further research has shown that interlocks, that is, overlaps in the membership of companies' boards of directors, are one of the main drivers of mimetic isomorphism (Davis and Greve, 1997). Third, normative isomorphism refers to the consequences of professionalization, namely, the fact that close and repeated interactions within professional groups give rise to common understandings about appropriate practices, where appropriateness may or may not be linked to effectiveness. For example, Fourcade (2006) described in detail how the development of economics was favourable to the establishment of global professional standards.

Other sociological research has focused even more directly on interdependence by looking at various channels of social influence, that is, ways in which individuals influence one another. Many studies have found that a surprisingly large number of phenomena spread like diseases, although, strictly speaking, they are not contagious. A famous (and controversial) study is Christakis and Fowler (2007), which uncovered social influence patterns in the case of obesity. The study leveraged data that enabled the researchers to reconstruct a large social network over 32 years and showed that a given person was significantly more likely to become obese if one of his or her friends had become obese in a previous period. Because the geographical distance between friends did not affect this influence, the authors argued that in this case social influence had more to do with the social acceptance of obesity than with more concrete behavioural effects such as eating habits or physical exercise. These arguments are powerful and have been applied to many other settings (Christakis and Fowler, 2009). However, they always tend to be vulnerable to the 'homophily' counterargument, that is, friends do not become more alike but, rather, people who are alike become friends. We return to this point below. In another study, Liu et al. (2010), using fine-grained individual and geographical data from California, demonstrated that children living very close to children previously diagnosed with autism were more likely to receive the same diagnosis. The analysis could rule out alternative explanations and highlighted the effects of geographical proximity on the diffusion of information among parents. Social network studies have become more prominent in recent years and have been conducted at the intersection of the social, natural and biological sciences (Watts, 2004; Christakis and Fowler, 2009). One reason for this trend has been the rise of online networks such as Facebook and Twitter, which not only create new and powerful channels for social interaction but also allow researchers to access an unprecedented wealth of data.

Interdependence is also at the core of many problems in international relations. War and peace themselves are, of course, a manifestation of the fact that nation states must coexist in an interdependent world. One of the largest literatures in international relations focuses on the so-called 'democratic peace', that is, the idea that democracies do not fight one another, which we have already met in Chapters 3 and 6. In recent decades, the claim has been tested empirically in a large numbers of studies. These have established that, in effect, the likelihood that two countries enter into conflict is much lower if they are both democratic (Maoz and Russett, 1993; Danilovic and Clare, 2007; Gartzke, 2007). Most and Starr (1980) have explored other channels through which international conflicts may spread, as well as the possibility of both positive and negative diffusion. Beyond international conflicts, the literature has examined the spread of various types of violent phenomena such as military coups (Li and Thompson, 1975), civil war (Salehyan and Gleditsch, 2006; Buhaug and Gleditsch, 2008) and terrorism (Horowitz, 2010). Another classic theory in international relations is that of 'democratic dominoes' (Starr, 1991; Leeson and Dean, 2009), whose relevance has been highlighted by the 'Arab Spring' of 2011, in which several dictatorships in north Africa and the Middle East were overturned or put under considerable pressure in a chain reaction triggered by a popular uprising in Tunisia. The domino metaphor was used by many commentators, such as the cartoonist

Figure 7.1 Democratic dominoes (© Chappatte in NZZ am Sonntag, Zurich: www.globecartoon.com)

Chappatte (Figure 7.1). It has also informed decision-making at critical historical junctures. For instance, US President Dwight Eisenhower used the metaphor to describe the possible spread of Communist regimes after World War II: 'You have a row of dominoes set up, you knock over the first one, and what will happen to the last one is the certainty that it will go over very quickly' (Eisenhower, 1954). President George W. Bush used the same argument as a rationale for the second Iraq war: 'The establishment of a free Iraq at the heart of the Middle East will be a watershed event in the global democratic revolution' (Bush, 2003). Research has demonstrated that, indeed, even with many confounding factors controlled for, democratization events tend to be clustered both in space and in time, such that the probability that a country will switch from autocracy to democracy increases significantly with the number of its democratic neighbours (Gleditsch and Ward, 2006). However, the causal mechanisms remain unclear. Work on the spread of democracy in nineteenth-century Europe suggests that the driving force could be that neighbouring transitions alter beliefs on the strength of the domestic autocracy (Weyland, 2010).

Similar to many sociological works, some international relations scholars have sought to measure interdependence with the tools of social network analysis. For example, Hafner-Burton and Montgomery (2006) constructed a network of membership in intergovernmental organizations and showed that the positions of states within this network affect the likelihood of conflict among them, while Cao (2010) used similar data to show that similar network positions increase the probability that two countries will enact similar capital taxation reforms. Other research has used social network analysis to measure the extent to which countries are in competition with one another, and whether this influences the diffusion of certain policies. For instance, Elkins et al. (2006) showed that the probability that a country will sign a bilateral investment treaty, intended to facilitate foreign investment, increases with the number of treaties signed by other countries with similar trade relationships, that is, that export similar goods to similar countries.

Public policy is another large social science sub-field where interdependence is considered an important phenomenon. The general idea here is that interdependence between countries, federal states, cities and so on causes policies to spread. There are several concepts denoting this phenomenon. The most important are 'transfer' and 'diffusion'. Policy transfer can be defined as 'the process by which knowledge about policies, administrative arrangements, institutions and ideas in one political system (past or present) is used in the development of policies, administrative arrangements, institutions and ideas in another political system' (Dolowitz and Marsh, 2000: 5), while (international) policy diffusion occurs 'when government policy decisions in a given country are systematically conditioned by prior policy choices made in other countries' (Simmons et al., 2006). A third concept that is often mentioned in this context is policy convergence, defined as the tendency of policies in different units to become more alike (Bennett, 1991). However, it is important to note that policies can converge for reasons unrelated to interdependence, for instance when different countries face similar problems.

Policy interdependence is a premise of classic defences of federalism. For instance, in *New State Ice Co.* v. *Liebmann* (1932),[1] US Supreme Court Justice Louis Brandeis famously defended the view that decentralization fosters innovation and the spread of best practices: 'It is one of the happy incidents of the federal system that a single courageous State may, if its citizens choose, serve as a laboratory; and try novel social and economic experiments without risk to the rest of the country.' This argument has been investigated empirically in a number of studies. Volden (2006), for instance, looked at the state-level implementation of the US federal Children's Health Insurance Program and found that policies that were more successful in increasing the insurance rate among poor children (a major objective of the programme) were more likely to be adopted in other states. In other words, states seemed to learn from one another, consistent with

---

[1]285 U.S. 262 (1932) (http://goo.gl/CZPmi).

the hopes of Justice Brandeis. Other studies, however, have argued that best practices spread only to the extent that they are compatible with the ideological predispositions of policy-makers, who, moreover, may also be more inclined to adopt policies that have proven beneficial for re-election rather than those that are most effective in solving social problems (Gilardi, 2010). Besides learning, competition is another powerful driver of policy diffusion or transfer. The prototypical example is tax competition, which has been shown to be a real phenomenon, but does not produce a race to the bottom in tax rates because of the many economic, political and institutional constraints faced by policy-makers (Genschel and Schwarz, 2011). Explicit tax coordination is seldom achieved. In the European Union, the weak legitimacy of supranational institutions, coupled with the lack of a clear best practice, has prevented the emergence of a common tax policy despite the disadvantages of competition (Radaelli, 2000). On the other hand, even in the absence of formal coordination, sustained interaction of policy-makers within networks can give rise to norms on acceptable levels of competition, as a comparison of tax rates in Swiss cantons has shown (Gilardi and Wasserfallen, 2012).

To conclude, interdependence is a central issue for many social science questions. But what kinds of research design allow us to study it empirically? We turn to this point in the next section.

How can we study interdependence empirically?

Measuring interdependence: Social network analysis

Social network analysis (SNA) is a major approach for the study of social relations. It focuses directly on relationships between actors rather than attributes of actors. The idea that units are interdependent is a crucial assumption here, whereas many statistical approaches, including those discussed in Chapter 3, make the opposite assumption. Thus, the underlying ontology (the fundamental characteristics of social phenomena) premised by SNA is that the social world cannot be understood from a methodological-individualist position, based solely on individual actors. Instead, it should be interpreted holistically, as an inherently interconnected web of relations.

Let us begin with a few definitions. A relation is a specific kind of contact, connection or association (or 'tie') between a given pair of actors (or 'nodes'). Relations may be either directed (or asymmetric), if one actor sends the link and the other receives it, or non-directed (or symmetric), if the link has a bidirectional nature. In addition, we can distinguish between dichotomous ties, which simply identify the presence or absence of a connection, and valued ties, which measure its intensity. These four types of connections are, in fact, quite intuitive, as these examples show:

- Symmetric and dichotomous ties: shared language or religion (Elkins et al., 2006); shared borders (Gleditsch and Ward, 2006).
- Symmetric and valued ties: number of directorate members that two companies have in common (Davis and Greve, 1997); number of events or organizations in which two actors co-participate (Hafner-Burton et al., 2009).
- Asymmetric and dichotomous ties: perceived friendship (Christakis and Fowler, 2007).
- Asymmetric and valued ties: export or import flows between two countries (Polillo and Guillén, 2005); commuting flows between cities or states (Gilardi and Wasserfallen, 2012).

Figure 7.2 shows how network data are structured and how they can be represented graphically. Specifically, the tables represent four socio-matrices, one for each type of tie. Each cell shows whether and, for valued ties, with what intensity each pair of actors is connected. The graphs display the same information visually and help to impart a first understanding of the properties of the network, such as its density, and which actors occupy a more central position.

Two main analytical perspectives can be applied to social networks. The first is holistic and is based on the properties of the networks ('global network analysis'), while the second focuses on the individual level and is based on actor-level measures ('ego-network analysis').

Global network analysis concentrates on the structural properties of one or, less frequently, more networks. This perspective examines questions such as how dense, bounded or clustered a network is; whether it is diversified or limited in its size and heterogeneity; how narrowly specialized or broadly based its relationships are; how direct and indirect connections and positions in networks affect behaviour; and what the structural contexts within which relationships operate are. For instance, Fowler (2006b) examined the legislative network in the US Congress by looking at co-sponsorship of legislation. In the US system, legislative bills must be presented by one, and only one, representative or senator (in the House of Representatives or Senate, respectively). However, other legislators can co-sponsor bills that they have contributed to drafting or that they want to support. Using data from 280,000 pieces of legislation and their corresponding 2.1 million co-sponsorships, Fowler (2006b) was able to measure the connections among legislators in the US House and Congress from 1973 to 2004 and construct the network that they produced. The Senate network is shown in Figure 7.3. Further, he highlighted some structural characteristics of the network, such as the density of the connections. One way to measure the density of a network is to look at the pairwise distances between the actors, which denote the shortest path connecting two actors. To illustrate, in the

Symmetric, dichotomous
(Example: shared language)

	A	B	C	D	E
A	0	1	0	1	1
B	1	0	1	0	0
C	0	1	0	0	0
D	1	0	0	0	1
E	1	0	0	1	0

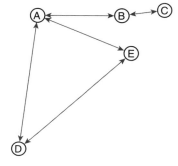

Asymmetric, dichotomous
(Example: perceived friendship)

	A	B	C	D	E
A	0	0	1	1	1
B	1	0	0	0	1
C	0	1	0	0	1
D	1	0	0	0	1
E	1	0	0	1	0

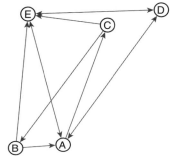

Symmetric, valued
(Example: co-participation in events)

	A	B	C	D	E
A	0	3	3	3	1
B	3	0	0	3	2
C	3	0	0	1	0
D	3	3	1	0	0
E	1	2	0	0	0

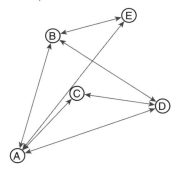

Asymmetric, valued
(Example: export flows)

	A	B	C	D	E
A	0	3	3	1	0
B	3	0	2	0	0
C	3	0	0	0	0
D	3	3	1	0	0
E	1	2	0	0	0

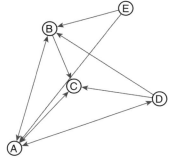

Figure 7.2 Socio-matrices and graphs

top-left panel of Figure 7.2 the distance between A and B is 1 because they have a direct relationship, while that between A and C is 2 because, to reach C, A has to go through B first. Using this idea, Fowler (2006b) showed that in the

2003–4 House the average distance between any two legislators was 1.67 and that more than 33 per cent of the relationships were direct. The 2003–4 Senate network was even denser, with an average distance of 1.27. The networks were also highly clustered, meaning that they were composed of groups of legislators who cooperated closely. The clustering coefficient measures the probability that two actors who are linked to a given actor also have a connection between them. To illustrate, again using the top-left panel of Figure 7.2, the clustering coefficient would be higher if not only D and E, which are connected to A, were linked, but also, for instance, B and E. In 2003–4, this coefficient was 0.6 in the House and as high as 0.9 in the Senate.

Ego-network analysis addresses the different roles played by the actors involved in various types of social relations. There are several methods to assess the relative importance of individuals and their status or rank, notably centrality and structural and role equivalence. The centrality of an actor can be measured in different ways. Degree centrality represents the number of direct ties between an actor and other actors in the network. (Often, this measure is normalized to the total number of ties available in the network, so that centrality

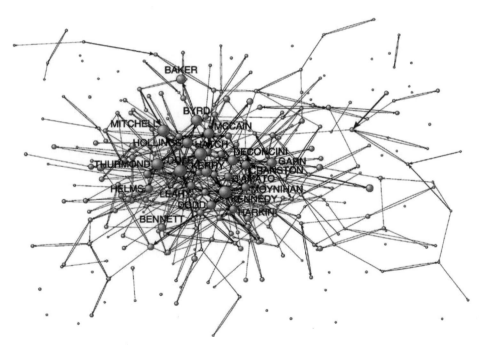

Figure 7.3 Legislative co-sponsorship network in the US Senate, 2003–4

Source: Fowler (2006b: 463)

DESIGNING RESEARCH IN THE SOCIAL SCIENCES

measures can be compared across networks of differing size.) For instance, in the top-left panel of Figure 7.2, A is the most central actor because it is directly connected to three other actors, whereas B, D, and E have two direct links and C only one. Closeness centrality assesses how close an actor is to all the other actors in the network by looking at the length of the paths that connect it to the other actors. For instance, still in the top-left part of Figure 7.2, both A and B can reach all other actors with a maximum of two steps, while the others need three steps. Third, betweenness centrality attempts to determine which actors have a 'mediating' role in assessments of the relational ties in the network. Actors are assigned values based on their probability of being a part of all communication paths. In our example, A is the gatekeeper for connecting D and E with B and C. Adapting these ideas to the specificities of co-sponsorship data, Fowler (2006b) was able to identify the best-connected legislators in the US Congress. The most central senators are highlighted in Figure 7.3. Interestingly, Fowler (2006a) found that a legislative proposal tends to receive stronger support in Congress if its sponsor is more connected, which suggests that legislators who occupy a more central position in the network are more influential.

Structural equivalence measures the similarity of actors' roles and positions within the network. Two actors are structurally equivalent if they share the same ties with the same actors. For instance, in the top-right panel of Figure 7.2, B and D are structurally equivalent because they are both connected with A and D but disconnected from B, C and D. On the other hand, role equivalence denotes the similarity of the types of relationships that actors have, whether they are with the same actors or not. As Polillo and Guillén (2005: 1779) illustrate:

> when countries A and B trade in the same products but with a different set of countries, they are role equivalent but may not be structurally equivalent. Conversely, countries may be structurally equivalent but not role equivalent if they trade in different types of products but with the same set of countries.

Many studies have found that actors tend to imitate others who are (role or structurally) equivalent to them, which is often interpreted as evidence of competitive pressures (Polillo and Guillén, 2005; Cao, 2010).

In sum, SNA offers a set of methods to measure the nature and structure of interdependencies. These methods are primarily descriptive in that they help uncover the characteristics of the network but do not establish connections between those characteristics and other variables of interest. However, network measures can also be used in combination with other approaches, which we discuss in the following subsections.

Measuring the consequences of interdependence

Spatial regression

The predominant quantitative strategy to analyse the effects of interdependence on some outcome of interest is spatial regression (Ward and Gleditsch, 2008). At the bottom, the method involves adding to regression models (for a brief definition of regression analysis, see Chapter 4) a variable, called a 'spatial lag', measuring the dependent variable in other units, weighted by their 'proximity'. Figure 7.4 shows how this works. The top panel shows the first component of a spatial lag, namely, the connectivity matrix, which contains information on how two units (in this case countries) are related. The example shows the easiest case, that is, geographical proximity coded in a binary manner, where 1 means that two countries share a border, and 0 that they do not. While this example is very simple, it is crucial that the connectivity matrix contains information that allows researchers to capture theoretically meaningful interdependencies. (We return to this point below.) Then the bottom panel of Figure 7.4 shows that the spatial lag is constructed by, first, row-standardizing the connectivity matrix and then multiplying it by the dependent variable, which in this example is

Connectivity matrix

	DEN	FRA	GER	ITA	SWI
DEN	0	0	1	0	0
FRA	0	0	1	1	1
GER	1	1	0	0	1
ITA	0	1	0	0	1
SWI	0	1	1	1	0

Row-standardized connecivity matrix					Dependent variable		Spatial lag
0	0	1	0	0	28.0		21.9
0	0	$1/3$	$1/3$	$1/3$	34.3		20.5
$1/3$	$1/3$	0	0	$1/3$	21.9	=	23.0
0	$1/2$	0	0	$1/2$	33.0		20.5
0	$1/3$	$1/3$	$1/3$	0	6.7		29.7

Figure 7.4 Construction of a spatial lag: corporate tax rates, 2006

Source: Cao (2010)

corporate tax rates. Row standardization means that each cell is divided by the sum of the corresponding row. This ensures that the sum of the row is 1, and the spatial lag can be interpreted very intuitively as the weighted average of the dependent variable in other units, where the weights are the values contained in the connectivity matrix.

For instance, for Italy the spatial lag is computed as follows:

$$0 \times 28 + 0.5 \times 34.3 + 0 \times 21.9 + 0 \times 33.0 + 0.5 \times 6.7 = 20.5$$

In other words, the spatial lag is the average corporate tax rate of two of its neighbours, France and Switzerland. Because spatial lags are fundamentally very intuitive, many researchers use them implicitly or without using this terminology. Any study with a variable measuring the (weighted) average of the dependent variable in other units includes, to speak technically, a spatial lag.

The spatial lag so constructed is then included in the analysis, just like another variable.[2] From the perspective of the research design, the most crucial step is the definition of the weights. These often range from relatively general types of geographical proximity, such as shared borders or distance between capital cities, to other measures of physical distance. For example, Buhaug and Gleditsch (2008) examined the spread of civil war by weighting conflict in other countries by the inverse of their distance as well as by a simpler measure, namely the presence of an ongoing conflict in at least one neighbouring state. Similarly, Berry and Berry's (1990) influential study of the diffusion of state lotteries in the US states relied on the number or share of lottery adoptions in neighbouring states as the main explanatory variable.

Geographical distance is in many cases a perfectly reasonable starting point for measuring interdependence. However, in the words of Beck et al. (2006), 'space is more than geography'. Weights should be defined for the purpose of measuring theoretically relevant connections among units. In this respect, geographical proximity is usually a proxy of many different types of interdependences and, consequently, it cannot be interpreted very precisely. Gilardi and Wasserfallen's (2012) study of tax competition in Switzerland illustrates the problem. Many analyses have found that the tax rates of one jurisdiction are positively correlated with those of its neighbours, which is often taken to support the argument that jurisdictions are in competition with one another. However, it could be that neighbours are not competitors but sources of valuable information about the consequences of different tax policies, or that neighbours develop common understandings of appropriate tax rates. Gilardi and Wasserfallen (2012) tried

---

[2]The model estimation needs to consider several complications that are beyond the scope of this book. We refer interested readers to Ward and Gleditsch (2008).

to improve the operationalization of competition by using the number of commuters instead of shared borders in the construction of the connectivity matrix, the idea being that competitive pressures increase with the feasibility of moving to another canton without switching jobs. Concretely, each cell in the connectivity matrix includes, instead of just 1 or 0 depending on whether two units are neighbours, the number of people commuting from the column unit to the row unit. Another example of the flexibility of the spatial lag set-up is given by Simmons and Elkins (2004), who analysed the world-wide diffusion of international economic policies with several connectivity matrices. One matrix is constructed with the correlation between countries' trade patterns, which is taken as a measure of competition; another gives more weight to countries that experience higher growth rates, which is a measure of success; others measure whether two countries share the same language, religion, and colonial heritage. Generally, all network measures discussed in relation to SNA can be used as weights in the connectivity matrix.

There are a few technical limits to the construction of spatial lags, for instance if a unit has no connections (hence, all 0s in the corresponding row of the connectivity matrix). In this case, the spatial lag will be 0, but this may or may not be meaningful depending on the specific application. Another problem arises if the weights can take both positive and negative values, in which case the spatial lag does not add up as expected. However, there is usually a fix for these technical hitches. The real problems are theoretical and, especially, practical. First, what is the best indicator of a specific type of interdependence? Second, can the required data be collected? While it is relatively easy to come up with good ideas, they often prove unfeasible because of data constraints.

In sum, the spatial regression approach provides clear guidelines for research design. Essentially, it builds on standard regression methods and adds one or more variables capturing theoretically relevant forms of interdependence through spatial lags. The key issue here is the construction of the connectivity matrix, which measures the connections among all units in the analysis. While there are some technical obstacles both to this step and to model estimation, the big issues are the theoretical definition of the weights and, in particular, the availability of appropriate data.

Dyadic approach

Another quantitative approach to interdependence is the dyadic approach, in which units are not actors but pairs of actors. This definition of the units of analysis makes it easy to take relational variables into account, which allows for a direct operationalization of various types of interdependence.

A dyadic data structure is well suited to the analysis of network data. In Christakis and Fowler's (2007: 376) study of the spread of obesity, for example, units are pairs of individuals, which makes it possible to incorporate directly in the data set whether the first person ('ego') perceives the second ('alter') as a friend, whether the two people are mutual friends, whether they are married to one another, and so on. Crucially, the dependent variable is the obesity of the first person, while the main explanatory variable is the obesity of the second. Figure 7.5 shows the results of the analysis. Generally, a person is more likely to become obese if his or her friends are obese, but the effect is stronger in the event of mutual friendship than if only the first person identifies the second as a friend, and the effect disappears if it is the other way round. Both people being of the same sex also seems to play an important role. As mentioned earlier, the authors think that these findings are driven by obesity becoming more socially accepted if it is widespread among friends, which makes it more likely that a person makes less effort to avoid becoming overweight. However, the results have been controversial, and we discuss the main issue below in the treatment of homophily.

The dyadic approach has been used extensively in the democratic peace literature, which can be used to illustrate its basic set-up. Gartzke (2007) used non-directed dyads to study the role of capitalism in explaining democratic peace. The dependent variable is the onset of a militarized interstate dispute between the two countries in the dyad. Democracy is measured by the highest and lowest values in the dyad, as well as by a dichotomous variable with a value of 1 if both countries are fully democratic. Because dyads are non-directed, 'high' and 'low' values cannot be attributed to a specific country. However, dyads can also be directed. For instance, Danilovic and Clare (2007) defined one country in the dyad as the 'initiator' and the other as 'target' of conflict. This means that each country enters

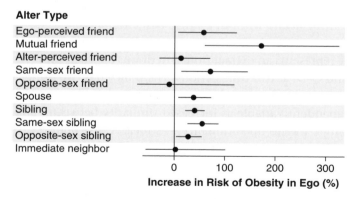

Figure 7.5 Increase in risk of obesity in ego (per cent)

Source: Christakis and Fowler (2007: 376)

the data set twice, once as (potential) initiator and once as (potential) target. This makes it possible to measure which country attacks and which is attacked in the dependent variable. Similarly, explanatory variables can distinguish between different combinations of the democratic status in the dyad, that is, whether only one, both, or none of the countries are democratic. The big advantage of this approach is that it makes it possible to test relational arguments directly. Thus, Gartzke (2007) found that conflict is significantly less likely when both countries in a dyad have high financial and trade openness, which suggests that economic policy is an important driver of democratic peace. Similarly, Danilovic and Clare (2007) refined the democratic peace argument by showing that respect for individual freedoms strongly influences the absence of conflict between countries.

Volden (2006) adapted the dyadic approach to the study of policy diffusion. This task is not straightforward because, unlike in the case of interstate conflict or trade, the dependent variable is not directly observable. That is to say, we are interested in whether one unit was influenced by other units, but such influence is essentially unobservable. Indeed, finding out whether there was any influence at all is one of the main goals of the analysis. Volden (2006) circumvented this problem by defining the dependent variable in terms of convergence between the two units in the dyad, and specifically in terms of the first unit becoming more similar to the second. The analysis, then, attempted to find whether there were any factors that made the first unit systematically more likely to alter its policies in ways that moved it closer to the second unit. As discussed earlier, Volden (2006) found that states were more likely to become more similar to other states that managed to increase health insurance rates among children, which was one of the main goals of the policy under study. The dyadic approach makes it possible to test this argument directly because it can easily include variables measuring characteristics of the first unit, of the second unit, and of the relationship between the two. This is its main advantage. However, the definition of the dependent variable is somewhat artificial and without a single best alternative.

Figure 7.6 shows four alternative operationalizations of the dependent variable. The table represents an extract from a fictitious data set, showing three dyads (A–D, B–D, and C–D) at two time periods. The policy has two dimensions, which are measured for both units of the dyad (i and j). Following Volden (2006), we define the dependent variable as increased similarity between i and j. However, there is no single way to operationalize this idea. A first option is simply to say that i becomes more similar to j if there is convergence on at least one dimension of the policy. If this is the case, DV_1 is coded 1 and 0 otherwise. With this definition, both A–D and B–D are coded 1. A second option is to require that the first unit becomes more similar to the second on at least one dimension and does not become more dissimilar on another (DV_2). If we apply this rule, A–D is still coded 1, but B–D must be coded 0 because B moves away from D on the second dimension of the policy. The third option is more complex. Here, we can situate the units in a multidimensional policy space and measure their distance continuously, as shown in the bottom panel of Figure 7.6. The dependent variable can use distance directly (DV_3), or we can further compute the difference in distance between the two time periods (DV_4). This list shows that, in the dyadic

$Unit_i$	$Unit_j$	t	DV_1	DV_2	DV_3	DV_4	$Policy_{1,i}$	$Policy_{2,i}$	$Policy_{1,j}$	$Policy_{2,j}$
A	D	1			0.36		0.90	0.30	0.70	0.60
A	D	2	1	1	0.22	−0.14	0.60	0.40	0.70	0.60
B	D	1			0.45		0.30	0.40	0.70	0.60
B	D	2	1	0	0.41	−0.04	0.60	0.20	0.70	0.60
C	D	1			0.21		0.65	0.80	0.70	0.60
C	D	2	0	0	0.34	0.13	0.55	0.90	0.70	0.60

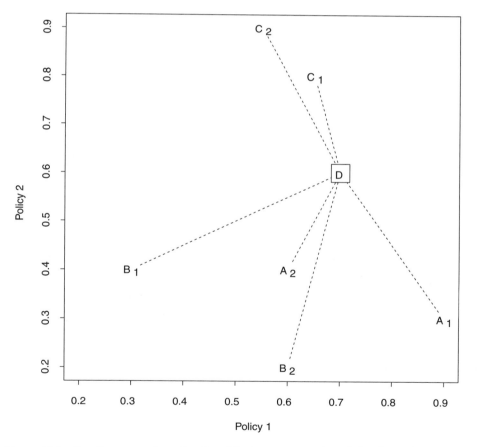

Figure 7.6 Dyadic approach and policy diffusion: construction of the dependent variable

approach, the operationalization of the dependent variable is not straightforward. Therefore, it is crucial that researchers discuss the alternatives in detail and try different implementations when there is no clear best option (that is, in the majority of cases).

A by-product of the dyadic approach is that the number of observations increases dramatically. This is not necessarily a good thing because the increase is due to a rather artificial manipulation, not to a real increase in the number of cases. Relatedly, complex interdependencies emerge between observations, which can complicate the analysis. Also, the construction of the dependent variable in policy diffusion applications creates its own set of problems. These methodological issues are beyond the scope of this volume, and interested readers are referred to specialized articles on the subject (Green et al., 2001; Gilardi and Füglister, 2008). Finally, we note that the spatial approach discussed above in the subsection on spatial regression can be implemented even within a dyadic data structure (Plümper and Neumayer, 2010).

In terms of research design, the essential point is that focusing on pairs of countries can provide considerable analytical leverage when the dependent variable itself is dyadic (conflict, trade and so forth) or, in a diffusion study, when it makes sense to redefine the dependent variable in dyadic terms. The latter is more likely to be the case when the policy has several dimensions, which are difficult to handle in a normal set-up. When these conditions hold, the dyadic approach allows researchers to integrate interdependences directly into the analysis, which is a significant advantage. However, the price to be paid is the increased complexity of the data structure and the methodological complications that come with it.

The problem of homophily

Evidence of diffusion has been uncovered by countless studies. However, such evidence could also be produced in cases where diffusion is extremely implausible, such as acne, height and headaches (Cohen-Cole and Fletcher, 2008). This problem points to the well-known 'homophily' principle, namely, 'that a contact between similar people occurs at a higher rate than among dissimilar people' (McPherson et al., 2001: 416). This phenomenon could be documented for socio-demographic characteristics such as race, ethnicity, and age; for acquired characteristics such as education, occupation, religion, and behaviour; and for internal characteristics such as attitudes, abilities, beliefs, and aspirations (McPherson et al., 2001: 419–29). Moreover, homophily pertains not only to friendship *formation*, but also to friendship *dissolution* (Noel and Nyhan, 2011). Thus, on the one hand, people who share some characteristics tend to become and to remain more connected (homophily). On the other hand, more connected people tend to take up each other's characteristics (diffusion, contagion). Distinguishing the two phenomena empirically is difficult, and some authors have argued that it is almost impossible with observational (that is, non-experimental) data (Shalizi and Thomas, 2011). At a general level, the problem is related to the distinction between descriptive and causal inference discussed in Chapter 4. To the extent that claims of diffusion or contagion are causal, it is paramount that homophily be ruled out. However, this is usually unfeasible because homophily can take so many different forms, some of which are latent, that is, cannot be observed. This leads Shalizi and Thomas (2011: 216) to conclude that 'there is just no way to separate selection from influence observationally', which is a rather bleak assessment. On the other hand, there is no consensus on the actual magnitude of the problem and scholars are actively researching ways to overcome or limit it.

The homophily critique is most directly relevant to studies of interpersonal networks because that is the context where the phenomenon is most likely to be an issue. However, more generally, it means that researchers should always consider carefully the extent to which the connections among units are exogenous or, conversely, can be influenced by the outcomes under study. Geographical proximity is an example of an exogenous connection (but, as mentioned earlier, these are difficult to interpret theoretically), while joint membership in (international) organizations is potentially endogenous. For instance, countries sharing many memberships in organizations could appear more likely to adopt similar policies, but they might be more likely to join the same organizations if they have similar policies. Here, the issue is less intractable than in the case of interpersonal networks because it is possible to find evidence that membership is exogenous. For instance, membership of some organizations has a pure geographical basis, or it can be shown that self-selection is unrelated to the specific policy under consideration. The qualitative methods discussed below in the subsection on qualitative approaches, especially within-case analysis, can be particularly helpful in this context. While always potentially problematic, homophily will generally be both less extensive and more manageable in interstate than in interpersonal networks. However, the usual complications of causal inference, discussed in Chapter 4, still apply.

Qualitative approaches

The majority of research designs for the study of interdependence rely on quantitative tools. However, it is obvious that quantitative methods alone cannot give a full picture of this (or any) phenomenon and that qualitative research designs can make a distinct contribution. In particular, two approaches seem particularly fruitful, namely cross-case analysis and process tracing (Starke, 2011). Both are well-established methods in the social sciences, and we have already discussed them in Chapter 3. However, their application to the specific question of interdependence has been examined in less depth than has been the case with the other methods presented in this chapter. Counterfactual approaches could also be useful for the analysis of interdependence (Starke, 2011) but, in practice, they have not been used as extensively as other methods. As we have seen in Chapter 3, this conclusion also applies to other areas of the social sciences. However, when used in combination with other methods, they can certainly help strengthen the analysis.

Following Starke (2011), we can usefully differentiate between two questions that are relevant for the study of interdependence and assess the various methods accordingly. First, how can we establish whether interdependence matters in a given context? Even if we can observe, descriptively, that a given phenomenon spreads, we need to make sure that interdependence drives it, and not other factors such as internal characteristics or common pressures. Second, what is the nature of interdependence? For instance, the diffusion literature discussed above distinguishes theoretically mechanisms such as learning, competition, and emulation. How can the different methods help us to differentiate them empirically?

To start with cross-case analysis, the most fruitful case selection strategy is probably the 'diverse cases' approach, which 'has as its primary objective the achievement of maximum variance along relevant dimensions' (Gerring, 2007c: 97). A traditional method of difference (or, equivalently, most-similar-systems design, MSSD) could in principle be adopted, by selecting cases with different outcomes, similar control variables, and different diffusion variables. Alternatively, the method of agreement (or most-different-systems design, MDSD) would require that cases differ on the outcome and on key diffusion variables, but are similar on the control variables. However, J.S. Mill's methods often do not work well in practice because cases seldom fit cleanly into the theoretical schemes. By contrast, the diverse-cases strategy, while no magic solution, gives more flexibility to select cases that vary on several interesting dimensions. Answering the first question ('does interdependence matter?') will be difficult because the small number of cases makes it very hard to control for alternative explanations, but cross-case analyses give more leverage to answer the second question ('what is the nature of interdependence?'). For instance, Weyland (2007) argued that bounded learning was the main driver of the spread of health and pension reforms in Latin America. His argument is that policy-makers strive to learn from the experience of other countries but rely on cognitive short cuts instead of analysing all the available evidence systematically. One piece of evidence in support of this idea comes from a cross-case comparison showing that the learning process was more superficial in countries that could not rely on extensive expertise (Weyland, 2007: 220):

> Countries with especially limited technical capacity, such as Bolivia and El Salvador, therefore imported most of the Chilean privatization scheme. Nations with ample, long-standing expertise, such as Costa Rica, introduced

substantial modifications but nevertheless instituted the core innovation of the Chilean model, namely, privately managed individual pension accounts in the obligatory social security system.

This quotation shows both the strengths and the weaknesses of qualitative cross-case analysis. On the one hand, the comparison highlights a covariation that can be directly linked to the theoretical expectations. On the other hand, alternative factors cannot be convincingly ruled out. This is why most qualitative studies combine cross-case comparisons and within-case analysis.

The analysis of interdependence within cases is definitely the strongest of qualitative approaches. This step corresponds to what is known as process tracing. As Bennett (2008: 704–5) explains (see also the discussion in Chapter 3):

> [p]rocess tracing involves looking at evidence within an individual case, or a temporally and spatially bound instance of a specified phenomenon, to derive and/ or test alternative explanations of that case. … [It] is the technique of looking for the observable implications of hypothesized causal processes within a single case.

Although there are few standard procedures for process tracing, which makes it difficult to outline clear prescriptions for researchers, there is no doubt that a fine-grained focus on process and mechanisms is the most important contribution that qualitative work can offer to the understanding of interdependence. Thus, qualitative research should strive to uncover crucial 'causal-process observations', that is, 'an insight or piece of data that provides information about context, process, or mechanism, and that contributes distinctive leverage in causal inference' (Brady and Collier, 2004: 277). For instance, Weyland (2007) showed in detail how pension privatization in Chile played an important role in promoting reforms in other Latin American countries. In Bolivia, a crucial event was the finance ministry's budget director attending a keynote speech by the architect of Chile's pension privatization. Similarly, in El Salvador the Chilean model was placed on the agenda by a consultant who was involved in the Chilean reform, and who was originally hired to assist with a smaller-scale project (Weyland, 2007: 101). By contrast, contacts with experts and policy-makers from Argentina and Colombia, which had also introduced reforms of the pension system, were much more limited (Weyland, 2007: 105–6). In some instances, researchers may even uncover 'smoking guns' supplying very strong evidence. For instance, in his study of national tax blacklists, Sharman (2010) provided examples of countries that literally copied and pasted legislation from others. The most striking case is Venezuela (Sharman, 2010: 625):

> [T]he Venezuelan legislation made reference to the wishes of the Mexican legislature and the need to be consistent with the Mexican constitution. Worse still, the original Mexican list had included Venezuela, and thus by copying the Mexican list, Venezuela succeeded in blacklisting itself.

Biedenkopf's (2011) study of the effects of EU environmental legislation on the United States is also a good example of how within-case analysis can yield insights into the relevance and nature of interdependence. For instance, like Weyland (2007), Biedenkopf (2011) is interested in whether policy-makers learn from the experience of other countries. One piece of evidence supporting the learning argument is that in many cases US policy-makers (at both the federal and state levels) were quite familiar with the details of EU rules and not just with the general concept. Another argument is that, under some circumstances, policy-makers may be more sensitive to the symbolic features of the policy than to the actual evidence of its effectiveness. Interviews found some support for this idea: '[A] number of interviewees described California as striving to be trendsetters. According to one interviewee: "They don't like falling behind" and according to another: "California does not want to be perceived as a laggard internationally"' (Biedenkopf, 2011: 220). These 'causal-process observations' are less dramatic than those uncovered by Sharman (2010), but they do help us to understand how and to what extent interdependence matters, and they are a distinctive contribution of qualitative approaches.

In sum, qualitative approaches to interdependence are less developed than their quantitative counterparts but have specific strengths that can yield unique insights into the nature of interdependence, especially when cross-case comparisons are combined with within-case analysis and, possibly, counterfactual reasoning. While they cannot measure interdependence as reliably as quantitative approaches, they allow us to uncover detailed elements of the phenomenon to which quantitative methods are almost completely blind.

Conclusion

Interdependence is a fundamental characteristic of the social world. Sometimes it is treated, under the 'Galton's problem' rubric, as a source of complications for comparative research. However, interdependence is an interesting subject of study in its own right, which can be and has been investigated in a wide range of social science sub-fields, including communication, sociology, international relations, public policy, and federalism. Moreover, the list of phenomena for which interdependence is a relevant angle for research is virtually unlimited. Research designs for the study of interdependence should pay attention to several dimensions. Descriptively, social network analysis is the method of choice to measure the connections among units and the structural properties of the network that they constitute. More explanatory research questions would ask what the consequences of interdependence are. Here, information on interdependence can be integrated in regression models through spatial or dyadic frameworks. As for other research questions, separating correlation and causation is not straightforward, but the problem is complicated here by 'homophily', that is, the fact that not only do actors who are more connected tend to become more alike, but also those who are more alike tend to become more connected in the first place. Qualitative approaches can make a distinct contribution to the study of interdependence through focused cross-case comparisons and, especially, within-case analysis. Even though they are currently less developed than quantitative options, they have an unparalleled capacity to test important assumptions and to uncover crucial pieces of information that can go a long way to confirm or disprove the relevance and nature of interdependence in a variety of contexts.

Students of interdependence face many methodological problems. However, ignoring interdependence is certainly not a better option than taking it into account as accurately as possible with the current methodological state of the art. The importance of the topic certainly justifies (indeed, it requires) further efforts to elucidate the nature and consequences of interdependence.

Checklist

- Interdependence is a phenomenon that is studied in most social science sub-fields, including sociology, political science, international relations, public policy, communication and economics.
- Social network analysis is a method that analyses connections ('ties') between units ('nodes'). It describes the patterns of these connections and can be used in combination with various research designs.
- Spatial regression and dyadic methods are quantitative approaches suitable for measuring interdependence. However, they usually cannot precisely establish its nature.
- 'Homophily' means that stronger contacts tend to be established among actors who are more similar. Therefore, it is difficult to establish whether actors become more alike because they are connected or become more connected because they are alike.
- Qualitative research designs tend to rely on 'diverse cases' approaches and within-case analysis. They are relatively weak when it comes to measuring interdependence, but they are quite strong in uncovering the nature of interdependence.

 **Questions**

1 Read closely five articles in your field of study. To what extent could interdependence be an interesting angle to complement or extend these works? What types of interdependence could matter? Develop a research question.
2 Try to formalize these interdependencies with a connectivity matrix/sociomatrix. What are the relevant units, and how could their relationships be measured?

3 Now think about the dependent variable, that is, the phenomenon that is subject to interdependence. How would you redefine it if you were to use a dyadic approach?
4 Make a list of causal-process observations that, ideally, you would like to find in a within-case analysis. Try to connect them with different types of interdependence as explicitly as possible.
5 Think about the ways in which qualitative and quantitative approaches could be combined to answer your research question.

▋▋ Further reading ▋

Christakis, N.A. and Fowler, J.H. (2009) *Connected: The Surprising Power of Our Social Networks and How They Shape Our Lives*. New York: Little, Brown. An overview of recent social networks research for the general public.
Gilardi, F. (2012). Transnational diffusion: Norms, ideas, and policies. In W. Carlsnaes, T. Risse and B.A. Simmons (eds), *Handbook of International Relations*, 2nd edn. Thousand Oaks, CA: Sage Publications. A review of diffusion research in public policy and international relations.
Scott, J. (2000) *Social Network Analysis: A Handbook*, 2nd edition. London: Sage Publications. A non-technical introduction to social network analysis.
Ward, M.D. and Gleditsch, K.S. (2008) *Spatial Regression Models*. Los Angeles: Sage Publications. An accessible introduction to statistical techniques for the analysis of interdependence.

EIGHT

Conclusions: Connecting the dots

At the conclusion of our journey across research traditions, approaches, and trade-offs, it is useful to ask what the core message is that emerges from this book. Granted that the previous chapters allow for diversity and reasoned, moderate, analytic eclecticism – which is the opposite of saying that 'anything goes' – how do we connect the dots? This is the topic of our last chapter.

A famous quote by Steve Jobs has it that we can only connect the dots backwards, not forwards. This concluding chapter is therefore the right place to try to accomplish this task. We argue that research is a process of learning. It is not a series of rigidly segmented tasks. Rather, it is a process of thinking, collecting evidence and writing that evolves and often mutates over time.

There are many ways to think about the research process: some are more realistic than others, some (as we said earlier) are closer to the shop-floor activities of researchers, and others are idealized. We suggest thinking about research in probabilistic terms. Our knowledge of the world is incomplete, especially (but not only) in the social sciences. We can only formulate conjectures that are valid in some temporal and geographical contexts. There are no universal laws valid in all societies and at all times. Given this presupposition about our knowledge of the world, the Bayesian concept of learning sheds light on the essence of the research process. Bayesian epistemologists think that research is a process through which we move from an uncertain, probabilistic, subjective knowledge of the world to new levels of knowledge, yet again probabilistic but informed by new evidence. This change is made possible by taking evidence to inform our probabilities.

In Bayesian epistemology, probabilities are not frequencies of events that happen out there, in the real world, but subjective conjectures about the states of the world. This is particularly useful because in some very important cases we investigate events that simply do not exhibit a frequency distribution because they are unique or very few in number. For example, as social scientists we may want to explore the reason why six countries gave birth to an international organization called the European Coal and Steel Community in 1952 and then upgraded it to the European Community five years later. Or why there is a single currency without an elected government in the Eurozone but not in the USA.

Thus researchers have their own subjective probabilities. Taken together, we can say that communities of researchers share collectively a set of prior probabilities about certain states of the world they are interested in – hence subjectivity does not necessarily mean 'individual'. Given this background, what is a project? What we call 'a project' is the process that, via appropriate methods, generates evidence that enables researchers to draw valid causal inferences. Evidence changes our prior probabilities. If evidence is used coherently to update our probabilistic knowledge of the world, the posterior probabilities are more informative than the priors. Bayesian probability theory provides some rules of coherence and a key theorem that shows how evidence creates convergence of probability distributions.

You do not have to go too deep into Bayesian theory. But you have to grasp the essence of this epistemological notion. Basically, what we are saying is that to research is to learn. But, as mentioned earlier, learning is very often a process that cannot be divided into neatly differentiated steps, like slicing a salami. The fiction of the researcher that starts with a blank page, distils the best theoretical propositions into observable implications and hypotheses, goes out to collect evidence and tests the hypotheses does not match the shop-floor practice of social science researchers. Our priors start from a blend of evidence and theory – rarely have we seen a professional researcher starting a project without having collected some evidence. Conceptual work is 'done' throughout the process. Sometimes the cases define the concept (Becker,1998) or become indispensable to make concepts and initial conjectures sharper and suitable to empirical analysis. The dialogue between conjectures, theories and observations is a two-way street.

Becker (1998), in his review of sociological research on 'prison culture', provides a wonderful example. Early research on the social life of men in prisons shed light on the presence of prison culture. Men deprived of individual freedom – this was the argument – are socialized into a convict code, including among other things the prohibition on snitching on other prisoners to prison staff. Men without sharp objects, belts, drugs and the goods they previously had in their ordinary lives create a shadow market in prison where all these goods are made available at certain costs and under certain conditions dictated by a clear, albeit illegal, political economy of prison markets. Sex deprivation led men to develop predatory homosexual relationships. The fact that they are predatory does not seem to threaten the self-conception of a macho man in prison.

This sociological knowledge of the time seemed to explain prison culture pretty well: prison culture – researchers reasoned – means deprivation of hierarchy, sex relationships, and the provision of certain goods. Observations seemed to fit the theoretical claim – until researchers started carrying out projects on women in prison. They did not find anything that looked like the concept of prison culture. They did not find a convict code. Neither did they find predatory sex relationships or a real underground market. Women in jail replicated family life: their pseudo-families had 'butches' who behaved like fathers and husbands of 'daughters' and 'wives'. Women were keen on having cosmetics and clothes – items for which there was no need to develop an underground market with its own political economy.

As Becker (1998: 141–2) shows, this kind of evidence did not mean the end of the concept of prison culture, but rather contributed to concept development. The key concept underlying the culture of men and women in prison was deprivation. But men were deprived of autonomy, hierarchical relations, and certain goods, whilst women, who never enjoyed autonomy in a male-dominated society, were deprived of protection. Hence they were re-creating protection by developing all-female pseudo-families in prisons. The key move to understand prison culture in the case of both men and women is thus a redefinition of the concept at a higher level of abstraction. Deprivation is key to the development of prison culture, but men are deprived of certain things, women of others.

We argued that research is a process that can mutate. However, we cannot say 'anything goes'. There is little dispute indeed in contemporary social sciences that Popper, Kuhn and Lakatos's rule-based views of methodology are more productive than Feyerabend's 'epistemological anarchism'. Methods are required to discover and/or test theories in the light of empirical results, and intersubjective criteria are needed to judge the methodological quality of research designs. At the same time, there is no research strategy that is intrinsically superior to others, and disciplines are distinguished primarily by their subject matter rather than by the application of distinctive methods (Hall, 2012).

In this book, we suggest that different research strategies coexist and sometimes intersect but share the need to be coherent with our research goals. The alignment of our ontological assumptions (about the nature of causation) with the theoretical framework and the methods used to explore or test these theories should be preserved throughout the research process (Hall, 2003), although exceptions inspired by analytic eclecticism have to be factored in (as explained in Chapter 1).

One example of a typical research strategy is the macro-comparative approach which is concerned with the correspondence between cross-case properties and macro-level phenomena. Macro-comparative research strategies are best suited for assessing probabilistic relationships about the effect of independent variables on dependent variables over the widest possible population of observations, following a homogeneous, linear and additive conception of causation. Another example is the mechanisms-centered perspective, which aims to explain how a cause produces its effect. This research strategy is in line with complex ontologies, that is, including the possibility that the same effect can follow multiple causal pathways. Actor-level theories and related methods are recommended to unravel the micro-foundations of mechanisms producing social phenomena. Many other coherent research strategies can be implemented in a research project, also transgressing the boundaries between qualitative and quantitative research.

What is more, research projects are virtually never finished, because our research continues even after the project and results are never definitive (Booth et al., 2008). Therefore, research strategies may combine different methods and tools and may evolve during or after the project, in the context of broader, hopefully cumulative, research programmes. In our own experience, we have seen the findings of our initial project feeding into a second, more ambitious, project. This is something to bear in mind if you are developing a doctoral dissertation. Doctoral students often feel that they have to answer 'all questions' that matter to them in the dissertation. But when we speak to them, we realize that they are after a research agenda that requires two or three projects, and hopefully can be developed beyond the doctoral dissertation.

There is a sense, however, in which projects are never finished. First, we write our conclusions for a given funding body (this can be the faculty or national research committee that has funded your doctoral dissertation). But at the same time we typically develop a string of articles arising out of the project. Since getting an article in print in a good journal takes time, the chances are that the 'final' article will already get some inspiration or even data from the next project. We can also be asked to write and disseminate our findings to different audiences, and this may happen months after we have formally concluded the project. To write for our press office or a blog is not the same as to write for the national research council. To present our findings to a conference of policy-makers, a civil society organization or the annual conference of a political party requires systematic rethinking about our findings and why they should matter to the particular audience we are about to address. It may well be the case that we need to explain very clearly when we have proved causation and when we only have correlation – to avoid misunderstandings about the nature of our conclusions. You may have to go back to your data and perform different types of analysis to answer the questions that your audience is most likely to ask. Next you may succeed in generating a book out of your project. And here research and writing start again, given the large differences between raw research outputs (such as a final report for a funding body) and a book that can be marketed and hopefully read by a wide audience in many different countries.

In any case, research strategies imply trade-offs. Let us quickly rehearse what we have found in this book and conclude on this important point. There is no single way to handle the problems of research design. Trade-offs are never absolute but should be considered as choices that 'cost' something. In our view, the most important trade-offs partially overlap with but do not exactly correspond to the four crucial issues mentioned by Adcock and Collier (2001), that is, the validity of measurement, the distinction between measurement and conceptual disputes, the generality of research strategies, and the assessment of validation procedures. Accordingly, and in no particular order, we can mention a foundational trade-off between the complexity of theories and the broad testability of hypotheses. This trade-off is directly connected with the choice of assuming a relatively simple causal structure of the social world or thinking in terms of complex causation (Ragin, 2008). The former choice facilitates comparative analysis while the latter enables richer, more detailed explanation. Another frequently cited trade-off is between internal validity and external validity. In preceding chapters we have shown that some methods such as actor-based simulations and strategic game analysis allow us to obtain 'non-trivial' results from artificial situations that are very useful for theory development but typically lack external validity. In this case, the tension is between the discovery and generation of new theories and the empirical test of existing theories. A similar trade-off is found also in statistical research for causal inference, which clearly prioritizes the latter. Then, there is a potential trade-off between conceptual formation and measurement, because sometimes in order to make our concept measurable we have to use crude proxies that are very distant from the underlying concept. This is the case of multi-faceted concepts such as 'social capital' or 'learning', which are difficult to measure directly and can be operationalized in very dissimilar or even contradictory ways. Statistical research tends to favour measurement over concept formation, while the reverse is true for qualitative case study and qualitative comparative analysis.

The quality of concept formation is crucial. For instance, the concept of 'free-riding' developed by Mancur Olson has powerful analytical leverage. It allows us to explain a wide array of social phenomena involving collective action with a very parsimonious argument: collective action – in social movements, civil society associations, trade unions, political parties and so on – is difficult for members of large groups in the absence of selective incentives. The last trade-off is about the tension between effects-of-causes and causes-of-effects designs (Goertz and Mahoney, 2005). The first is centred on explanatory variables and aims to estimate the net effect of independent variables on the dependent variables. In other words, explanatory variables are considered as independent competitors in explaining the result. The second design is centred on the explanandum and aims to fully explain individual cases. The goal is to account for all different factors that combine to produce the result under investigation. Because of this trade-off we have to choose between the partially generalizable understanding of specific cases, for example the outbreak of World War I, and constant relationships among variables. If we go for the latter, we won't have any particular concern for substantial cases. In the first design, variables are contextualized and contingently bounded to the cases under study; in the second, cases are considered as collections of variables. Another way to see this issue is that there is a trade-off between reliable answers to very specific questions and less precise answers to bigger questions. The 'effects-of-causes' perspective is designed to achieve the former, while the 'causes-of-effects' perspective tends to produce the latter.

To conclude, we agree with Brady and Collier (2004) that different research strategies and research tools should have in common similar standards of quality. As anticipated in Chapter 4 following Gerring's criteria-based approach, to escape any possible essentialist conundrum that would reify the scope of causal analysis, the quality of causal propositions should be judged with reference to their formal properties: specification, precision, breadth, boundedness, completeness, parsimony, differentiation, priority, independence, contingency, mechanism, analytic utility, intelligibility, relevance, innovation and comparison (Gerring, 2001, 2005). Quite obviously, given the presence of trade-offs in research strategies, some of these criteria are conflicting or are incompatible. Therefore, quality standards must also be aligned with specific research strategies in terms of their goals, ontologies, theories and methods. For instance, when we apply Gerring's framework to our examples, we see that macro-comparative approaches should be judged foremost with reference to their breadth ('what range of instances are covered by the proposition?'), completeness ('how many features, or how much variation, is accounted for by the proposition, how strong is the relationship?'), parsimony ('how parsimonious is the proposition?') and analytic utility ('does the proposition fit with what we know about the world, does it help to unify that knowledge?'). Mechanism-oriented research strategies should instead, above all, comply with different criteria, such as precision ('how precise is the proposition?'), differentiation ('is the X differentiable from the Y, is the cause separate, logically and empirically, from the outcome to be explained?'), contingency ('is the X contingent, relative to other possible Xs, does the causal explanation conform to our understanding of the normal course of events?') and, above all, causal narrative ('is there a plausible mechanism connecting X to Y?').

We wish to close with what really fuels our research. To carry out research is a disciplined, analytically controlled activity. But it can flourish only if there is fundamental freedom and a desire to find out something genuinely new. Research design is not about conformism. Quite the opposite, conformism – producing findings that merely confirm that what has been said up until now is correct – does not respond to the *so what* question introduced in Chapter 1. So we hope you will find that research is liberating in the sense of allowing you to challenge our many conventional wisdoms. Discipline at the level of choices that can be intersubjectively controlled by a community of scholars can and should go hand in hand with passion, motivation, fun and emotional 'fire'.

References

Abbott, A. (1995) Sequence analysis: new methods for old ideas. *Annual Review of Sociology,* 21 (1): 93–113.

Abbott, A. and Hrycak, A. (1990) Measuring resemblance in sequence data: An optimal matching analysis of musicians' careers. *American Journal of Sociology,* 96 (1): 144–85.

Acemoglu, D., Johnson, S. and Robinson, J.A. (2001) The colonial origins of comparative development: an empirical investigation. *American Economic Review,* 91 (5): 1369–1401.

Adcock, R. and Collier, D. (2001) Measurement validity: a shared standard for qualitative and quantitative research. *American Political Science Review,* 95 (3): 529–46.

Ahn, W., Kalish, C.W., Medin, D.L. and Gelman, S.A. (1995) The role of covariation versus mechanism information in causal attribution. *Cognition,* 54 (3): 299–352.

Angrist, J.D. and Pischke, J. (2009) *Mostly Harmless Econometrics: An Empiricist Companion.* Princeton, NJ: Princeton University Press.

Angrist, J.D. and Pischke, J. (2010) The credibility revolution in empirical economics: how better research design is taking the con out of econometrics. *Journal of Economic Perspectives,* 24 (2): 3–30.

Axelrod, R.M. (1997) *The Complexity of Cooperation: Agent-Based Models of Competition and Collaboration.* Princeton, NJ: Princeton University Press.

Barabas, J. and Jerit, J. (2010) Are survey experiments externally valid? *American Political Science Review,* 104 (2): 226–42.

Barro, R.J. (1996) Democracy and growth. *Journal of Economic Growth,* 1 (1): 1–27.

Barro, R.J. (1999) Determinants of democracy. *Journal of Political Economy,* 107 (S6): 158–83.

Barro, R.J. and Sala-i-Martin, X. (2004) *Economic Growth.* Cambridge, MA: MIT Press.

Bartolini, S. (1993) On time and comparative research. *Journal of Theoretical Politics,* 5 (2): 131.

Bates, R.H., Greif, A., Levi, M. and Rosenthal, J.-L. (1998) *Analytic Narratives.* Princeton, NJ: Princeton University Press.

Bauman, Z. (2000) Time and space reunited. *Time and Society,* 9 (2–3): 171–85.

Beck, N. (2010) Causal process 'observation': oxymoron or (fine) old wine. *Political Analysis,* 18 (4): 499–505.

Beck, N., Gleditsch, K.S. and Beardsley, K. (2006) 'Space is more than geography: Using spatial econometrics in the study of political economy'. *International Studies Quarterly,* 50: 27–44.

Becker, H.S. (1998) *Tricks of the Trade: How to Think about Your Research While You're Doing It.* Chicago: University of Chicago Press.

Bellucci, P. and Lewis-Beck, M. (2011) A stable popularity function? Cross-national analysis. *European Journal of Political Research,* 50 (2):190–211.

Bennett, A. (2008) Process tracing: A Bayesian perspective. In D. Collier, H.E. Brady and J.M. Box-Steffensmeier (eds), *The Oxford Handbook of Political Methodology.* Oxford: Oxford University Press, pp. 702–21.

Bennett, A. (2010) Process tracing and causal inference. In H. E. Brady and D Collier (eds.), *Rethinking Social Inquiry*: Rowman and Littlefield.

Bennett, A. and Elman, C. (2006a) Complex causal relations and case study methods: The example of path dependence. *Political Analysis*, 14 (3): 250.

Bennett, A. and Elman, C. (2006b) Qualitative research: recent developments in case study methods. *Annual Review of Political Science*, 9: 455–76.

Bennett, C.J. (1991) Review article: What is policy convergence and what causes it? *British Journal of Political Science*, 21 (2): 215–33.

Benoit, K. (2001) Simulation methodologies for political scientists. *Political Methodologist*, 10: 12–16.

Berg-Schlosser, D., De Meur, G., Rihoux, B. and Ragin, C.C. (2009) Qualitative comparative analysis (QCA) as an approach. In B. Rihoux and C.C. Ragin, *Configurational Comparative Methods. Qualitative Comparative Analysis (QCA) and Related Techniques*. Thousand Oaks, CA: Sage, pp. 1–18.

Berry, F.S. and Berry, W.D. 1990. State lottery adoptions as policy innovations: an event history analysis. *American Political Science Review*, 84 (2): 395–415.

Besserman, L.L. (ed.) (1996) *The Challenge of Periodization: Old Paradigms and New Perspectives*. New York: Garland.

Betsill, M.M. and Corell, E. (2001) NGO influence in international environmental negotiations: a framework for analysis. *Global Environmental Politics*, 1 (4): 65–85.

Bhavnani, R.R. (2009) Do electoral quotas work after they are withdrawn? Evidence from a natural experiment in India. *American Political Science Review*, 103 (1): 23–35.

Biedenkopf, K. (2011) Policy recycling? The external effects of EU environmental legislation on the United States. Doctoral dissertation, Vrije Universiteit Brussel.

Blalock, H. (1982) *Conceptualization and Measurement in the Social Sciences*. London: Sage.

Bloch, M. (1992) *The Historian's Craft*. Manchester: Manchester University Press.

Blumer, H. (1954) What is wrong with social theory? *American Sociological Review*, 18: 3–10. Available at http://www.brocku.ca/MeadProject/Blumer/Blumer_1954.html.

Blyth, M. (2006) Great punctuations: Prediction, randomness, and the evolution of comparative political science. *American Political Science Review*, 100 (4): 493–8.

Booth, W.C., Colomb, G.C., and Williams, J.M. (2008) *The Craft of Research*, 3rd edn. Chicago: University of Chicago Press.

Bourdieu, P. (1984) *Distinction* (trans. R. Nice). London: Routledge.

Box-Steffensmeier, J.M. and Jones, B.S. (2004) *Event History Modeling: A Guide for Social Scientists*. Cambridge: Cambridge University Press.

Brady, H.E. and Collier, D. (eds) (2004) *Rethinking Social Inquiry. Diverse Tools, Shared Standards*. Lanham, MD: Rowman and Littlefield.

Brady, H.E. and Collier, D. (eds) (2010) *Rethinking Social Inquiry: Diverse Tools, Shared Standards*, 2nd edn. Lanham, MD: Rowman and Littlefield.

Brady, H.E., Collier, D. and Seawright, J. (2006) Toward a pluralistic vision of methodology. *Political Analysis*, 14 (3): 353–68.

Braithwaite, J. and Drahos, P. (2000) *Global Business Regulation*. Cambridge: Cambridge University Press.

Brams, S.J. (2003) *Negotiation Games: Applying Game Theory to Bargaining and Arbitration*, 2nd edn. London: Routledge.

Brandt, P.T. and Williams, J.T. (2007) *Multiple Time Series Models*. Thousand Oaks, CA: Sage Publications.

Braudel, F. (1958) Histoire et sciences sociales: La longue durée. Annales. Histoire, Sciences Sociales, 13, 4, 725–53.

Bray, J.H. and Maxwell, S.E. (1985) *Multivariate Analysis of Variance*. Beverly Hills, CA: Sage Publications.

Buhaug, H. and Gleditsch, K.S. (2008) Contagion or confusion? Why conflicts cluster in space. *International Studies Quarterly*, 52 (2): 215–33.

Bush, G.W. (2003) President Bush Discusses Freedom in Iraq and Middle East. Remarks at the 20th Anniversary of the National Endowment for Democracy, United States Chamber of Commerce, 6 November. http://georgewbush-whitehouse.archives.gov/news/releases/2003/11/20031106-2.html (accessed 17 January 2010).

Byrne, D. and Ragin, C.C. (2009) *The Sage Handbook of Case-Based Methods*. Los Angeles: Sage Publications.

Cao, X. (2010) Networks as channels of policy diffusion: Explaining worldwide changes in capital taxation, 1998–2006. *International Studies Quarterly*, 54 (3): 823–54.

Caren, N. and Panofsky A., (2005) TQCA: A technique for adding temporality to Qualitative Comparative Analysis, *Sociological Methods & Research*, 34, 2, 147.

Chan, T.W. (1995) Optimal matching analysis: a methodological note on studying career mobility. *Work and Occupations*, 22 (4): 467–90.

Checkel, J.T. (2006) Tracing causal mechanisms. *International Studies Review*, 8 (2): 362–70.

Christakis, N.A. and Fowler, J.H. (2007) The spread of obesity in a large social network over 32 years. *New England Journal of Medicine*, 357 (4): 370–9.

Christakis, N.A. and Fowler, J.H. (2009) *Connected: The Surprising Power of Our Social Networks and How They Shape Our Lives*. New York: Little, Brown.

Cohen-Cole, E. and Fletcher, J.M. (2008) Detecting implausible social network effects in acne, height, and headaches: longitudinal analysis. *British Medical Journal*, 337: a2533.

Coleman, J.S. (1990) *Foundations of Social Theory*. Cambridge, MA: Belknap Press of Harvard University Press.

Collier, D. (2011) Understanding Process Tracing, PS Political Science and Politics, 44, 4, 823.

Collier, D. and Levitsky, S. (1997) Democracy with adjectives: Conceptual innovation in comparative research. *World Politics*, 49 (3): 430–51.

Collier, D. and Mahon, J.E. (1993) Conceptual stretching revisited: Adapting categories in comparative analysis. *American Political Science Review*, 87 (4): 845–55.

Collier, P. and Vicente, P. (2008) Votes and violence: Evidence from a field experiment in Nigeria. Centre for the Study of African Economies Working Paper Series 296.

Collins, J.D., Hall, E.J. and Paul, L.A. (2004) *Causation and Counterfactuals*. Cambridge, MA: MIT Press.

Correll, S.J. (2004) Constraints into preferences: Gender, status, and emerging career patterns. *American Sociological Review*, 69: 93–113.

Creswell, J.W. (2008). *Research Design: Qualitative, Quantitative and Mixed-Method Approaches*, 3rd paperback edn. London: Sage.

Creswell, J.W. (2009) *Research Design: Qualitative, Quantitative, and Mixed Methods Approaches*. Los Angeles: Sage Publications.

Danilovic, V. and Clare, J. (2007) The Kantian liberal peace (revisited). *American Journal of Political Science*, 51 (2): 397–414.

Davis, G.F. and Greve, H.R. (1997) Corporate elite networks and governance changes in the 1980s. *American Journal of Sociology*, 103 (1): 1–37.

DiMaggio, P.J. and Powell, W.W. (1983) The iron cage revisited: Institutional isomorphism and collective rationality in organizational fields. *American Sociological Review*, 48: 147–60.

Dimitrova, D.V. and Strömbäck, J. (2005) Mission accomplished? Framing of the Iraq War in the elite newspapers in Sweden and the United States. *Gazette*, 67 (5): 399.

Dixit, A.K. and Skeath, S. (1999) *Games of Strategy*. New York: Norton.

Dolowitz, D.P. and Marsh, D. (2000) Learning from abroad: The role of policy transfer in contemporary policy-making. *Governance*, 13 (1): 5–24.

Doucouliagos, H., and Ulubaşoğlu, M.A. (2008) Democracy and economic growth: a meta-analysis. *American Journal of Political Science*, 52 (1): 61–83.

Dowe, P. and Noordhof, P. (2004) *Cause and Chance: Causation in an Indeterministic World*. Abingdon: Routledge.

Druckman, J.N., Green, D.P., Kuklinski, J.H. and Lupia, A. (2006) The growth and development of experimental research in political science. *American Political Science Review*, 100 (4): 627–35.

Dunlop, C. and Radaelli, C.M. (2013) Systematizing policy learning: from monolith to dimensions. *Political Studies*, forthcoming.

Dunning, T. (2008) Improving causal inference: Strengths and limitations of natural experiments. *Political Research Quarterly*, 61 (2): 282–93.

Dunning, T. and Harrison, L. (2010) Cross-cutting cleavages and ethnic voting: an experimental study of cousinage in Mali. *American Political Science Review*, 104 (1): 21.

Eckstein, H. (1975) Case study and theory in political science. In F.I. Greenstein and N.W. Polsby (eds), *Handbook of Political Science*, Vol. 7. Reading, MA: Addison-Wesley, pp. 79–137.

Eggers, A. and Hainmueller, J. (2009) MPs for sale? Returns to office in postwar British politics. *American Political Science Review*, 103 (4): 513–33.

Eisenhower, D. (1954) The President's news conference. http://www.presidency.ucsb.edu/ws/index.php?pid=10202#axzz1lV6Qq7hV (accessed 17 January 2010).

Elias, N. (1992) *Time: An Essay*. Oxford: Blackwell.

Elkins, Z., Guzman, A. and Simmons, B. (2006) Competing for capital: The diffusion of bilateral investment treaties, 1960–2000. *International Organization*, 60 (4): 811–46.

Elman, C. (2005) Explanatory typologies in qualitative studies of international politics. *International Organization*, 59 (2): 293–326.

Elster, J. (1978) *Logic and Society: Contradictions and Possible Worlds*. New York: Wiley.

Epstein, J.M. and Axtell, R. (1996) *Growing Artificial Societies: Social Science from the Bottom Up*. Washington, DC: Brookings Institution Press.

Epstein, J., Duerr D., Kenworthy L., and Ragin C. (2008) Comparative employment performance: A fuzzy-set analysis. In L. Kenworthy and A. Hicks (eds.), *Method and Substance in Macrocomparative Analysis*. Houndmills: Palgrave Macmillan.

Exadaktylos, T. and Radaelli, C.M. (2009) Research design in European studies: the case of Europeanization. *Journal of Common Market Studies*, 47 (3): 507–30.

Exadaktylos, T. and Radaelli, C.M. (eds) (2012) *Research Design in European Studies: Establishing Causality in Europeanization*. Basingstoke: Palgrave.

Eysenck, M.W. and Keane, M.T. (2005) *Cognitive Psychology: A Student's Handbook*. Hove: Psychology Press.

Fearon, J.D. (1991) Counterfactuals and hypothesis testing in political science. *World Politics*, 43 (2): 169–95.

Feyerabend, P. (1975) *Against Method*. London: Verso.

Field, A. (2009) *Discovering Statistics Using SPSS*, 3rd edn. Los Angeles: Sage Publications.

Fligstein, N. (1985) The spread of the multidivisional form among large firms, 1919–1979. *American Sociological Review*, 50: 377–91.

Flyvbjerg, B. (2006) Five misunderstandings about case-study research. *Qualitative Inquiry*, 12 (2): 219.

Fourcade, M. (2006) The construction of a global profession: The transnationalization of economics. *American Journal of Sociology*, 112 (1): 145–94.

Fowler, J.H. (2006a) Connecting the Congress: A study of cosponsorship networks. *Political Analysis*, 14 (4): 456–87.

Fowler, J.H. (2006b) Legislative cosponsorship networks in the US House and Senate. *Social Networks,* 28 (4): 454–65.

Franck, I. (1982) Psychology as a science: Resolving the idiographic-nomothetic controversy. *Journal for the Theory of Social Behaviour,* 12 (1): 1–20.

Gaines, B.J., Kuklinski, J.H. and Quirk, P.J. (2007) The logic of the survey experiment reexamined. *Political Analysis,* 15 (1): 1–20.

Gallotti, M. (2012) A naturalistic argument for the irreducibility of collective intentionality. *Philosophy of the Social Sciences,* 42 (1): 3–30.

Gamst, G., Meyers, L.S. and Guarino, A.J. (2008) *Analysis of Variance Designs: A Conceptual and Computational Approach with SPSS and SAS.* Cambridge: Cambridge University Press.

Gartzke, E. (2007) The capitalist peace. *American Journal of Political Science,* 51 (1): 166–91.

Geertz, C. (1973) *The Interpretation of Cultures: Selected Essays.* New York: Basic Books.

Gelman, A. (2011) Causality and statistical learning. *American Journal of Sociology,* 117 (3): 955–66.

Genschel, P. and Schwarz, P. (2011) Tax competition: a literature review. *Socio-Economic Review,* 9 (2): 339–70.

George, A.L. and Bennett, A. (2005) *Case Studies and Theory Development in the Social Sciences.* Cambridge, MA: MIT Press.

Gerber, A.S. and Green, D.P. (2008) Field experiments and natural experiments. In J.M. Box-Steffensmeier, H.E. Brady and D. Collier (eds), *The Oxford Handbook of Political Methodology.* Oxford: Oxford University Press, pp. 357–81.

Gerber, A.S., Gimpel, J.G., Green, D.P. and Shaw, D.R. (2011) How large and long-lasting are the persuasive effects of televised campaign ads? Results from a randomized field experiment. *American Political Science Review,* 105 (1): 135–50.

Gerber, E.R. and Hopkins, D.J. (2011) When mayors matter: Estimating the impact of mayoral partisanship on city policy. *American Journal of Political Science,* 55 (2): 326–39.

Gerring, J. (2001) *Social Science Methodology: A Criterial Framework.* Cambridge: Cambridge University Press.

Gerring, J. (2004) What is a case study and what is it good for? *American Political Science Review,* 98 (2): 341–54.

Gerring, J. (2005) Causation: A Unified Framework for the Social Sciences, *Journal of Theoretical Politics,* 17, 2, 163–98.

Gerring, J. (2006) Single-outcome studies. *International Sociology,* 21 (5): 707–34.

Gerring, J. (2007a) The mechanismic worldview: Thinking inside the box. *British Journal of Political Science,* 38 (1): 161–79.

Gerring, J. (2007b) Is there a (viable) crucial-case method? *Comparative Political Studies,* 40 (3): 231.

Gerring, J. (2007c) *Case Study Research: Principles and Practices.* Cambridge: Cambridge University Press.

Gerring, J., Bond, P., Barndt, W.T. and Moreno, C. (2005) Democracy and economic growth. *World Politics,* 57: 323–64.

Gilardi, F. (2005) The same, but different. Central banks, regulatory agencies and the politics of delegation to independent authorities. Paper presented to Credibility Through Delegation? Independent Agencies in Comparative Perspective, Norwich, 28–29 June.

Gilardi, F. (2008) Delegation in the regulatory state: independent regulatory agencies in Western Europe. Northampton, MA: Edward Elgar.

Gilardi, F. (2010) Who learns from what in policy diffusion processes? *American Journal of Political Science,* 54 (3): 650–66.

Gilardi, F. and Füglister, K. (2008) Empirical modeling of policy diffusion in federal states: the dyadic approach. *Swiss Political Science Review,* 14 (3): 413–50.

Gilardi, F. and Wasserfallen, F. (2012) How socialization attenuates tax competition. University of Zurich.

Glaser, B.G. and Strauss, A.L. (1967) *The Discovery of Grounded Theory: Strategies for Qualitative Research*. Chicago: Aldine.

Gleditsch, K.S. and Ward, M.D. (2006) Diffusion and the international context of democratization. *International Organization*, 60 (4): 911–933.

Goertz, G. (2006a) *Social Science Concepts: A User's Guide*. Princeton, NJ: Princeton University Press.

Goertz, G. (2006b) Assessing the trivialness, relevance, and relative importance of necessary or sufficient conditions in social science. *Studies in Comparative International Development*, 41 (2): 88–109.

Goertz, G. and Mahoney, J. (2005) Two-level theories and fuzzy-set analysis. *Sociological Methods and Research*, 33 (4): 497–538.

Goldstein, J.S. and Pevehouse, J.C. (1997) Reciprocity, bullying, and international cooperation: Time-series analysis of the Bosnia conflict. *American Political Science Review*, 91 (3): 515–29.

Goldthorpe, J.H. (2001) Causation, statistics, and sociology. *European Sociological Review*, 17 (1): 1–20.

Graves, R. and Hodge, A. (1944) *The Reader over Your Shoulder: A Handbook for Writers of English Prose*. New York: Macmillan.

Green, D.P., Kim, S.Y. and Yoon, D.H. (2001) Dirty pool. *International Organization*, 55 (2): 441–68.

Green, D.P., Leong, T.Y., Kern, H.L., Gerber, A.S. and Larimer, C.W. (2009) Testing the accuracy of regression discontinuity analysis using experimental benchmarks. *Political Analysis*, 17 (4): 400–17.

Greenacre, M.J. and Blasius, J. (2006) *Multiple Correspondence Analysis and Related Methods*. Boca Raton, FL: Chapman & Hall/CRC.

Grice, J.W. and Iwasaki, M. (2009) A truly multivariate approach to MANOVA. *Applied Multivariate Research*, 12 (3): 199–226.

Hacker, J.S. (2004) Privatizing risk without privatizing the welfare state: The hidden politics of social policy retrenchment in the United States. *American Political Science Review*, 98 (2): 243–60.

Hafner-Burton, E.M. and Montgomery, A.H. (2006) Power positions. International organizations, social networks, and conflict. *Journal of Conflict Resolution*, 50 (1): 3–27.

Hafner-Burton, E.M., Kahler, M. and Montgomery, A.H. (2009) Network analysis for international relations. *International Organization*, 63: 559–92.

Hainmueller, J. and Hiscox, M.J. (2010) Attitudes toward highly skilled and low-skilled immigration: evidence from a survey experiment. *American Political Science Review*, 104 (1): 61.

Hall, P.A. (2012) Tracing the progress of process tracing, European Political Science, Advance online publication: http://www.palgrave-journals.com/eps/journal/vaop/ncurrent/pdf/eps20126a.pdf.

Hall, C., Scott C. and Hood C., (2000) Telecommunications regulation: culture, chaos and interdependence inside the regulatory process: Routledge.

Hansford, T.G. and Gomez, B.T. (2010) Estimating the electoral effects of voter turnout. *American Political Science Review*, 104 (2): 268–88.

Harrington, D. (2008) *Confirmatory Factor Analysis*. New York: Oxford University Press.

Harvey, A. (1997) Trends, cycles and autoregressions. *Economic Journal*, 107 (440): 192–201.

Hassig, R. (2001) Counterfactuals and revisionism in historical explanation. *Anthropological Theory*, 1 (1): 57–72.

Hedström, P. (2005) *Dissecting the Social. On the Principles of Analytical Sociology.* Cambridge: Cambridge University Press.

Hedström, P. and Swedberg, R. (1998) *Social Mechanisms. An Analytical Approach to Social Theory.* Cambridge: Cambridge University Press.

Hempel, C.G. (1965) *Aspects of Scientific Explanation and Other Essays in the Philosophy of Science.* New York: Free Press.

Hendry, D.F. (1986) Econometric modelling with cointegrated variables: an overview. *Oxford Bulletin of Economics and Statistics*, 48 (3): 201–12.

Hesslow, G. (1976) Two notes on the probabilistic approach to causality. *Philosophy of Science*, 43 (2): 290–2.

Ho, D.E., Imai, K., King, G. and Stuart, E.A. (2007) Matching as nonparametric preprocessing for reducing model dependence in parametric causal inference. *Political Analysis*, 15: 199–236.

Holland, P. W. (1986) Statistics and causal inference. *Journal of the American Statistical Association*, 81 (396): 945–60.

Hornik, J. (1984) Subjective vs. objective time measures: A note on the perception of time in consumer behavior. *Journal of Consumer Research*, 11: 615–18.

Horowitz, M.C. (2010) Nonstate actors and the diffusion of innovations: the case of suicide terrorism. *International Organization*, 64: 33–64.

Hume, D.A. (2003) *Treatise of Human Nature.* New York: Dover.

Humphreys, M. and Weinstein, J.M. (2009) Field experiments and the political economy of development. *Annual Review of Political Science*, 12 (1): 367–78.

Hyde, S.D. (2007) The observer effect in international politics: Evidence from a natural experiment. *World Politics*, 60: 37–63.

Inglehart, R. (1997) *Modernization and Postmodernization.* Princeton, NJ: Princeton University Press.

Jackson, G. (2005) Employee representation in the board compared: a fuzzy sets analysis of corporate governance, unionism, and political institutions. *Industrielle Beziehungen*, 12: 1–28.

Jensen, J.L. and Rodgers, R. (2001) Cumulating the intellectual gold of case study research. *Public Administration Review*, 61: 236–46.

Kaufman, L. and Rousseeuw, P.J. (1990) *Finding Groups in Data: An Introduction to Cluster Analysis.* New York: Wiley.

Kelemen, R.D. and Capoccia, G. (2007) The study of critical junctures: Theory, narrative, and counterfactuals in historical institutionalism. *World Politics*, 59 (3): 341–69.

Kenny, D.A., Kashy, D.A. and Cook, W.L. (2006) *Dyadic Data Analysis.* New York: Guilford Press.

Kerckhoff, A.C., Campbell, R.T. and Winfield-Laird, I. (1985) Social mobility in Great Britain and the United States. *American Journal of Sociology*, 91 (2): 281–308.

Kern, H.L. and Hainmueller, J. (2009) Opium for the masses: How foreign free media can stabilize authoritarian regimes. *Political Analysis*, 17 (4): 377–399.

King, G., Keohane, R.O. and Verba, S. (1994) *Designing Social Inquiry: Scientific Inference in Qualitative Research.* Princeton, NJ: Princeton University Press.

Krebs, D., Berger, M. and Ferligoj, A. (2000) Approaching achievement motivation-comparing factor analysis and cluster analysis. In A. Ferligoj and A. Mrvar (eds), *New Approaches in Applied Statistics*, Metodoloski zvezki 16. Ljubljana: FDV.

Kuehn, D., and Rohlfing, I. (2009) Causal explanation and multi-method research in the social sciences. APSA 2009 Toronto Meeting Paper. Available at SSRN: http://ssrn.com/abstract=1451631.

Kurki, M. (2008) *Causation in International Relations: Reclaiming Causal Analysis.* Cambridge: Cambridge University Press.

Kvist, J. (2006) Diversity, ideal types and fuzzy sets in comparative welfare state research. In B. Rihoux and H. Grimm (eds), *Innovative Comparative Methods for Policy Analysis*. New York: Springer, pp. 167–84.

Lalive, R. and Zweimüller, J. (2009) How does parental leave affect fertility and return to work? Evidence from two natural experiments. *Quarterly Journal of Economics*, 124 (3): 1363–1402.

Landman, T. (2003) *Issues and Methods in Comparative Politics. An Introduction*. London: Routledge.

Latour, B. and Woolgar, S. (1979) *Laboratory Life: The Social Construction of Scientific Facts*. London: Sage.

Lazarsfeld, P. and Barton, A.H. (1951). Qualitative measurement in the social sciences: Classification, typologies, and indices. In D. Lerner and H. D. Laswell (eds), *The Policy Sciences: Recent Developments in Scope and Method*. Stanford, CA: Stanford University Press, pp. 155–192.

Lebow, R.N. (2000) What's so different about a counterfactual? *World Politics*, 52 (4): 550–85.

Leeson, P.T. and Dean, A.M. (2009) The democratic domino theory: an empirical investigation. *American Journal of Political Science*, 53 (3): 533–51.

Levi, M. (2002) Modeling complex historical processes with analytic narratives. In R. Mayntz (ed.), *Akteure – Mechanismen – Modelle. Zur Theoriefähigkeit makro-sozialer Analysen*. Frankfurt am Main: Campus, pp. 108–127.

Levi, M. (2004) An analytic narrative approach to puzzles and problems. In I. Shapiro, R.M. Smith and T.E. Masoud (eds), *Problems and Methods in the Study of Politics*. Cambridge: Cambridge University Press, pp. 201–26.

Lewis, D. (1973) Causation. *Journal of Philosophy*, 70 (17): 556–67.

Li, R.P.Y. and Thompson, W.R. (1975) The 'coup contagion' hypothesis. *Journal of Conflict Resolution*, 19 (1): 63–84.

Lieberman, E. S. (2005) Nested analysis as a mixed-method strategy for comparative research. *American Political Science Review*, 99 (3): 435–51.

Lijphart, A. (1971) Comparative politics and the comparative method. *American Political Science Review*, 65 (3): 682–93.

Linos, K. (2011) Diffusion through democracy. *American Journal of Political Science*, 55 (3): 678–95.

Lipset, S.M. (1959) Some social requisites of democracy: Economic development and political legitimacy. *American Political Science Review*, 53 (1): 69–105.

Lipset, S.M. (1963) *Political Man: The Social Bases of Politics*. Garden City, New York: Anchor Books.

Little, D. (1991) *Varieties of Social Explanation*. Boulder, CO: Westview Press.

Liu, K.-Y., King, M. and Bearman, P.S. (2010) Social influence and the autism epidemic. *American Journal of Sociology*, 115 (5): 1387–1434.

Macal, C.M. and North, M.J. (2010) Tutorial on agent-based modelling and simulation. *Journal of Simulation*, 4 (3): 151–62.

Mackie, J.L. (1965) Causes and condition. *American Philosophical Quarterly*, 2: 245–64.

MacKinlay, A.C. (1997) Event studies in economics and finance. *Journal of Economic Literature*, 35 (1): 13–39.

Mahoney, J. (2004) Comparative-historical methodology. *Annual Review of Sociology*, 30: 81–101.

Mahoney, J. (2008) Toward a unified theory of causality. *Comparative Political Studies*, 41 (4–5): 412.

Mahoney, J. and Goertz, G. (2004) The possibility principle: Choosing negative cases in comparative research. *American Political Science Review* 98 (4): 653–69.

Mahoney, J. and Goertz, G. (2006) A tale of two cultures: Contrasting quantitative and qualitative research. *Political Analysis* 14 (3): 227–49.

Mahoney, J. and Rueschemeyer, D. (2003) *Comparative Historical Analysis in the Social Sciences*. Cambridge: Cambridge University Press.

Mahoney, J., Kimball, E. and Koivu, K.L. (2009) The logic of historical explanation in the social sciences. *Comparative Political Studies*, 42 (1): 114–46.

Majone, G. (1980) An anatomy of pitfalls. In G. Majone and E.S. Quade (eds), *Pitfalls of Analysis*. Chichester: Wiley, pp. 7–22

Majone, G. (1996) *Regulating Europe*. London: Routledge.

Maoz, Z. and Russett, B. (1993) Normative and structural causes of democratic peace, 1946–1986. *American Political Science Review*, 87 (3): 624–38.

Marland, P., Patching, W. and Putt I., (1992) Thinking while studying: A process tracing study of distance learners, *Distance education*, 13, 2, 193–217.

Marsh, D. and Stoker, G. (eds) (2010) *Theory and Methods in Political Science*, 3rd edn. Basingstoke: Palgrave.

Mason, M.K. (2011) *Analysis of Variance (ANOVA)*, Unpublished paper.

McCarty, N.M. and Meirowitz, A. (2007) *Political Game Theory: An Introduction*. Cambridge: Cambridge University Press.

McPherson, M., Smith-Lovin, L. and Cook, J.M. (2001) Birds of a feather: Homophily in social networks. *Annual Review of Sociology*, 27: 415–44.

Mezias, S.J. (1990) An institutional model of organizational practice: Financial reporting at the Fortune 200. *Administrative Science Quarterly*, 35: 431–57.

Mill, J.S. (2002) *A System of Logic*. Honolulu: University Press of the Pacific.

Minier, J.A. (1998) Democracy and growth: alternative approaches. *Journal of Economic Growth*, 3 (3): 241–66.

Moehler, D.C. (2010) Democracy, governance, and randomized development assistance. *Annals of the American Academy of Political and Social Science*, 628 (1): 30–46.

Moore, B. (1966) Social origins of democracy and dictatorship, Boston: Beacon.

Morgan, S.L. and Winship, C. (2007) *Counterfactuals and Causal Inference. Methods and Principles for Social Research*. Cambridge: Cambridge University Press.

Morton, R.B. and Williams, K.C. (2008) Experimentation in political science. In J.M. Box-Steffensmeier, H.E. Brady and D. Collier (eds), *The Oxford Handbook of Political Methodology*. Oxford: Oxford University Press, pp. 339–56.

Morton, R.B. and Williams, K.C. (2010) *Experimental Political Science and the Study of Causality: From Nature to the Lab*. Cambridge: Cambridge University Press.

Most, B.A. and Starr, H. (1980) Diffusion, reinforcement, geopolitics, and the spread of war. *American Political Science Review*, 74 (4): 932–46.

Noel, H. and Nyhan, B. (2011) The 'unfriending' problem: The consequences of homophily in friendship retention for causal estimates of social influence. *Social Networks*, 33 (3): 211–18.

Olken, B.A. (2010) Direct democracy and local public goods: evidence from a field experiment in Indonesia. *American Political Science Review*, 104 (2): 243–67.

Olsen, J.P. (2001) Garbage cans, new institutionalism, and the study of politics. *American Political Science Review*, 95 (1): 191–8.

Peterson, R.A. and Kern, R.M. (1996) Changing highbrow taste: from snob to omnivore. *American Sociological Review*, 61 (5): 900–7.

Pevehouse, J.C. and Brozek, J.D. (2008) Time-series analysis. In J.M. Box-Steffensmeier, H.E. Brady and D. Collier (eds), *The Oxford Handbook of Political Methodology*. Oxford: Oxford University Press.

Pierson, P. (2000) Increasing returns, path dependence, and the study of politics. *American Political Science Review*, 94 (2): 251–67.

Plümper, T. and Neumayer, E. (2010) Spatial effects in dyadic data. *International Organization*, 64 (1): 145–66.

Polillo, S. and Guillén, M.F. (2005) Globalization pressures and the state: The worldwide spread of central bank independence. *American Journal of Sociology*, 110 (6): 1764–1802.

Przeworski, A. and Limongi, F. (1997) Modernization: theory and facts. *World Politics*, 49 (1): 155–75.

Przeworski, A. and Teune, H. (1970) *The Logic of Comparative Social Inquiry*. New York: Wiley.

Punj, G. and Stewart, D.W. (1983) Cluster analysis in marketing research: review and suggestions for application. *Journal of Marketing Research*, 20: 134–48.

Putnam, R.D., Leonardi, R. and Nanetti, R.Y. (1993) *Making Democracy Work*. Princeton, NJ: Princeton University Press,

Radaelli, C.M. (2000) Policy transfer in the European Union: Institutional isomorphism as a source of legitimacy. *Governance*, 13 (1): 25–43.

Radaelli, C.M. (2005) Diffusion without convergence: How political context shapes the adoption of regulatory impact assessment. *Journal of European Public Policy*, 12 (5): 924–43.

Ragin, C.C. (1987) *The Comparative Method. Moving beyond Qualitative and Quantitative Strategies*. Berkeley: University of California Press.

Ragin, C.C. (2000) *Fuzzy-Set Social Science*. Chicago: University of Chicago Press.

Ragin, C.C. (2006a) Set relations in social research: evaluating their consistency and coverage. *Political Analysis*, 14 (3): 291–310.

Ragin, C.C. (2006b) The limitations of net-effects thinking. In B. Rihoux and H. Grimm (eds), *Innovative Comparative Methods for Policy Analysis*. New York: Springer.

Ragin, C.C. (2008) *Redesigning Social Inquiry: Fuzzy Sets and Beyond*. Chicago: University of Chicago Press.

Riemer, Frances Julia (2009) Ethnography Research. In Stephen D. Lapan and MaryLynn T. Quartaroli (eds.), *Research Essentials: An Introduction to Designs and Practices*. San Francisco, CA: Jossey-Bass.

Rihoux, B. and Lobe, B. (2009) The case for qualitative comparative analysis (QCA): Adding leverage for thick cross-case comparison. In D. Byrne and C.C. Ragin (eds), *The Sage Handbook of Case-Based Methods*. Los Angeles: Sage Publications, pp. 222–42.

Rihoux, B. and Ragin, C. (2008) *Configurational Comparative Analysis*. Thousand Oaks, CA: Sage Publications.

Robson, K. and Sanders, C. (2009) *Quantifying Theory: Pierre Bourdieu*. Dordrecht: Springer.

Rogers, E.M. (2003) *Diffusion of Innovations*, 5th edn. New York: Free Press.

Ross, M. (2008) Oil, Islam, and women. *American Political Science Review*, 102 (2): 107–23.

Rothstein, B. (2000) Trust, social dilemmas and collective memories. *Journal of Theoretical Politics*, 12 (4): 477–501.

Rubin, D.B. (1974) Estimating causal effects of treatments in randomized and nonrandomized studies. *Journal of Educational Psychology*, 66 (5): 688.

Salehyan, I. and Gleditsch, K.S. (2006) Refugees and the spread of civil war. *International Organization*, 60 (2): 335–66.

Sartori, G. (1970) Concept misformation in comparative politics. *American Political Science Review*, 64 (4): 1033–53.

Sartori, G. (1991) Comparing and miscomparing. *Journal of Theoretical Politics*, 3 (3), 243–57.

Schelling, T. (1978) *Micromotives and Macrobehavior*. New York: Norton.

Schneider, C.Q. and Wagemann, C. (2010) Standards of good practice in qualitative comparative analysis (QCA) and fuzzy-sets. *Comparative Sociology*, 9 (3): 397–418.

Schwert, G.W. (1981) Using financial data to measure effects of regulation. *Journal of Law and Economics*, 24 (1): 121–58.

Searle, J. (1995) *The Construction of Social Reality*. London: Penguin.

Seawright, J. and Gerring, J. (2008) Case selection techniques in case study research: a menu of qualitative and quantitative options. *Political Research Quarterly*, 61 (2): 294.

Sewell, W.H. (1996) Three temporalities: Toward an eventful sociology. In T.J. McDonald (ed.), *The Historic Turn in the Human Sciences*. Ann Arbor: University of Michigan Press, pp. 245–80.

Shalizi, C.R. and Thomas, A.C. (2011) Homophily and contagion are generically confounded in observational social network studies. *Sociological Methods and Research*, 40 (2): 211–39.

Sharman, J.C. (2010) Dysfunctional policy transfer in national tax blacklists. *Governance*, 23 (4): 623–39.

Sil, R. and Katzenstein, P. (2010) *Beyond Paradigms: Analytic Eclecticism in the Study of World Politics*. Basingstoke: Palgrave Macmillan

Simmons, B.A. and Elkins, Z. (2004) The globalization of liberalization: Policy diffusion in the international political economy. *American Political Science Review*, 98 (1): 171–89.

Simmons, B., Dobbin, F. and Garrett, G. (2006) Introduction: The international diffusion of liberalism. *International Organization*, 60 (4): 781–810.

Sirowy, L. and Inkeles, A. (1990) The effects of democracy on economic growth and inequality: a review. *Studies in Comparative International Development*, 25 (1): 126–57.

Sovey, A.J. and Green, D.P. (2010) Instrumental variables estimation in political science: a readers' guide. *American Journal of Political Science*, 55 (1): 188–200.

Sraffa, P. (1960) *Production of Commodities by Means of Commodities: Prelude to a Critique of Economic Theory*. Cambridge: Cambridge University Press.

Starke, P. (2011) Sir Francis Galton's stepchildren: Qualitative methods for the study of policy diffusion. University of Bremen.

Starr, H. (1991) Democratic dominoes: Diffusion approaches to the spread of democracy in the international system. *Journal of Conflict Resolution*, 35 (2): 356–81.

Stock, J.H. and Watson, M.W. (1988) Testing for common trends. *Journal of the American Statistical Association*, 83: 1097–1107.

Strauss, A.L. and Corbin, J. (eds) (1997) *Grounded Theory in Practice*. London: Sage.

Suppes, P.C. (1970) *A Probabilistic Theory of Causality*. Amsterdam: North-Holland.

Tetlock, P. and Belkin, A. (1996) *Counterfactual Thought Experiments in World Politics: Logical, Methodological, and Psychological Perspectives*. Princeton, NJ: Princeton University Press.

Thelen, K. (1999) Historical institutionalism in comparative politics. *Annual Reviews in Political Science*, 2 (1): 369–404.

Tilly, C. (2006) How and why history matters. In R.E. Goodin and C. Tilly (eds), *The Oxford Handbook of Contextual Political Analysis*. Oxford: Oxford University Press.

Tripp, A.M. and Kang, A. (2008) The global impact of quotas: On the fast track to increased female legislative representation. *Comparative Political Studies*, 41 (3): 338–61.

Tylor, E.B. (1889) On a method of investigating the development of institutions: applied to laws of marriage and descent. *Journal of the Anthropological Institute of Great Britain and Ireland*, 18: 245–72.

Vicente, P.C. and Wantchekon, L. (2009) Clientelism and vote buying: lessons from field experiments in African elections. *Oxford Review of Economic Policy*, 25 (2): 292.

Volden, C. (2006) States as policy laboratories: Emulating success in the Children's Health Insurance Program. *American Journal of Political Science* 50 (2): 294–312.

Wallerstein, I. (1987) World-systems analysis. In A. Giddens and J. Turner (eds), *Social Theory Today*. Stanford, CA: Stanford University Press, pp. 309–24.

Ward, M.D. and Gleditsch, K.S. (2008) *Spatial Regression Models.* Los Angeles: Sage Publications.

Watts, D.J. (2004) The 'new' science of networks. *Annual Review of Sociology,* 30: 243–70.

Welzel, C. and Inglehart, R. (2003) The theory of human development: a cross-cultural analysis. *European Journal of Political Research,* 42: 341–79.

Weyland, K. (2007) *Bounded Rationality and Policy Diffusion: Social Sector Reform in Latin America.* Princeton, NJ: Princeton University Press.

Weyland, K. (2010) The diffusion of regime contention in European democratization, 1830–1940. *Comparative Political Studies,* 43(8–9): 1148–76.

Whitehead, T.L. (2005) *Basic Classical Ethnographic Research Methods,* EICCARS Working Paper Series, University of Maryland, Maryland, 1–29.

Windrum, P., Fagiolo, G. and Moneta, A. (2007) Empirical validation of agent-based models: alternatives and prospects. *Journal of Artificial Societies and Social Simulation,* 10 (2): 8.

Wolcott, H.F. (2005) *The art of fieldwork.* Walnut Creek, CA: Altamira Press.

Woodward, J. (2001) Causation and manipulability. In *Stanford Encyclopedia of Philosophy.* http://plato.stanford.edu/entries/causation-mani/ (accessed 6 June 2012).

Woodward, J., and Hitchcock, C. (2003) Explanatory generalizations, Part I: A counter-factual account. *Noûs,* 37 (1): 1–24.

Yin, R.K. (2003) *Case Study Research: Design and Methods.* Thousand Oaks, CA: Sage.

Zadeh, L.A. (1965) Fuzzy sets. *Information and Control,* 8 (3): 338–53.

Zakay, D. (1990) The evasive art of subjective time measurement: some methodological dilemmas. In R.A. Block (ed.), *Cognitive Models of Psychological Time.* Hillsdale, NJ: Lawrence Erlbaum Associates, pp. 59–84.

Index

Eckstein, H., 133
econometrics, 103
effects-of-causes and causes-of effects, 69–70, 165–6
Eggers, A., 85
ego-network analysis, 144–7
Eisenhower, Dwight, 141
Elias, N., 94
elimination in experimental design, 54
Elkins, Z., 142
Elman, Colin, 36–7
Elster, J., 48
epistemic learning and epistemic communities, 37–8
epistemology, 7, 14
Epstein, J., 62–3
equifinal explanations of social phenomena, 18, 116, 124
ethical issues, 10–11
ethnographic research, 22, 50–1, 134–5
event history analysis, 108–9, 113
event studies, 100–1, 113
'exclusion restriction', 86
experiments, 17, 54–6, 66–7, 77–85, 91
    definition of, 78
    design of, 49
    see also quasi-experiments
explanatory arguments in the social sciences, 13–14
extension of conceptual categories, 29–32, 39, 116
extreme cases, 132, 134

factor analysis (FA), 26, 118–21
family resemblances, 35–6, 39
Feyerabend, P., 163
field experiments, 55, 81–3, 89
    definition of, 81
fieldwork, 134
'fixation' in cognitive psychology, 54–5
Fligstein, N., 139
Fourcade, M., 139
Fowler, J.H., 139–40, 144, 147, 151
'free riding', 165
fuzzy-set analysis, 62, 105–6, 127–8

Galton, Sir Francis (and 'Galton's problem'), 138, 158

game theory, 106–8, 112
Gartzke, E., 151–2
Geertz, Clifford, 50–1
Gelman, A., 71–2
generalization, 21–2, 27, 49–50
    context-bound and *law-like*, 22
Gerber, E.R., 82
Gerring, John, 10, 14–15, 64, 102, 130–3, 156, 166
gestalts, 32
Gilardi, F. (co-author), 128, 149–50
Glaser, Barney, 22
Gleditsch, K.S., 149
global network analysis, 144–6
Goertz, Gary, 23–6, 31–2, 34, 44, 57
Goldstein, J.S., 104
Gomez, B.T., 87
Greenpeace, 60
Grice, J.W., 122
grounded theory, 22, 25
grouping of variables and cases, 118
Guillén, M.F., 147

Hafner-Burton, E.M., 141–2
Hainmueller, J., 55, 80, 85, 87
Hall, Claire, 135
Hansford, T.G., 87
Harrison, L., 79
Hedström, P., 13
Hempel, Carl, 3–4
Hendry, David, 45
heterogeneity, 18, 115–36
    of causal relations, 135–6
    confirmatory, 118
    in kind and *in degree*, 116–18
    research designs for the study of, 136
Hiscox, M.J., 80
historical analysis, 95–9
Holland, P.W., 74
homophily, 19, 140, 154–5, 159
'homophily principle', 154
Hrycak, A., 105
Hume, D.A., 46
Hyde, S.D., 83
hypothesis testing, 60, 66

idiographic research, 21, 27
'ignorability assumption', 86

incommensurability between different approaches to research, 2, 14
increasing returns processes, 109
inductive thinking, 42
inference *see* causal inference
influential cases, 132, 134
Inglehart, R., 99
institutional isomorphism, 139
instrumental variables, 86–8
intension of conceptual categories, 29, 31, 39, 116–17
interdependence, 18–19, 138–59
  dyadic approach to the study of, 150–4
  measuring the consequences of, 148–54
  qualitative approaches to the study of, 155–9
  in the social sciences, 139–43
international relations, 140–2
interval measurement, 117–18
INUS conditions, 44, 64, 125
isomorphism, types of, 139
Iwasaki, M., 123

Jobs, Steve, 161
Jones, B.S., 108

Kang, A., 76, 88
Katzenstein, P., 8
Kennedy, John F., 107
Kenny, D.A., 109
Kerckhoff, A.C., 57
Kern, H.L., 55, 87
Kern, R.M., 58
Khrushchev, Nikita, 107
King, G., 50
Krebs, D., 119
Kuhn, T., 163
Kyoto Protocol, 116

laboratory experiments, 54, 78–80
'ladder of abstraction', 29–31, 34–6, 39
Lakatos, I., 163
Lalive, R., 85
latent variables, 26, 121
Lazarsfeld, P., 37
least-likely research designs, 133

level variables in the social sciences, 102, 113
Levitsky, S., 32
Limongi, F., 99
Linos, K., 81
Liphart, A., 57
Lipset, S.M., 99, 110
Liu, K.-Y., 140
local average treatment effects, 88
'logical distance' between cases, 119
longue durée of history, 96

Macal, C.M., 97
Mackie, J.L., 44
Mahon, J.E., 32–6
Mahoney, J., 44, 57, 131
Majone, G., 31
manipulability perspective, 48–9, 51–2
Mao Zedong, 2
marketing research, 118
Marsh, D., 142
Marxian theory, 96
matching, 50, 54, 77; *see also* optimal matching
Maxwell, S.E., 122
Mead, George Herbert, 7
Mead, Margaret, 135
measurement
  and concept formation, 165
  and conceptual analysis, 24–5, 39
Mill, John Stuart, 43, 56, 156
Minier, J.A., 103
minimal-rewrite rule, 47
modernization theory, 99
Montgomery, A.H., 141–2
Moore, B., 111
Morton, R.B., 78, 81
Most, B.A., 140
most-different-systems design (MDSD) and most-similar-systems design (MSSD), 56–7, 156
multi-method research, 6, 66
multiple causation, 62
multiple correspondence analysis (MCA), 120
multivariate analysis of variance (MANOVA), 122–3

narratives, analytical, 111–12
natural experiments, 55, 83–5
necessary conditions, 125–7
necessity, test of, 62
nested analysis, 66, 131
nominalism, 23–4, 39
nomothetic sciences, 21, 27
non-compliance in experiments, 78
'normal performance' models, 100
North, M.J., 97

observational studies, 50, 55, 83
Olken, B.A., 82
Olson, Mancur, 165
omitted-variable bias, 50, 76–7, 111
ontology, 7, 24
optimal matching, 105
ordinal measurement, 117
outliers, 125
overdetermination, 71

Panofsky, A., 106
paradigm-bound thinking, 2, 9
path dependence, 18, 109–13
pay-offs from games, 107–8
peer review, 9–10
periodization of historical phenomena, 95
Peterson, R.A., 58
Pevehouse, J.C., 104
Pierson, P., 109
Pischke, J., 89–90
'pitfalls' (Majone), 31
pluralism, 2, 14, 31
   methodological, 16, 42, 64–5
policy transfer, policy diffusion and *policy convergence*, 142
Polillo, S., 147
Popper, Karl, 163
positivism, 15
potential-outcomes framework, 46–9, 54, 69, 72–5
Powell, W.W., 139
Princip, Gavrilo, 47
principal component analysis (PCA), 119–20
prison culture, 162–3
probabilistic approaches to causal analysis, 45–6, 51–3, 69, 161

process analysis, 58–60, 66–7, 111
process tracing, 59–60, 106, 131, 155, 157
projectability, criterion of, 47–8
propensity scores, 77
Przeworksi, A., 56, 99, 138
publication of research findings, 12, 164
purposive sampling, 131

qualitative comparative analysis (QCA), 18, 62–3, 65, 105–6, 116, 124–5, 135–6
   procedure for, 127–30
   see also temporal qualitative comparative analysis
qualitative and quantitative research, 6, 16–19, 64–5, 70, 83, 89, 117, 155, 164–5
quasi-experiments, 17, 54, 64, 83, 86, 91
quasi-randomization, 85–6
QWERTY keyboard, 110

Radaelli, C.M. (co-author), 36–7
radial categories and concepts, 32–3, 39
Ragin, C.C., 62, 124–8
'random walks', 100
randomization, 17, 54–5, 77–84, 88–91;
   see also quasi-randomization
reflexive learning, 37
regression analysis, 75–7, 90–1, 99–100, 103
   conditions for yielding of unbiased estimates, 76
   see also spatial regression
regularity approaches to causal analysis, 43–5, 51–2
regulatory quality, 23
relational concepts in the social sciences, 29, 143–4
reliability of research, 15
research design, 4–6, 9–18, 64, 166
   ex post and *ex ante* corrections to, 88
   minimalistic definition of, 10
   paramount importance of, 69, 91
   status of methods in, 11
Research Excellence Exercise, 12

responsible researchers, choices to be made by, 5–6
'results' in the social sciences, 13
revolutions, 115, 126
Rogers, E.M., 139
Rothstein, B., 8

sampling, 28
Sartori, Giovanni, 29–36, 116
Seawright, J., 131–2
segmentation of markets, 118
sensitizing concepts, 27
sequencing of events, 112–13
sequential processes, 103–8
set-relations analysis, 60–3, 66–7
set-theoretic analysis, 125–8, 135–6
Shalizi, C.R., 155
Sharman, J.C., 157–8
Sil, R., 8
Simmons, B., 142
'simulated shocks', 104
simulation, 97–8
sine qua non conditions, 47
Skocpol, Theda, 43–4, 126
so what question, 12–13
social constructionism, 7
social network analysis (SNA), 18, 65, 140–50, 158
social ontology and social representations, 7
social sciences as an autonomous field of knowledge, 13–16
sociological research, 139
spatial regression, 148–50, 154
'special case study', use of term, 130–1
special cases, analysis of, 130–6
spillovers, 83
spurious relationships, 45
Sraffa, Piero, 12
stable unit treatment value assumption (SUTVA), 73, 83
Starke, P., 156
Starr, H., 140
statistical analysis, 17, 57–8, 64–7, 69–91, 165
  lessons for research design, 88–90
  methods of, 75–88

stochastic movements, 99–100
stock variables in the social sciences, 102–3, 113
Strauss, Anselm, 22
structural equivalence within networks, 147
subjectivity of researchers, 162; *see also* double subjectivity
sufficiency, analysis of, 62
sufficient conditions, 125–7
survey experiments, 80–1
Sutherland, Edwin, 28
systematic case comparisons, 111

tax competition and *tax coordination*, 143
temporal qualitative comparative analysis (TQCA), 105–6
temporality, 93–113
  research goals and research designs related to the study of, 96–112
tendency, analysis of, 112–13
Tetlock, P., 47
Teune, H., 56, 138
'thick' analysis, 111
Thomas, A.C., 155
Tilly, C., 96–7
time, different conceptualizations of, 94–6, 112
time-series analysis, 99–100, 103–4
time span of social phenomena, 96–8, 112–13
  simulative approaches to, 97–8
timing of events, 108–9
Titanic, 44
trade-offs in research design, 6, 9, 89, 91, 130, 164–6
treatment effects, 73–4; *see also* local average treatment effects
treatment groups, 16, 50, 77–8, 91
trend analysis, 98–101, 112
Tripp, A.M., 76, 88
truth tables, 127, 129
typical cases, 131, 134
typological analysis, 16, 36–7

unique cases, 161

validity of research, 15
  internal and *external*, 17, 89–90, 98, 108, 165
value-laden nature of social sciences, 6–7
variance, *within-group* and *between-group*, 122
vector autoregressions (VARs), 103–5
Velázquez de Cuéllar, Diego, 48
Vicente, P., 55
Volden, C., 142, 152

Wallerstein, I., 96
Wasserfallen, F., 149–50

Weber, Max, 29
Welzel, C., 99
Weyland, K., 156–8
who cares question, 12–14
Williams, J.T., 103
Williams, K.C., 78, 81
within-case analysis, 157–9
within-group variance, 122
Wittgenstein, Ludwig, 35
Woodward, J., 49
world systems theory, 96

Zadeh, L.A., 127
Zweimüller, J., 85